丛书主编 吕中舌
丛书副主编 何福胜 张文霞 孙建民

读写译 学生用书
第 2 册

Reading, Writing & Translation
Student's Book
Book Two

主编：邢如
编者：沈明波 杨芳 覃学岚 张文霞

清华大学出版社
北京

内 容 简 介

《新英语教程(第四版)》以教育部最新颁布的《大学英语课程教学要求》为编写原则,分为"听说"和"读写译"两大系列。本书为"读写译"系列第二册,包括8个单元。每个单元分 Part A、Part BI、Part BII 和 Part C。Part A 包括精读、写作和翻译三大版块。Part B 为泛读,用来扩大阅读量和训练阅读流利程度。Part C 为阅读技巧的讲解。三部分都配有各种形式的练习,以提高学习者的语言运用能力。

本书适合大学英语一年级的学生及同等水平的广大英语爱好者。

版权所有,侵权必究。举报:010-62782989,beiqinquan@tup.tsinghua.edu.cn。

图书在版编目(CIP)数据

新英语教程读写译学生用书. 第2册/吕中舌主编;邢如等编. —4版. —北京:清华大学出版社,2005.9(2024.8重印)
ISBN 978-7-302-11778-0

Ⅰ. 新… Ⅱ. ①吕… ②邢… Ⅲ. ①英语—阅读教学—高等学校—教材 ②英语—写作—高等学校—教材 ③英语—翻译—高等学校—教材 Ⅳ. H31

中国版本图书馆 CIP 数据核字(2005)第 103491 号

责任编辑:蔡心奕
责任印制:丛怀宇

出版发行:清华大学出版社
网　　址:https://www.tup.com.cn,https://www.wqxuetang.com
地　　址:北京清华大学学研大厦 A 座　　邮　编:100084
社 总 机:010-83470000　　邮　购:010-62786544
投稿与读者服务:010-62776969,c-service@tup.tsinghua.edu.cn
质 量 反 馈:010-62772015,zhiliang@tup.tsinghua.edu.cn
印 装 者:涿州市般润文化传播有限公司
经　　销:新华书店总店北京发行所
开　　本:185×230　　印　张:19.75　　字　数:400 千字
版　　次:2005 年 9 月第 1 版　　印　次:2024 年 8 月第 17 次印刷
定　　价:68.00 元

产品编号:018662-06/H

PREFACE
第四版前言

第四版《新英语教程》(*New English Course*) 是一套全国通用的大学英语教材,由清华大学外语系根据2004年教育部颁发的《大学英语课程教学要求》主持编写。它总结了清华大学及一些兄弟院校近二十年的教学实践经验,经广泛征求学生和教师意见,对原教材进行了多方面的修改与完善,是我们对现代语言教学理论、教学方法以及《大学英语课程教学要求》理解的具体体现。希望我们的第四版《新英语教程》对兄弟院校的大学英语教学、语言测试和评估能尽绵薄之力。

《新英语教程》是我国大学外语界具有广泛影响的教材之一。《新英语教程》第一版在1987年首次由清华大学出版社出版,1992年荣获国家教委优秀教材奖。为体现语言的时代性,我们先后对此教材作过多次修订。第二版面世于1994年。第三版出版于1999年。第三版的《新英语教程》荣获两项大奖:2001年北京市政府颁布的北京市教育教学成果二等奖;2002年教育部颁布的全国普通高等学校优秀教材二等奖。目前,《新英语教程》系列教材是清华大学大学英语国家级精品课的主干教材。

随着我国改革开放的不断深入,大学英语教学也经历了无数次的变革。无论是学校或社会用人单位都对大学生的英语水平有很高的期待,这就促使大学英语教学必须不断改进、不断提高。2004年教育部颁布的《大学英语课程教学要求》又对大学英语教学提出了新的目标。为全面贯彻《大学英语课程教学要求》的主旨,我们再次对《新英语教程》进行修订,编写出版了此套第四版《新英语教程》。

第四版《新英语教程》主要有以下两方面大的变动:

➢ 新的《大学英语课程教学要求》在教学目标中指出大学英语应注重培养学生的语言综合运用能力,为贯彻执行这一精神,我们将

PREFACE

培养学生的语言"综合运用能力"作为第四版《新英语教程》的主要突出的特点，我们在指导思想和编写原则方面都将围绕这一特点展开。通过一段时间的调研，我们发现以往教材对说、写、译重视不够，对语言的五种技能（听、说、读、写、译）衔接不够。因此我们对《新英语教程》（第三版）系列教材重新整合：将写作与阅读紧密地结合在一起，扩展了翻译部分，从而形成主干教材为读写译和听说两部分。听说部分也在原有基础上加大了口语交流和表达的比例。这样，我们一方面淡化培养学生被动接受的能力，将重点放在培养学生的产出能力，注重学生口笔头交际能力的培养，从而提高学生语言的各项技能和综合运用语言的能力。

➢ 在经过对部分任课教师及学生调研的基础上，保留了第三版比较受欢迎的文章，补充了一些精选的内容，补充新课文数量在30%—50%左右，各册不同：第一册新增课文多达50%，目的是让用户有耳目一新的感觉；其余各册均在30%以上。听说教材增加了说的比例，且替换内容也在30%以上。教参不但指出各课的重点和难点，并给出比较详尽具体的教学参考步骤。更值得一提的是我们在翻译和写作部分加大了力度。我们不仅提供了范文，而且还提供了相当一部分学生真实的翻译和写作样本，并对这些样本作了大量的分析和评论。目的是让老师在教学过程中有的放矢；学生在学习过程中引以为戒，取长补短。

第四版《新英语教程》有以下几个显著特点：

1. "综合运用能力"是此教材强调和突出的特点。我们不仅强调听说读写译五项技能全面发展，同时还强调五项技能的衔接性和互补性。

2. 英语教学不仅要教授学生语言的技能，同时也要教授学生世界文化方面的知识，以开阔学生的眼界，拓宽学生的知识面。同时，为体现"授人以渔"，我们在传授国际文化的同时，特别注重培养学生的文化意识，以提高学生的文化素养，更好地做好国际交流工作。

3. 在教学方法和教学模式方面我们主要采用传统教学法与交际法，既有知识输入的环节，又有输出操练的环节，同时我们也不摈弃其他模式，如：增加了利用网络查询知识点等网络自主化学习的模式，使学生在使用语言中获得技能。

4. 该套教材倡导学生自主学习。我们不仅在每册目录中，为学生提供了一份内容框架图，其中包括每一单元文章的主题、体裁、语言难点、语法重点、阅读技能、翻译技能及写作技能的要求。同时，还在每单元开始之前列出本单元具体的教学目标和课文导读，学生既可以有目的地去学习，也可在每一单元学习结束后检查自己对所要求内容掌握的情况。

5. 坚持选材的真实性、趣味性和前瞻性。阅读图文并茂，听力材料有真实背景音，使学生置身于更真实的语言环境中。注重将知识性和趣味性相结合，充分调动学生的学习热情和主观能动性。将替换掉的文章用最新的时文来取代，以体现语言的时代感，与时俱进。

6. 在课文选材的长度和词汇要求方面，严格按《大学英语课程教学要求》的尺度来衡量。对积极词汇有标示和演练。

7. 练习在总体设计方面以国内外外语教学理论为指导，形式采用流行的 task-based approach，并力求最大限度地培养学生的思维能力即：thinking skills。

8. 学练结合，强调可操练性，让学生在学中练，练中学。练习紧密结合课文内容合理编排设计。课文是范例，是学生模仿的对象，在掌握课文的基础上，学生要举一反三，直至掌握范例中的语言技巧。听、说、读、写、译各项技能既独立操作又互相渗透，以培养学生综合的语言技能和语言运用的能力。

9. 翻译和写作不仅有简明扼要的知识点讲解，还提供了与课文紧密结合的练习、学生真实译作的实例。并且，我们还在教参中提供了范文及比较详尽的评语和解释。

10. 教参具有较强的针对性和操作性，对每一教学步骤我们都提供了具体的参考意见。

11. 在配套 CD-ROM 中，适当扩充趣味性内容，以及学习方法的引导。

教材内容：

本套第四版《新英语教程》包含《读写译》学生用书、教师用书；《听说》学生用书、教师用书。

PREFACE

《读写译》学生用书共 4 册,每册 8 个单元。每个单元包括 5 部分内容:

  1) 课文 A 及综合练习

  2) 翻译技巧及练习

  3) 写作技巧及练习

  4) 2 篇课文 B 及练习

  5) 阅读技巧

《读写译》教师用书共 4 册,内容包括:

  1) 课文背景知识介绍

  2) 课堂组织建议

  3) 语言难点解析

  4) 练习答案

  5) 写作范文及解析

  6) 翻译参考答案及解析

  7) 精泛读课文参考译文

《听说》学生用书共 4 册,每册 16 个单元,两套测试题。《听说》除更换了 30% 的内容外,还相当程度地增加了说的比重。《听说》教师用书分为四册,内容包括:

  1) 课文背景知识介绍

  2) 课堂组织建议

  3) 语言难点解析

  4) 练习答案

  5) 听力原文资料

  第四版《新英语教程》在编写过程中得到了清华大学外语系、清华大学教务处及清华大学出版社的大力支持,也得到了一些兄弟院校的鼓励和非常有建设性的意见和建议。在此我们谨向有关单位和同仁表示最衷心的感谢!在《新英语教程》第四版出版之际,编委会特向《新英语教程》第一版、第二版及第三版的编者们表示最诚挚的谢意，感谢他们近二十年来为《新英语教程》所付出的关爱、劳动和智慧。

最后，我们真诚地欢迎我们的前辈、同行对这套教材的缺点和不足提出宝贵的意见和建议。

《新英语教程》（第四版）编写委员会

2005年5月于清华园

使用说明

《新英语教程——读写译》(第四版)第二册供大学英语一年级下学期的学生使用。本教程除了着重培养阅读能力外,还分别增加了写、译的指导和练习,以期加强对学生读写译综合应用能力的培养。

第四版保持了第三版的基本框架和主要特点。本册共8个单元,每个单元由 PART A, PART B 和 PART C 三个部分组成,一般可安排4—6个学时完成。

PART A 为精读部分,课文有一定的难度,课文长度约在350—950词之间,生词率在6%上下,主要用来训练学生准确理解的能力(READING FOR ACCURACY),培养学生准确无误地进行书面交际的本领,同时也是扩大学生词汇量、进一步熟悉各种句型和语法规则、掌握语言技能及提高、培养学生语言表达能力的重要途径。

PART B 为泛读部分。各单元的 PART B 在文体和内容上与 PART A 有密切联系,其中大部分文章难度有所降低,生词密度较小,趣味性较强。该部分的主要目的是扩大学生阅读量和训练学生阅读的流畅性(READING FOR FLUENCY),同时对精读部分所学知识和能力起到巩固、加深和检验的作用,是 PART A 的重要补充和延伸。

PART C 为阅读中学习方法或技能指导部分。本册侧重复合词、识别段落和语篇的中心思想、转换词、获取隐含信息等。

第四版阅读第二册修订的主要内容如下:
1. 第二册中的8个单元更新了30%的课文,用具有时代感、趣味性、知识性和思想性更强的材料替代了第三版的部分内容。其中 Unit 1BI, Unit 2BII, Unit 3BI, Unit 6A, BI 和 Unit 8A, BI, BII 为新内容。
2. 根据全国大学外语教学指导委员会英语组 2004 年 7 月审定的《高

等学校本科用)《大学英语课程教学要求》(试行)的精神,同时也参照了中学英语大纲(2005年版)中对词汇的新要求,适当增加和调整了各单元的词汇量。

本书对重点词汇采用英汉双解,对于其他难于用简易英语注释的词则只用汉语注释。纲内一般要求词汇为黑体,要求掌握。词汇前加星号的为较高要求词汇,加三角的为更高要求词汇。纲外词为斜体,不要求掌握。本书对积极词汇进行了特殊标注,为彩色粗体。在总词汇表中对不同的词汇的注解与课文中一致,尤其突出对积极词汇的注解。整个注音体系与中学教材一致。英美语在读音和拼写上有明显区别的词均加以注明,此外书中还附有英美语读音区别表,供使用者参考。分课词汇表按课文中出现的先后列出,书后总词汇表则按字母顺序排列,并在词后注明出现的课次。

纲内词组在本书的词组表中用黑体标记,纲外词组未做特殊标记。

全册共计567个新出现的一般要求词汇(中学除外),其中本册首次出现的积极词汇达248个,较高要求词汇83个,更高要求词汇48个。符合大纲要求,其分布情况详见表1。

表1 各单元大纲一般要求词汇(不包括中学词汇)分布情况

Unit \ PART	A	BI	BII	Total
1	29	28	19	76
2	30	27	31	88
3	19	32	16	67
4	30	12	29	71
5	20	20	18	58
6	15	24	20	59
7	20	29	10	59
8	39	22	28	89
∑	202	194	171	567

3. 重新设计全书的练习，根据《大学英语课程教学要求》的精神，增加了主观练习题的分量，尤其是根据课文内容，充实了紧密联系生活中阅读技巧的练习内容，提高了练习的质量和实用性。完善了练习的形式，使每个练习的教学目的明确，有的放矢。

   A. 学生用书设计了 Pre-Read Activities 并沿用了 While-Reading Questions，放在相应行后的页边空白处，这样的设计有助于培养学生良好的阅读习惯，同时也使他们对课文的理解更深入、更透彻。需要指出的是：这些问题不仅仅局限于对内容的理解，还涉及对语言本身的理解和把握。因为我们认为作为精读教材，我们的课本不仅要培养学生的阅读能力，更重要的是要帮助他们打下坚实的语言基础。

   B. PART A 后面的练习分为：Pre-Reading、Reading Comprehension、Vocabulary、Grammar、Writing 和 Translation 等。

   C. Vocabulary 一项中新增加了利用重点词汇和短语造句、完成句子等练习，大大提高了对词汇掌握的要求。

   D. Translation 和 Writing 两项为本版的全新内容。分别系统地介绍了翻译和写作技巧，并结合课文内容配有相应练习。翻译技巧系统且理论联系实际，趣味性强。写作练习则从学生的实际水平出发，重点讲解了为什么学生的原文有缺陷，怎么改，尤其是为什么作这些改动。这使得写作练习突出了教与学之间的沟通，是第四版教材的一个主要特色。

各单元阅读量分布情况如表 2 所示。

表2 各单元阅读量分布情况

PART Unit	A	BI	BII	C	Total
1	695	510	407	150	1762
2	937	1067	683	750	3437
3	711	819	498	750	2778
4	703	714	549	1160	3126
5	458	604	527	500	2089
6	618	702	547	530	2397
7	631	1587	1130	530	3878
8	855	848	687	400	2790
∑	5608	6851	5028	4770	22257

　　本册是在第三版《新英语教程——阅读》的基础上修订的。本版编者为邢如、沈明波、杨芳、覃学岚、张文霞。程慕胜教授、刘平梅教授、罗力胜教授、吕中舌教授、陈永国教授及在清华大学外语系工作的美籍教师 David Peck 审阅了全部书稿，对本书指出了不少宝贵的建议和指导。

　　在《新英语教程》第四版出版之际，谨向上述专家和所有参与样课讨论的校内外的同事们和专家以及支持本版修订工作的专家、学者表示衷心地感谢。对第三版第二册的编者温少霞和周允程老师表示最诚挚的谢意。

　　由于编写时间仓促，编者热忱欢迎兄弟院校的使用者对本书的缺点和不足之处提出批评和指正。

编　者

2005 年 5 月

符号说明

1. 圆括号( )

    1) 是词义的一部分。例如：现实（主义）的。意思是"现实的"或"现实主义的"。

    2) 圆括号内是词形变化。例如：knit (knitted 或 knitting)。

    3) 圆括号内是该词要求的介词搭配。例如：frown 不满，不赞成 (on)。

    4) 加注语法或使用说明等方面的补充说明。例如：(常用被动语态)。

2. / / 内是国际音标。例如：vain /vein/。

3. 代字号（~）用于代表词条的本词。

4. 斜线号（/）用于表示其前后两部分是任选关系。例如：progress *vi. /n.* 表示该词条可用作不及物动词（*vi.*）或名词（*n.*）。

5. 连词符 -

    连词符用于表示省略了前面相同的部分，如：criterion (*pl.*) -ria, -rions

SHORT FORMS

缩略语对照表

a.	adjective
ad.	adverb
AmE.	American English
&	and
aux.	auxiliary verb
BrE.	British English
cap.	capitalized
cf.	compare
conj.	conjunction
e.g.	for example
esp.	especially
etc.	et cetera; and so on
fml	formal
i.e.	that is
infml	informal
interj.	interjection
n.	noun
num.	numeral
pl.	plural
par.	paragraph
prep.	preposition
pron.	pronoun
sing.	singular
sb.	somebody
sth.	something
usu.	usually
v.	verb
vi.	verb intransitive
vt.	verb transitive

DIFFERENCES BETWEEN RP[1] & GA[2]

英音与美音音标对照表

RP	GA	EXAMPLES
[ɑː]	[æ]	'after, half, dance, 'answer, staff, fast, pass, past, bath, 'rather
[ɔ]	[ɑ]	got, box, 'dollar, 'obstacle, 'colonist, 'colleague, 'constant, 'content
[ʌ]	[ə]	love, son, done, young, 'worry, cut, fun, sun, re'sult, 'hurry
	[i]	'missile, 'fragile
[ai]	[ə]	civili'sation(AmE civili'zation), moderni'sation(AmE moderni'zation)
[w]	[hw]	what, when, where, 'whether, 'somewhere
[juː]	[uː]	do due, pro'duce, re'duce, tube, tune, 'student, en'thusiasm, as'sume, pre'sume, new, news, knew
[ɑː]	[ar]	car, 'farmer, dark
[ɔː]	[ɔːr]	or, for, more, sort, re'corder, ac'cording
[əː]	[əːr]	'certain, 'thermos bird, sir, firm fur, 'surface, 'urgent
[ə]	[ər]	'smaller, 'sister, dis'coverer 'dollar 'doctor, in'ventor
[iə]	[ir]	ear, hear, year, here
[eə]	[er]	air, hair, fair, there, dare, care, aware
[uə]	[ur]	poor, tour, 'tourist
[əri]	[ˌeri]	'neces'sary, 'ordi'nary, 'pri'mary, 'secon'dary
[əni]	[ˌouni]	'cere'mony, 'har'mony

1. **RP (Received Pronunciation):** a form of *BrE* accent which may be regarded as standard and as a model for foreign learners.
2. **GA (General American):** a form of American pronunciation which may be taken as a model, comparable with RP in *BrE*.

CONTENTS

Unit

1 On English Language — 1

Readings
A: Speech Communities
BI: Graduates Spoil Job Chances with Spelling Mistakes
BII: Our Crazy Language

Genre/Style
Exposition

Word Power
The Usage of "As"

Grammar Focus
Gerund
Partial Negation

Reading Skill
Compound Words

Writing Skill
Classification

Translation Skill
Splitting and Combining (1)

2 Campus Life — 33

Readings
A: University Days
BI: The Real Test
BII: Students Learn to Cheat

Genre/Style
Narration
Description

Word Power
Figures of Speech

Grammar Focus
The Usages of "Would"

Reading Skill
Reading for the Main Idea

Writing Skill
Description (2)

Translation Skill
Splitting and Combining (2)

3 Cultural Differences   67

Readings
A: Space
BI: US-French Bickering: Tradition, Not News
BII: Getting Along Verbally and Nonverbally

Genre/Style
Exposition
Argumentation

Word Power
"To" Used as a Preposition

Grammar Focus
Prepositions
Adverbs

Reading Skill
Reading for the Implied Main Idea

Writing Skill
Exemplification

Translation Skill
Splitting and Combining (3)

4 On Relations   99

Readings
A: Thanksgiving
BI: Why I Want a Wife
BII: October and June

Genre/Style
Exposition

Word Power
Antonyms

Grammar Focus
The Word "While"
Parallelism

Reading Skill
The Organization of a Discourse

Writing Skill
Comparison and Contrast

Translation Skill
Shift/Conversion (2)

Contents

Unit 5 Living a Full Life 133

Readings
A: Dreams
BI: How to Live Beautifully
BII: The Lost Gold Piece

Genre/Style
Exposition
Argumentation

Word Power
Antonyms

Grammar Focus
Subjunctive Mood

Reading Skill
Transition Words (1)

Writing Skill
Simple Definitions

Translation Skill
Shift/Conversion (3)

Unit 6 On Personal Qualities 163

Readings
A: Man at His Best
BI: Emotions Help with Success
BII: What Is Intelligence, Anyway?

Genre/Style
Exposition
Narration

Word Power
Phrasal verbs

Grammar Focus
Past Continuous Tense

Reading Skill
Transition Words (2)

Writing Skill
Cause and Effect

Translation Skill
Translation of English Pronouns

7 Stories of a Pet, a Young Writer 191

Readings
A: The Capybara
BI: The Luncheon
BII: After Twenty Years

Genre/Style
Narration
Description

Word Power
The Word "Wake" and Its Synonyms

Grammar Focus
Introductory "It" in Cleft Sentences

Reading Skill
Transition Words (3)

Writing Skill
The Beginning of an Essay

Translation Skill
Translation of English Prepositions

8 Enthusiasm for Work 227

Readings
A: How to Be True to You
BI: Michael Jordan's Farewell Letter to Basketball
BII: A Pair of Socks

Genre/Style
Exposition
Narration

Word Power
Measure Word

Grammar Focus
Noun Clauses

Reading Skill
Inferring the Author's Views and Attitudes

Writing Skill
The Ending of an Essay

Translation Skill
Repetition

Unit 1

On English Language

Aims and Objectives

In this unit you will learn:
1. Genre/Style: Exposition
2. Word Power: The Usage of "As"
3. Grammar Focus: Gerund/Partial Negation
4. Writing Skill: Classification
5. Translation Skill: Splitting and Combing (1)
6. Reading Skill: Compound Words

Brief Introductions to the Texts

The passages in this unit deal with the English language.

The first passage talks about speech communities, especially the English speech community, and emphasizes the significance of learning a second language.

The second passage alerts readers to a serious problem facing UK higher education: the falling standard in graduate literacy, which is revealed in spelling and grammar mistakes in CVs.

In the third passage, the author discusses, with a sense of humor, some very interesting points in English to show that language cannot be judged merely according to rules of logic.

On English Language

Part A — Intensive Reading

Pre-Reading

Task 1

Learning English is very popular among Chinese people. Why do they put in so much time and effort to improve English? Here are a list of reasons:

- With increasing cultural contact, English has become an important means of communication with foreigners.
- English is one of the most important qualifications in the job market.
- English is one of the biggest barriers to going abroad and studying in English-speaking countries.
- A knowledge of English is crucial if one wants to keep up-to-date with the literature (printed in English) in his/ her field.
- English is a required subject at school.

What's your purpose for learning English? Have a discussion with your partner about it.

Task 2

How long have you been studying English? Do you enjoy it? Look back on your study of English and decide which of the following words best describes your feeling.

A. interesting   B. boring   C. painful   D. _____ (your own answer)

Like it or not, English is of vital importance to us. Have a discussion with your partner about the strategies you use to learn English.

English Learning Strategies			
Listening	Speaking	Reading	Writing
English videos	go to an English corner	newspapers	keep a journal in English

Part A

Intensive Reading

Reading and Thinking

Speech Communities

There is no denying that English is a useful language. The people who speak English today make up the largest speech community in the world with the exception of speakers of Chinese. Originally they were small tribes of people living in northern Europe who left
5 their homelands and settled in England. Isolated in their island community, the various tribes used languages which became more and more similar to each other and less and less like the other languages of Europe. Eventually, the language had enough uniformity to be used by all speakers in England. The people were united into a speech
10 community through their shared language. In time, people moved from the small island to many parts of the world, taking their language with them and thus still remaining members of the English speech community wherever they settled.

Do you think English is a useful language? Why?

A speech community is similar to other kinds of communities.
15 The people who make up the community share a common language. Often they live side by side, as they do in a neighborhood, a village, or a city. More often they form a whole country. Many nations are

How does the author define a speech community?

composed of a single major speech community, for example, Italy, Sweden[1], and Japan. National boundaries, however, are not always
20 the same as the boundaries of a speech community. Some nations (for example, Russia[2] and India) are made up of many speech communities. Some speech communities (for example, Arabic[3], Spanish, and

---

1. **Sweden** /ˈswiːdn/ a country in northern Europe 瑞典
2. **Russia** /ˈrʌʃə/ a country in eastern Europe and northern Asia 俄罗斯
3. **Arabic** /ˈærəbik/ language of the Arabs 阿拉伯语

Unit 1 On English Language

English) extend across national boundaries. A speech community, then, is any group of people who speak the same language no matter where they happen to live.

We may say that anyone who speaks English belongs to the English speech community. For convenience, we may classify the speakers into two groups: one in which the speakers use English as their native language, the other in which the speakers learn English as a second language for the purposes of education, commerce, and so on. In the former group we, obviously, would include England, Canada, the United States, Australia[1], and New Zealand[2]. Naturally, not all people in these countries speak English natively, but a large majority do. In the latter groups we would include among many others, India, Denmark[3], Kenya[4], Turkey, Ethiopia[5], and the Philippines[6]. Not all these countries use English for the same purpose or to the same extent, but each uses English for important social and commercial activities.

English serves as a functional alternative language in several areas of public activity for the many nations of the world which use it as an international second language. Because of its widespread use geographically, and because of the large number of people who speak it, it has been adopted as the language of aviation and air traffic. English has continued as one of the important languages of commerce, as the sphere of political and economic influence of the English-speaking nations has extended beyond the boundaries of England. The use of English in international diplomacy is strengthened by its acceptance as one of the official languages of the United Nations. And as a final example, English is the language of the majority of published materials in the world so that education, especially specialised higher education, has come to rely heavily on an understanding of English. In no sense

> According to the author, in how many fields does English play an important role? What are they?

---

1. **Australia** /ɔsˈtreiljə/ a country and continent in the southern half of the globe 澳大利亚；澳洲
2. **New Zealand** /njuːˈziːlənd/ a country in the south Pacific 新西兰
3. **Denmark** /ˈdenmɑːk/ a country in northern Europe 丹麦
4. **Kenya** /ˈkenjə/ a country in East Africa 肯尼亚
5. **Ethiopia** /ˌiːθiˈəupjə/ a country in northeast Africa 埃塞俄比亚
6. **Philippines** /ˈfilipiːnz/ a country in eastern Asia 菲律宾

does English replace the cultural heritage and emotional ties of the first language, but for many speakers throughout the world, it provides a means of communication with people of similar training and interests who would otherwise not comprehend them.

Learning a second language extends one's vision and expands the mind. Looking at the world or oneself through a different language system shows the limits of one's own perception and adds new dimensions to familiar objects or events. A second language teaches us different ways of labeling and organizing our experiences. The history and literature of a second language record the real and fictional lives of a people and their culture; a knowledge of them adds to our ability to understand and to feel as they feel. Learning English as a second language provides another means of communication through which the window of the entire English speech community becomes a part of our heritage. (695 words)

> What do "who" and "them" refer to respectively?

> What does "people" mean here?

NEW WORDS

community	/kəˈmjuːniti/	n.	a group with shared origins or interest 团体，界；社区，社会；（动植物的）群落
deny	/diˈnai/	vt.	to say that sth. is not true 否认；拒绝给予，拒绝……的要求
exception	/ikˈsepʃən/	n.	sb. or sth. that is not included 例外
★ tribe	/traib/	n.	a group of people united by race and customs under the same leader 部落；族（生物分类）
homeland	/ˈhəumlænd/	n.	one's native land 祖国，故乡
eventually	/iˈventjuəli/	ad.	at last 终于，最后
uniformity	/juːniˈfɔːmiti/	n.	all parts being the same 同样，一致，均匀
neighborhood	/ˈneibəhud/	n.	a district or an area with distinctive characteristics 邻近地区，附近；四邻，街坊
compose	/kəmˈpəuz/	v.	to make up, to form (sth.) by putting sth. together 组成；创作（乐曲、诗歌等）；使平静，使镇静
boundary	/ˈbaundəri/	n.	border, the limiting or dividing line of surfaces or

Unit 1 On English Language

			spaces 边界，界线
convenience	/kən'viːnjəns/	n.	the state or quality of being easily accomplished 方便，合宜；便利设施
classify	/'klæsifai/	vt.	to divide according to class, to arrange or place into classes 把……分类，把……分级
obviously	/'ɔbviəsli/	ad.	it can be easily seen (that), plainly 明显地，显而易见地
latter	/'lætə/	a.	second (of two people or things just spoken of) 后者的；末了的
		n.	后者
extent	/iks'tent/	n.	the degree to which a thing extends 程度，范围；广度，宽度
commercial	/kə'məːʃəl/	a.	of commerce 商业的,商务的
		n.	商业广告
activity	/æk'tiviti/	n.	movement or action 活动，行动；活跃，活力
functional	/'fʌŋkʃənl/	a.	of a function; having, designed to have, functions 职责的，功能的，机能的；有作用的，有功能的
alternative	/ɔːl'təːnətiv/	a.	(of two or more things) that may be used, had, done, etc., instead of another 两者择一的，供选择的，供替代的
		n.	取舍，抉择；选择的自由
widespread	/'waidspred/	a.	spread over a large area or among many people 分布广的，普遍的
geographically	/ˌdʒiə'ɡræfikli/	ad.	地理地
★aviation	/ˌeivi'eiʃən/	n.	(art and science of) flying an aircraft 航空，飞行；飞机制造业
sphere	/sfiə/	n.	range of activities 范围，领域；球体
economic	/ˌiːkə'nɔmik/	a.	connected with trade, industry, and wealth; of or concerning economics 经济的；经济学的
diplomacy	/di'pləuməsi/	n.	management of a country's affairs by its official representatives abroad 外交
strengthen	/'streŋθən/	vt.	to make or become strong or stronger 加强，巩固
acceptance	/ək'septəns/	n.	the act of accepting, taking sth. offered 接受，接纳；承认；容忍

Part A
Intensive Reading

rely	/ri'lai/	vi.	(*on, upon*) to depend on with confidence 依赖，依靠；对……有信心
replace	/ri'pleis/	vt.	to take the place of 代替，取代；把……放回原处
★heritage	/'heritidʒ/	n.	that has been or may be received from one's ancestors 遗产，传统
emotional	/i'məuʃənl/	a.	of or directed to the emotions 情感的, 情绪的, 诉诸情感的
▲comprehend	/ˌkɔmpri'hend/	vt.	to understand fully 理解
vision	/'viʒən/	n.	ability to see 视力，视觉，视野；想象力，幻想
perception	/pə'sepʃn/	n.	process by which we become aware of changes (through the sense of sight, hearing, etc.) 感觉，知觉；认识，观念，看法
dimension	/di'menʃən/	n.	size; aspect 尺寸，大小; 方面
label	/leibl/	vt.	to classify, put into classes 将……分类；贴标签于
		n.	标签，标记；称号
fictional	/'fikʃənəl/	a.	of sth. invented or imagined, not real 虚构的, 想象的
ability	/ə'biliti/	n.	power to do sth. physically or mentally 能力；才能

PHRASES

make up	to make by putting things together 构成，组成
with the exception of	except, not including 除……以外
settle in	to (cause to) start living in (a place) (使)定居在……
in time	eventually, after a while; soon enough 后来，最后；及时
side by side	one beside the other in a row 一个接一个
be composed of	be made up of 由……组成
for convenience	in order to save trouble 为了方便起见
come to	to begin to 开始……
rely on	to depend on 依靠
in no sense	绝不（是）

7

Unit 1 On English Language

EXERCISES

Reading Comprehension

Task 3

Complete the following diagram to make a brief outline of the article.

Par. 1 Formation of _____	Par. 2 Definition of a _____
Par. 3 Classification of English speakers into two groups. 1._____ 2._____	Par. 4 _____ of English in many fields of public activity in the world: 1. as the language of aviation and air traffic 2. as _____ 3. in _____ 4. as _____

Par. 5 (Concluding paragraph) Learning a second language _____ and _____

Task 4

Are the following statements true or false? Mark "T" before a true statement and "F" before a false one.

_____ 1. There is no doubt that speakers of English form the largest speech community in the world.

_____ 2. Early settlers in England came from northern Europe.

_____ 3. All the nations in the world are made up of a single speech community.

_____ 4. A speech community is made up of people who speak the same language.

_____ 5. All people in England and the United States use English as their native language.

_____ 6. Because of its widespread use internationally, English will take the place of other languages and become the only language in the world.

_____ 7. Like national boundaries, there exist the boundaries of speech communities.

_____ 8. Just as speakers of English belong to the English speech community, all Chinese people belong to the Chinese speech community.

Part A
Intensive Reading

_____ 9. Having been accepted as one of the official languages of the United Nations, English is widely used in international diplomacy.

_____ 10. Whether English serves as a second language or a foreign language, learning English extends one's vision and expands the mind.

vocabulary

Task 5

Choose from Column B words or phrases that are close in meaning to those in Column A. There are some extra items in Column B.

A	B
1. refuse to accept	a. isolate
2. shut off	b. classify
3. depend on	c. boundary
4. take the place of	d. comprehend
5. understand	e. major
6. label	f. commerce
7. trade	g. widespread
8. border	h. deny
9. general	i. eventually
10. formerly	j. rely on
11. finally	k. replace
	l. obviously
	m. originally

Task 6

Match the following phrases with their Chinese equivalents.

1. walk side by side	a. 高等教育
2. leave one's homeland	b. 定居南美
3. for convenience	c. 背井离乡
4. official language	d. 并肩而行
5. extend one's vision	e. 为了方便起见
6. national boundary	f. 开阔视野
7. higher education	g. 官方语言
8. settle in South America	h. 国界

Unit 1 On English Language

Task 7

Using its proper form, choose the correct word to fit each sentence.

1. late, later, latest, latter
   a. Better _____ than never.
   b. Peter has a brother and a sister: the former is studying at Cambridge University, the _____ is in primary school.
   c. Have you heard the _____ news about the Smiths?
2. economic, economical, economy
   a. There's an increasing demand for cars which are more _____ on fuel.
   b. Tourism contributes millions of pounds to the country's _____.
   c. The country has been in a very poor _____ state ever since the decline of its two major industries.
   d. She writes with such _____ — I've never known a writer to say so much in so few words.
3. to strengthen, to sharpen, to widen, to enrich, to lengthen
   a. The wind _____ during the night.
   b. Learning foreign languages _____ our mind and extends our vision.
   c. Cold weather _____ the pain in my knee.
   d. Our culture has been _____ by immigrants from many other countries.
4. except, exception, to expect, expectation
   a. All healthy men between 18 and 45, without _____, are expected to serve in the army during the war.
   b. The house is in perfect condition, _____ for a few scratches on one of the doors.
   c. I _____ him home after five o'clock.
5. to rely, reliable
   a. John is very _____ — if he says he'll do something he'll do it.
   b. The success of this project _____ on everyone making an effort.
   c. Nowadays we _____ increasingly on computers to regulate the flow of traffic in the town.
6. to compose, composer, composition
   a. The music was specially _____ for the film.
   b. Air _____ mainly of nitrogen and oxygen.
   c. The _____ has to be at least three pages long.
   d. She had to sit down a moment and _____ herself before going on.
   e. A _____ is a person who writes music, especially classical music.

7. to accept, acceptable, acceptance, accepted
   a. Clearly we need to come to an arrangement that is _____ to both parties.
   b. It is doubtful whether this proposal will obtain general _____.
   c. He asked her to marry him and she _____ his proposal.

Task 8

Choose from among words and expressions listed below to replace the underlined ones, making necessary changes.

| with the exception of | classify | serve as | compose |
| there is no denying | in no sense | community | ability |

1. <u>Everyone must admit that</u> this has been a difficult year for the company.
2. <u>Except</u> for the weather it was a perfect holiday.
3. At the end of the Vietnam war, women <u>made up</u> only 1.6% of the US forces, but the percentage is much higher now.
4. The judge said that the fine would <u>function as</u> a warning to other motorists who drove without due care and attention.
5. The job of a politician is to serve the <u>society</u>.
6. She is fond of playing basketball, but <u>by no means</u> does she wish to become a professional athlete.
7. She has the <u>capacity</u> to summarize an argument in a few words.
8. The books in the library are <u>grouped</u> according to subject.

Task 9

Cloze: Fill in the blanks with appropriate words. The first letter(s) of each expected word is given to help you.

English is spoken as a native language by more than 300 million people, most of them living in North America, the British Isles (群岛), Australia, New Zealand, the Caribbean, and South Africa. In several (1) o___ these regions (地区), English is not the only (2) l___. But those whose (3) n___ language is not English will have English as their (4) s___ language for certain governmental, (5) co___, social, or educational (6) ac___ within their own country. English is also a second language in many countries (7) w___ only a small (8) pr___ of the people have English (9) a___ their native language. In about twenty-five countries, English has been (10) le___ designated (指定) as an (11) o___ language: in about ten of them, it is the (12) on___ official language, and in some fifteen (13) ot___ it shares that (14) st___ with one or more other languages. Most of these countries are (15) f___ British territories (领土).

Unit 1 On English Language

Task 10

Translate the following sentences into English, using the words or phrases given in the brackets.

1. 讲英语和汉语的人构成了世界上最大的两个言语群体，不过就人数而论，后者要比前者大得多。言语群体是指无论居住在何地而讲同一种语言的任何人群。为（叙述）方便起见，我们可将讲英语的人分成两部分：一部分以英语为母语，另一部分以英语为第二语言。(make up / compose, as far as ... be concerned, classify)

2. 无可否认，学习外语既能扩大视野，又能拓宽思路。因此校学生会决定每逢周末举办"英语角"。(deny, vision, the Students' Union)

Grammar

Task 11

Identify the usage of "as" in the following sentences and translate them into Chinese.

1. As he grew older he lost interest in everything except gardening.
2. As I was just saying, I think the proposal needs further consideration.
3. With modern technology, even babies weighing as little as 1 kilogram at birth can survive.
4. Talented as he is, he is not yet ready to turn professional.
5. They entered the building disguised as cleaners.
6. As you weren't there I left a message.
7. The earth pulls things to it just as a magnet pulls needles.
8. They used the same type of machines as we did.

Task 12

Fill in the blanks with the words listed below, using their "-ing" forms, and translate the sentences into Chinese.

deny, talk, know, reason (with), try

Model: There is no denying the fact that modern cars are simply not built to last.

1. There's no _____ with him when he is in that sort of mood (心情).
2. She's completely unpredictable; there's no _____ what she will do next.
3. There's no _____ that recent inventions and discoveries have greatly affected our society.
4. It's no use _____ to escape — no one has ever gotten away before.
5. It's no good _____ to him, because he never listens.

Part A

Intensive Reading

Extra Reading

Task 13

Read the following two introductions and answer the six questions that follow for both a. and b.

a.

A Survey of Modern English

Stephan Gramley and **Michael Paetzold**, both at Bielefeld University, Germany

'This second edition of *A Survey of Modern English* is an admirable achievement in providing its readers with concise, but nevertheless comprehensive and clearly written introductions to the main areas of English linguistics. Its coverage is most impressive, and this text is warmly recommended as an indispensable study companion and reference work.' – *Bas Aarts, University College London*

'An indispensable companion for university students of English Language and Linguistics, with an accessible style and impressive range of subject matter.' – *Howard Jackson, University of Central England*

Fully revised and updated, the second edition of this authoritative guide is a comprehensive, scholarly and systematic review of modern English. In one volume the book presents a description of both the linguistic structure of present-day English and its geographical, social, gender and ethnic variations. Covering new developments such as the impact of email on language and corpus-based grammars, this accessible text has been extensively rewritten and brings the survey of modern English right up to date. Offering new examples and suggestions for further reading, the book is essential reading for all students of English language and linguistics.

2003: 234x156: 416pp
Hb: 0-415-30034-7: **£60.00**
Pb: 0-415-30035-5: **£19.99**
eB: 0-203-40855-1: **£19.99**

• AVAILABLE AS AN INSPECTION COPY

b.

A History of the English Language

Albert C. Baugh, formerly of the University of Pennsylvania, USA and **Thomas Cable**, University of Texas at Austin, USA

'The fifth edition of *A History of the English Language* will continue to be the standard reference work on the history of English.'
– *Peter Erdmann, Technische Universität Berlin*

'Baugh & Cable's classic is still an absolute must for everyone interested in the development of English in its socio-historical context. Revised and updated, this edition continues to provide an engaging biography of a living and dynamic language.' – *Ishtla Singh, Kings College, London*

A History of the English Language is a comprehensive exploration of the linguistic and cultural development of English, from the Middle Ages to the present day. The book provides students with a balanced and up-to-date overview of the history of the language.

The fifth edition has been substantially revised and updated to keep students up to date with recent developments in the field.

Enhanced features include:

• revised first chapter: 'English present and future'
• new section on gender issues and linguistic change
• updated material on African-American vernacular English.

2002: 234x156: 464pp: illus. 3 line drawings and 3 b+w photos
Hb: 0-415-28098-2: **£60.00**
Pb: 0-415-28099-0: **£17.99**

• AVAILABLE AS AN INSPECTION COPY

Unit 1 On English Language

1. Where are the authors from? _____
2. Who offered favourable comments on the book? _____
3. Who are the target readers of the book? _____
4. How many pages does it have? _____
5. How much is the hardcover? _____
6. How much is the paperback? _____

分类法 (Classification)

分类就是按照事物的不同特点将它们划成多个类别。事物可以按照不同的标准进行分类,标准则取决于分类的成因。例如,在分析某系学生的构成情况时,如果想了解他们的学习情况,可以将他们根据考试成绩划分为若干组;如果想研究是否有可能组织一场足球比赛或是篮球比赛,可以根据对足球和篮球的爱好程度把学生划分成若干组。

不管分类的目的是什么,分类的标准必须具有普适性和排他性,也就是说分类标准必须覆盖分类样本集中的所有样本元素,而且样本集中的任一元素只能隶属于分类标准项次中的惟一一项。例如,把学生分成男生、女生和运动员是不合适的,这一标准违反了排他性原则,因为某个学生可能是男生的同时又是运动员,他占据了两个分类项次。再如,把学生分成中学生和大学生在有些情况下也不一定合适,该标准违反了普适性原则,即有些学生既不是中学生也不是大学生(如小学生)。

表示分类的名词:
种:kind, sort, type
类:group, classification, category
组成成员:member
分部/分支:division/branch
纲:class   目:order   科:family   属:genus   种:species

Part A
Intensive Reading

表示分类的动词和动词短语：
将……按……分类（排序）：class, classify, divide, categorize, group, place, arrange
属于某一类：belong to, fall into, be classed with
包括若干类：there be, contain, consist of, comprise, include, be composed of, be comprised of
组成……类：make up, constitute, compose

Task 14

1. Read the following passages and discuss whether they follow the classification criterion of exclusiveness and inclusiveness.

Passage 1:

There are two main branches of electrical engineering. One is concerned with the generation of electricity to meet the power and light needs of cities and industries. The other covers the application of small amounts of power for communication and various other purposes.

Passage 2:

We usually think of bees as being sociable insects which live in communities, but this is not always true. One way of classifying bees is by "social" and "solitary" species, and there are many of the latter. Bumble bees (野蜂) and honey bees are social species. Among solitary bees there are primitive wasp like bees, medium-sized solitary mining bees, so-called sweat bees, carpenter bees and cuckoo bees.

2. Read the following passage, and fill in the blanks with appropriate words.

In Britain, state schools can be classified according to the age range of the pupils and the type of education provided. Basically, there are two types of schools: primary and secondary. Primary schools cater to (满足需要) children age 5—11 and secondary schools ages 11—16 (and up to 19). Primary schools can be sub-divided into infant schools (for age 5—7) and junior schools (for age 7—11). Secondary schools may be one type for all abilities, viz.(即) comprehensive schools; most secondary schools are of this kind. Alternatively, pupils may be grouped according to their ability and selected by means of an examination at age 11 (known as the "11-plus exam"). Thus, grammar schools cater to those with academic ability; modern schools for those with less academic ability; and technical schools for those with more practical skills.

1) Schools _____ the pupils' ages and the types of education.
2) There are _____ schools: primary and secondary.
3) Primary schools _____ into infant and junior schools.

Unit 1 On English Language

4) Secondary schools pupils _____ their ability.

5) The criterion (标准) for classifying secondary schools is whether or not there is _____.

Task 15

2. There are thousands of languages in the world. Languages are classified into different families according to their common attributes. Do you know which family English belongs to? Below is a language tree proposed by German linguistic August Schleicher (1821 — 1868). Please describe it using the classification method:

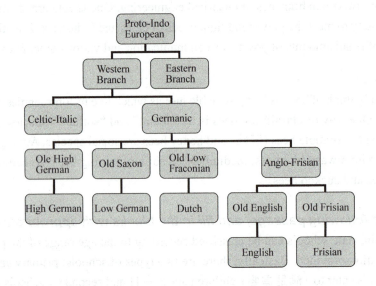

拆合法 (Splitting and Combining) (1)

拆合法实际上是拆译法和合译法的合称,拆译法是针对英译汉而言的,汉译英则多半与之背道而驰,采取合译法。

汉语强调意合，结构较松散，多用松散句、紧缩句、无主句、省略句、流水句或并列形式的复句（composite sentence），以中短句居多。书面语虽也用长句，但常用标点把句子切开，因而读起来舒缓、简短、轻松、活泼，无冗长之感，较之英语，仍属短句；英语强调形合，结构较严密，因此长句较多。所以汉译英时要根据需要注意利用连词、分词、介词、不定式、定语从句、独立结构等把汉语短句连成长句；而英译汉时又常常要在原句的关系代词、关系副词、主谓连接处、并列或转折连接处、后续成分与主体的连接处，以及意群结束处将长句切断，译成汉语分句。这样就可以基本保留英语语序，顺译全句，顺应现代汉语长短句相替、单复句相间的句法修辞原则。

拆合法是英汉互译的一项基本功。一般说来，英译汉时，如果长句不能很好地拆译成地道的中文短句，那么到了汉译英时，中文的短句也势必不可能翻译成地道的英文长句，这是一个相辅相成的问题。

拆合法，笼统地讲，就是在充分理解原文的基础上，摆脱原文的拘束，打破原文的句式结构，按照译入语的行文习惯重新组织句子，换言之，就是英译汉时把长句拆开来译，汉译英时则在分清主次的前提下，将分散的短语按照其在句中的功能和英语的组句规律合起来译。拆译法又可分为顺拆、倒拆、抽拆等多种方法，我们先从顺拆法谈起：

所谓顺拆法，就是把原句大致上按意群分成一个个片段，然后把这些片段按原来的顺序译出，适当垫进一些动词或虚词（补足语气或使上下文更好地得到衔接）或者根据需要加入一些标点，如：

- His delegation agreed with the executive director that the fund should continue working for a better understanding of the relationship between economic, social and demographic factors.

不会拆译法的译者笔下的译文可能是这样的：

他的代表团同意执行主任的关于该基金会应继续为更好地了解经济、社会和人口的相互关系而努力的意见。

有经验的译者碰到这样的原文，一般都会想办法将原文拆开来译：

他的代表团赞同执行主任的意见，认为该基金会应继续努力，以求更好地了解经济、社会和人口这三方面的相互关系。

两相比较，我们发现后一种译文只不过将前一种译文中的"关于"换成了动词"认为"，将"为"改成了"以求"，另外加入了"这三方面"和两个逗号，就将一个不太符合

Unit 1 On English Language

目的语（汉语）行文习惯的译文变成了一句地道的中文。像这种将原句按意群分成一个个片段，然后把这些片段基本按原来的顺序译出来的拆译法，可以称为顺拆法。顺拆法的要点是：片段之间往往需要填进一些词语或者标点，如本例中的"认为"等。

Task 16

Translate the following sentences into idiomatic Chinese, using the method you've learned.

1) There is no denying that English is a useful language.
2) A speech community, then, is any group of people who speak the same language no matter where they happen to live.
3) For convenience, we may classify the speakers into two groups: one in which the speakers use English as their native language, the other in which the speakers learn English as a second language for the purposes of education, commerce, and so on.
4) Because of its widespread use geographically, and because of the large number of people who speak it, it has been adopted as the language of aviation and air traffic.
5) Learning English as a second language provides another means of communication through which the window of the entire English speech community becomes a part of our heritage.

Quotation

Since no two languages are identical, either in the meanings given to corresponding symbols or in the ways in which such symbols are arranged in phrases and sentences, it stands to reason that there can be no absolute correspondence between languages. Hence there can be no fully exact translations.

— *Eugene Nida*

无论是就字符的意义而言，还是就遣词造句规则方式而言，世上都没有两种完全相同的语言，既如此，语言之间自然也就不可能存在完全的对应，所以，也就不可能有完全准确的翻译了。

——尤金·奈达

Part B Extensive Reading

I. Graduates Spoil Job Chances with Spelling Mistakes

By Helen Nugent

NINE out of ten graduates are turned down for a job because their CVs[1] are full of errors of spelling and grammar, according to a study released today.

Graduates and final-year students who are willing to get into debt by up to £21,000 in order to study at university are ill-equipped to get a job that will enable them to pay off their loans, Lewis, a public relations and marketing company, has found. It analysed more than 1,000 applications from undergraduates and graduates seeking trainee positions. More than 90 per cent of applicants had disqualified themselves before the end of the first page of the CV.

The worst application contained 17 spelling mistakes in the covering letter. Other graduates and students addressed their letters to the wrong person or referred to the wrong job.

Toni Castle, human resources director at Lewis, said: "In many ways the best educated people in this country are also the greenest when they leave higher education."

In an effort to capture the attention of a potential employer, many applicants had tried too hard, Lewis found. One graduate wrote: "I exist! I live! Seize me!" Another had burnt the edges of the CV, saying "As you can see from the singe marks on my application, I'm red-hot."

Lewis receives about 100 CVs each week, but contacts only a handful of applicants.

Even those selected for interview rarely secure a job. The survey found that many graduates had done little or no research into their chosen company. Miss Castle said: "This week a Swedish applicant demonstrated a better understanding of the UK media than his UK counterpart by knowing facts such as the differences in readership of *The Times*[2] and other national newspapers."

The poor standard of graduates attempting to enter the

---

1. **CV:** curriculum vitae 的缩写，履历，简历
2. ***The Times:*** 《泰晤士报》(英国)

Unit 1 On English Language

workforce will come as a blow to the Government, which wants to get 50 per cent of young
25 people into higher education by 2010. The survey's findings also undermine government assertions that degree-holders receive better pay later in life: ministers say that over their working lives graduates stand to earn £400,000 more than workers who did not attend university.

Lewis says that falling standards in graduate literacy also cast doubt on plans to increase tuition fees to £3,000 a year from 2006. Margaret Hodge[1], the Higher Education Minister, has
30 said that increased student debt is justified by graduates' higher incomes.

"On our evidence students are needlessly acquiring debt at university," Miss Castle said. "They're simply not acquiring the skills worthy of a job that will enable them to pay off their loans."

Chris Lewis, the founder of Lewis, added: "The falling standard of literacy is a most alarm-
35 ing development. In an age of increased course fees, this needs to be urgently addressed. How else can you explain this introduction from an arts graduate: 'I'm looking for a career in public relations.'"

A spokeswoman for the Department for Education and Skills[2] said: "Going to university is a shrewd investment for young people to make. The UK is renowned for the quality of higher
40 education." (510 words)

NEW WORDS

spoil /spɔil/	vt.	to destroy the value, quality or pleasure of, to ruin 损坏，破坏；宠坏，溺爱
	vi.	（食物）变质
	n.	[pl.] 战利品，掠夺物，赃物
error /ˈerə/	n.	a mistake 错误，差错
grammar /ˈɡræmə/	n.	语法（书）
loan /ləun/	n.	money lent at interest 贷款
	vt.	借出，贷给

---

1. **Margaret Hodge:** 玛格丽特·霍奇，现任英国教育技能部部长（Minister of State at the Department for Education and Skills）
2. **Department for Education and Skills:** 英国教育技能部

Part B
Extensive Reading

application /ˌæpliˈkeiʃən/	n.	formal request 申请，申请表；应用，实施；敷用，涂抹
trainee /treiˈniː/	n.	person being trained 受训者，实习生
applicant /ˈæplikənt/	n.	person who applies for sth. 申请人
disqualify /disˈkwɔlifai/	vt.	to prevent sb. from doing sth., usually because they have broken a rule 取消……的资格
capture /ˈkæptʃə/	vt.	to take by force, to win, to gain 夺得，占领；俘虏，捕获
	n.	俘获，捕获
potential /pəˈtenʃəl/	a.	possible but not yet actual 潜在的，可能的
	n.	潜力，潜能
singe /sindʒ/	n.	a slight burn 烧焦，烤焦
red-hot /ˌredˈhɔt/	a.	hot enough to glow, very hot 炽热的
contact /ˈkɔntækt/	vt.	to get in touch with 与……取得联系，与……接触
	n.	接触，联系；熟人，社会关系；（电路的）触点，接头
handful /ˈhændful/	n.	small number 少数，少量；一把
select /siˈlekt/	vt.	to pick out or choose 选择，挑选
	a.	精选的；优等的，第一流的
secure /siˈkjuə/	vt.	to obtain 得到，获得；使安全，保卫；缚牢
	a.	安全的，可靠的；牢固的；安心的
demonstrate /ˈdemənstreit/	vt.	to express sth. by one's action 显示，表露；论证，证明，说明，演示
	vi.	举行示威游行（或集会）
media /ˈmiːdjə/	n.	the newspapers, television and radio 新闻媒介，传播媒介
★ **counterpart** /ˈkauntəpɑːt/	n.	person or thing complementary to or corresponding to another 与对方地位相当的人，与另一方作用相当的物
readership /ˈriːdəʃip/	n.	readers of a publication collectively 读者群
workforce /ˈwəːkfɔːs/	n.	the total number of workers actively employed in, or available for work in a nation, region, plant, etc. 劳动力，劳动大军

Unit 1 On English Language

finding /ˈfaindiŋ/	n.	sth. learned as the result of an official inquiry [常 *pl.*] 调查（或研究的）结果；（陪审团的）裁决
undermine /ˌʌndəˈmain/	vt.	to weaken gradually 暗中破坏，逐渐削弱；侵蚀……的基础
assertion /əˈsəːʃən/	n.	a forceful statement or claim 主张，断言，声明
literacy /ˈlitərəsi/	n.	ability to read and write 识字，有文化，读写能力
fee /fiː/	n.	charge paid to be allowed to do sth. 费，酬金
acquire /əˈkwaiə/	vt.	to get or gain by one's own effort or action 学到；取得，获得
worthy /ˈwəːði/	a.	deserving 值得的，配得上的；有价值的，可尊敬的
urgently /ˈəːdʒəntli/	ad.	迫切地，急切地
spokeswoman /ˈspəuksˌwumən/	n.	女发言人
★ **shrewd** /ʃruːd/	a.	clever and perceptive 敏锐的，精明的，机灵的
▲ **renowned** /riˈnaund/	a.	famous 有名的，有声誉的

PHRASES

turn down	to refuse to accept 拒绝，驳回
get into	to put (oneself or someone else) into (a state) 使（自己、某人）进入（某状态）
up to	as much as （数目上）一直到，多达
in order to	with the purpose or intention of 为了
pay off	to pay the whole of (a debt) 还清（债务）
refer to	to mention 提到，谈到
in many ways	在许多方面
a handful of	a small number of 少数的
cast doubt on / upon	对……产生怀疑
worthy of	deserving 值得的，应得的

Part B

Extensive Reading

EXERCISES

Reading Comprehension

Task 1

A. Find answers from the text to the following questions.

1. All of the following are findings of the survey EXCEPT _____.
    a. Before the interview, many applicants hadn't done their homework about the chosen company.
    b. Most applicants' CVs are full of spelling and grammar mistakes.
    c. College graduates don't seem to have a firm grounding in literacy.
    d. Compared with UK applicants, foreign applicants are more competitive in the job market.
2. What does Lewis specialize in?
3. What does "green" mean in the sentence "In many ways the best educated people in this country are also the greenest when they leave higher education."?
4. Why did an applicant burn the edges of the CV?
5. Why does Margaret Hodge think increasing tuition fees is reasonable?
6. What does the falling standards of graduate literacy call into question?

B. Paraphrase the italicized part in each sentence.

1. Graduates and final-year students ... *are ill-equipped to get a job* that will enable them to pay off their loans.
2. Lewis receives about 100 CVs each week, but contacts only *a handful of* applicants.
3. This week a Swedish applicant demonstrated a better understanding of the UK media than *his UK counterpart* by knowing facts ...
4. ... ministers say that over their working lives graduates *stand to earn* £400,000 more than workers who did not attend university.
5. In an age of increased course fees, this needs *to be urgently addressed*.

Vocabulary

Task 2

Find in the text the words and phrases which fit the following definitions.

1. _____ : a request, especially officially and in writing form
2. _____ : to get in touch or communication with
3. _____ : to finish paying money owed for sth.

Unit 1 On English Language

4. _____: to weaken
5. _____: to speak about
6. _____: sth. found or discovered
7. _____: to show, make clear
8. _____: television, radio, and newspapers regarded as a group
9. _____: to damage sth.
10. _____: mistake
11. _____: possible when the necessary conditions exist
12. _____: the ability to read and write

II. Our Crazy Language

English is the most widely-used language in the history of our planet. One in every seven human beings can speak it. More than half of the world's books and three-quarters of international mail are in English. Of all languages, English has the largest vocabulary—perhaps as many as two million words — and one of the noblest bodies of literature.

5 Nevertheless, let's face it: English is a crazy language. There is no egg in eggplant, neither pine nor apple in pineapple and no ham in a hamburger. Sweetmeats are candy, while sweetbreads, which aren't sweet, are meat.

We take English for granted. But when we explore its
10 paradoxes, we find that quicksand can work slowly, boxing rings are square, public bathrooms have no baths in them.

And why is it that a writer writes, but fingers don't fing, grocers don't groce, and hammers don't ham? If the plural of tooth is teeth, shouldn't the plural of booth be beeth? One goose, two geese—so one moose, two
15 meese?

If the teacher taught, why isn't it true that the preacher praught? If a horsehair mat is made from the hair of horses and a camel-hair coat from the hair of camels, from what is a mohair coat made? If a vegetarian eats vegetables, what does a humanitarian eat?

In what other language do people drive on a parkway and park in a driveway? Ship by truck
20 and send cargo by ship? Have noses that run and feet that smell?

How can a slim chance and a fat chance be the same, while a wise man and a wise guy are opposites? How can overlook and oversee be opposites, while quite a lot and quite a few are alike? How can the weather be hot as hell one day and cold as hell the next?

You must be shocked at a language in which your house can burn up as it burns down, in which you fill in a form by filling it out and in which your alarm clock goes off by going on.

English was invented by people, not computers, and it reflects the creativity of the human race (which, of course, isn't really a race at all). That is why, when stars are out they are visible, but when the lights are out they are invisible. And why, when I wind up my watch I start it, but when I wind up this essay I end it. (407 words)

NEW WORDS

nevertheless /ˌnevəðə'les/	ad.	however, in spite of, still 然而，虽然如此，依然
eggplant /'egplɑ:nt/	n.	茄子
pine /pain/	n.	松树
	vi.	(*away*)（因悲哀等）消瘦，衰弱，憔悴；(*for*) 渴望，思念
▲ *pineapple* /'painæpl/	n.	菠萝
▲ *hamburger* /'hæmbə:gə/	n.	a flat round cake of finely cut beef, cooked and eaten in a round bread roll; ground beef 汉堡包；碎牛肉
sweetmeat /'swi:tmi:t/	n.	[*BrE.*] any sweet food or delicacy prepared with sugar or honey 甜食，糖果，蜜饯
candy /'kændi/	n.	(a shaped piece of) various types of boiled sugar, sweets, or chocolate 糖果
sweetbread /'swi:tbred/	n.	[*BrE.*]（供食用的）牛、羊胰脏
grant /grɑ:nt/	vt.	to give formally; to agree to fulfill or allow to be fulfilled 授予；同意
	n.	拨款，授予物
explore /iks'plɔ:/	vt.	to examine carefully in order to find out more 仔细察看，探索，探究；探险
★ *paradox* /'pærədɔks/	n.	statement that seems to say something opposite to common sense or the truth, but which may contain a truth (e.g., "More haste, less speed") 逆说，反论（如"欲速则不达"）；自相矛盾的人（或事物）
quicksand /'kwiksænd/	n.	流沙（区）
grocer /'grəusə/	n.	a storekeeper who sells food and various household

Unit 1 On English Language

			supplies 食品杂货商
hammer /ˈhæmə/	n.		锤，榔头
	v.		锤击，敲打
plural /ˈpluərəl/	n.		(a word or form) that expresses more than one 复数
	a.		复数的
★ **booth** /buːθ/	n.		（隔开的）小房间，公用电话亭；货摊, 售货亭
moose /muːs/	n.		麋（长有粗毛及厚角的一种大鹿，产于北美洲森林地带，北欧及北亚，在北欧及北亚被称为 elk）
★ *preacher* /ˈpriːtʃə/	n.		one who preaches (esp. sermons) 说教者，鼓吹者，（尤指）传教者；讲道者
horsehair /ˈhɔːsheə/	n.		马毛, 马毛织品
mat /mæt/	n.		a piece of rough, strong material, used for covering part of a floor 席子，垫子
camel /ˈkæməl/	n.		骆驼
mohair /ˈməuheə/	n.		安哥拉山羊毛，安哥拉山羊毛仿制品
vegetarian /ˌvedʒiˈtɛəriən/	n.		a person who does not eat meat or fish, but only vegetables, grains, fruit, eggs, etc. 素食者
humanitarian /hjuːˌmæniˈtɛəriən/	n.		人道主义者，慈善家，博爱主义者
parkway /ˈpɑːkwei/	n.		[*BrE.*] a wide road divided by or bordered with an area of grass and trees 公路，大路，林阴干道，风景区干道
driveway /ˈdraivwei/	n.		a road for vehicles that connects a private house or garage with the street 车道
cargo /ˈkɑːgəu/	n.		load of goods carried by a ship, plane, or vehicle（船、飞机或车辆所载的）货物
slim /slim/	a.		very small, slight（机会）少的，小的；苗条的；薄的
	v.		（用运动、节食等）减轻体重，变苗条
guy /gai/	n.		a man 家伙，伙计
overlook /ˌəuvəˈluk/	vt.		to look at from above; to fail to notice; to pretend not to see; to forgive 俯瞰，俯视；忽略，看漏；宽容
oversee /ˌəuvəˈsiː/	vt.		to control (work, workmen) 监视，监督
alike /əˈlaik/	a.		similar, like one another 相似的，同样的

Part B
Extensive Reading

	ad.	相似地；同样程度地
hell /hel/	n.	地狱；极不愉快的经历(或事)
visible /'vizəbl/	a.	able to be seen 看得见的，可见的，有形的
invisible /in'vizəbl/	a.	看不见的，无形的
essay /'esei/	n.	a piece of writing on one subject 散文，随笔

PHRASES

take...for granted	to accept...as certain without discussion 认为……理所当然
a slim chance	可能性很小的机会
a fat chance	实际上不存在的机会
a wise guy	自以为聪明的人
cold/hot as hell	冷 / 热得要命
burn up	to destroy completely by fire 烧光，烧尽
burn down	to destroy (usu. a building) or be destroyed by fire 烧毁，焚毁
fill out	[*AmE*] = fill in 填写
go off	to proceed; to explode; to ring loudly 进行；爆炸；（闹钟）响起来
wind up	to tighten the spring of a watch or a clock 上（钟）弦；结束

EXERCISES

Reading Comprehension

Task 1

Are the following statements true or false? Mark "T" before a true statement and "F" before a false one.

_____ 1. More than half of the books written every year all over the world are translated into English.

Unit 1 On English Language

_____ 2. According to the author, the meanings of English words are always in agreement with their spelling.

_____ 3. The meaning of the word "**hamburger**" comes from the combination of the meanings of the words **ham** and **burger**.

_____ 4. Although the word "**sweetbread**" is the combination of the words **sweet** and **bread**, in fact, sweetbread isn't sweet at all.

_____ 5. The word "**ring**" in the sentence "...boxing rings are square" means an enclosed space for boxing.

_____ 6. **Ham-** has the same meaning in both **hamburger** and **hammer**.

_____ 7. When we go on studying English words we come to find that, if the singular form of a noun contains **-oo**, its plural form contains **-ee**.

_____ 8. The author implies that English is not worth learning as it is a language that drives you crazy.

_____ 9. From the passage we can infer that, as English is such a crazy language, there are no rules to follow and, therefore, there is no way to learn it well.

_____ 10. The author's style in this passage can best be described as persuasive.

vocabulary

Task 2

Using its proper form, choose the correct word to fit each sentence.

explore	alike	grocer	plural	essay
visible	overlook	slim	grant	wind

1. Mary treats all her children _____.
2. I think it's about time we _____ this meeting up.
3. A _____ sells tea, sugar, butter, bottled food and many other household necessities.
4. How do you keep so _____ — is it all the exercise you do?
5. Mice is the _____ form of the word "mouse".
6. Columbus discovered America but did not _____ the new continent.
7. Her bedroom has large windows _____ a lake.
8. I didn't realize that Lisa hadn't been to college — I suppose I just took it for _____.
9. The house is _____ from the road, being surrounded by trees.
10. His last book was a collection of literary _____.

Part C ▶ Reading Skill

Compound Words

Words can be combined to make new words. Compound words are a combination of two or more words in which the spelling does not change and the meaning becomes a combined meaning of the parts.

For example, the word HEAD and ACHE combine to form HEADACHE. So we can say "I've got a headache." Similarly, we can guess the meaning of the words stomachache and toothache with no difficulty.

Sometimes a hyphen (-) separates the two (or three) parts of compound words.

For example, "a little-used railway station" is a railway station which is little used.

There are no rules in regard to the correct spelling of compound words. You may have to consult the dictionary to see if they are one word, two words or hyphenated words.

Note:
1. Compound words are hyphenated if they form a single adjective that modifies a noun, for example, a middle-aged man.
2. Numbers under one hundred are also hyphenated when spelled out, e.g. thirty-five, sixty-two.
3. The stress is normally on the first word.

EXERCISES

Task 1

Match compound words and their meanings. Put the letter of the definition in the left blank.

____ 1. Blind date   ____ 2. Gas fire
____ 3. Birth control   ____ 4. Travel agency
____ 5. Free-market economy   ____ 6. Lifeguard
____ 7. A window-dresser   ____ 8. Window-shopper
____ 9. A heart-breaking story ____ 10. An outlaw
____ 11. A househusband   ____ 12. A housekeeper

Unit 1 On English Language

a. an economic system that allows supply and demand to regulate (调节) prices, wages, etc., rather than government policy
b. a person present at a beach or pool to guard people against the risk of drowning
c. a heating-stove in which gas is burned
d. a story which makes one extremely sad as if one's heart would break
e. a married man whose principal occupation is managing a household and taking care of domestic affairs
f. a social meeting between a man and a woman who haven't met before
g. a person who commits crimes
h. a person, esp. a woman, employed to run a household
i. an agency that arranges flights, vacations, etc., for travelers
j. a person employed to design and build up a display in a shop window
k. a person who looks at goods in shop windows without buying them
l. limitation on child-bearing

Task 2

Choose from among words listed below to fill in each blank.

| part-time | milkman | breakdown | airtight | extra-long |

1. There was a _____ on the railway and all trains were delayed several hours.
2. Mr. Wright told the _____ that Wilt was only seven, and he shouldn't be lifting those heavy milk boxes.
3. He is so tall that he has a special, _____ bed to sleep in and a special car with enough space for his long legs.
4. The cloth is so tightly woven that it's almost _____.
5. Many young people cannot afford to pay the expenses of full-time college. Many students have _____ jobs in the evenings or on weekends.

Task 3

The following compound words should (A) be written as one word or (B) be hyphenated or (C) remain separate. Put them into the right column. Three of them have been done for you as examples.

drug store, shop keeper, poverty stricken, grammar school, half way, print out, public library, town hall, sit in, mile stone, secret agent, peace loving, time table, foot steps, sound waves, weather beaten, draw back, the next to last step, door knob, over shadow, rest room, drawing room, dining room, second year students, water proof, son in law, bank statement, bank loan, a middle income family, car park

A	B	C
drugstore	poverty-stricken	grammar school

Unit 2

Campus Life

Aims and Objectives

In this unit you will learn:
1. Genre/Style: Narration/Description
2. Word Power: Figures of Speech
3. Grammar Focus: The Usages of "Would"
4. Writing Skill: Description (2)
5. Translation Skill: Splitting and Combing (2)
6. Reading Skill: Reading for the Main Idea

Brief Introductions to the Texts

The first and second passages are about the authors' personal experiences as university students.

The third passage talks about the serious problem of cheating in US schools.

Unit 2 Campus Life

Part A — Intensive Reading

Reading

Task 1

The following is what some college students think of campus life. Have a discussion with your partner about it.

The reasons behind attending a college are quite simple.

1) Get a good education
2) Get a good job

Obviously, though, there is more to college than books and exams. While attending college you will find out what life is like in the "real world". You have the opportunity, possibly for the first time, to really know what it is like to be on your own. Mom won't be around to wake you up for school or check your homework. You're an adult with responsibilities.

However, at a university you will find a new family that is looking out for your best interests. From the dorms to the classrooms to administration you will find people genuinely concerned about you as an individual!

Student Life can be very rewarding. You will make friends here that will truly last a lifetime.

Task 2

Use the following expressions with a partner to talk about your studies.

pass a course on/in
take a course on/in
sit in on a course
enroll/register/sign up for a course
complete a course

drop a course/class
a demanding/difficult course
keep up in one's studies
it's one's turn to do sth.
keep up with the class

University Days

By **James Thurber**[1]

I passed all the other courses that I took at my University, but I could never pass botany. This was because all botany students had to spend several hours a week in a laboratory looking through a microscope at plant cells, and I could never see through a microscope.
5 I never once saw a cell through a microscope. This used to anger my instructor. He would wander around the laboratory pleased with the progress all the students were making in drawing the interesting structure of flower cells, until he
10 came to me. I would just be standing there. "I can't see anything," I would say. He would begin patiently enough, explaining how anybody can see through a microscope, but
15 he would always end up in violent anger, claiming that I could too see through a microscope but just pretended that I couldn't.

Bolenciecwcz Was Trying to Think

What is the usage of "would"?

Which sentences are the most humorous?

"It takes away from the beauty of flowers anyway," I used to tell
20 him. "We are not concerned with beauty in this course," he would say. "We are concerned solely with what I may call the mechanics of flowers." "Well," I'd say, "I can't see anything." "Try it just once again," he'd say, and I would put my eye to the microscope and see nothing at all, except now and again a cloudy milky substance. "I see
25 what looks like a lot of milk," I would tell him. This, he claimed, was the result of my not having adjusted the microscope properly, so he

---

1. **James Thurber:** a famous American writer of humor (1894—1961). His books include *The Night the Bed Fell*, *The Secret Life of Walter Mitty* and *My Life and Hard Times*, from which this story is taken.

Unit 2 Campus Life

would readjust it for me, or rather, for himself. And I would look again and see milk.

I finally took a deferred pass, as they called it, and waited a year and tried again. (You had to pass one of the biological sciences or you couldn't graduate.) The professor had come back from vacation brown as a berry, bright-eyed, and eager to explain cell-structure again to his classes. "Well," he said to me cheerily. "We're going to see cells this time, aren't we?" "Yes, sir," I said, but I didn't see anything.

"We'll try it," the professor said to me, sternly. So we tried it with every adjustment of the microscope known to man. To my pleasure and amazement, I saw some dots. These I hastily drew. The instructor, noting my activity, came to my desk, a smile on his lips and his eyebrows high in hope. He looked at my cell drawing. "What's that?" he demanded. "That's what I saw," I said. "You didn't, you didn't, you didn't!" he screamed, losing control of his temper and he bent over and looked into the microscope. "That's your eye!" he shouted. "You've fixed the lens so that it reflects! You've drawn your eye!"

> Can you feel the humor in this paragraph?

Another course that I didn't like, but managed to pass, was economics. I went to that class straight from the botany class, which didn't help me any in understanding either subject. I used to get them mixed up. But not as mixed up as another student in my economics class who came there direct from a physics laboratory. He was a tackle on the football team, named Bolenciecwcz. At that time Ohio State University[1] had one of the best football teams in the country, and Bolenciecwcz was one of its outstanding stars. In order to be qualified to play it was necessary for him to keep up in his studies, a very difficult matter, for while he was not dumber than an ox, he was not any smarter. Most of his professors were lenient and helped him along. None gave him more hints, in answering questions, or asked him simpler ones than the economics professor, a thin, kind-hearted man named Bassum.

---

1. **Ohio State University:** 俄亥俄州立大学

One day when we were on the subject of transportation and distribution, it came Bolenciecwcz's turn to answer a question. "Name one means of transportation," the professor said to him. No light came into the big tackle's eyes. "Just any means of transportation," said the professor. Bolenciecwcz sat staring at him. "That is," the professor pursued, "any medium, agency, or method of going from one place to another." Bolenciecwcz had the look of a man who is being led into a trap. "You may choose among steam, horsedrawn, or electrically propelled vehicles," said the instructor. "I might suggest the one which we commonly take in making long journeys across land." There was a profound silence in which everybody stirred uneasily, including Bolenciecwcz and Mr. Bassum. Mr. Bassum suddenly broke this silence in an amazing manner. "Choo-choo-choo[1]," he said, in a low voice, and turned instantly red. He glanced appealingly around the room. All of us, of course, shared Mr. Bassum's desire that Bolenciecwcz should keep up with the class in economics, for the Illinois game, one of the hardest and most important of the season, was only a week off. "Toot, toot, tootooooot[2]," some student with a deep voice said, and we all looked encouragingly at Bolenciecwcz. Somebody else gave a fine imitation of a locomotive letting off steam. Mr. Bassum himself rounded off the little show. "Ding, dong, ding, dong[3]," he said, hopefully. Bolenciecwcz was staring at the floor, trying to think, his huge hands rubbing together, his face red.

"How did you come to college this year, Mr. Bolenciecwcz?" asked the professor. "Chuffa chuffa, chuffa chuffa[4]."

"My father sent me," said the football player.

"What on?"[5] asked Bassum.

"I get an allowance," said the tackle, in a low voice, obviously embarrassed.

"No, no," said Bassum. "Name a means of transportation. What did you ride here on?"

> How is this paragraph connected with the previous one?

> Is this a common way to each college students?

1-4. **choo, toot, ding, dong and chuffa:** imitative words (拟声词) of trains

5. **This could be understood in two ways:** a. What money did you have to support you? b. On what means of transportation did you come here?

Unit 2 Campus Life

"Train," said Bolenciecwcz.

"Quite right," said the professor. "Now, Mr. Nugent, will you tell us —" (937 words)

NEW WORDS

★ **botany** /ˈbɒtəni/		n.	the scientific study of plants 植物学
laboratory /ləˈbɔrətəri/ (*US*) /ˈlæbərɔːri/		n.	a special room where scientists work 实验室
microscope /ˈmaikrəskəup/		n.	an instrument with lenses for making very small objects appear larger than they are 显微镜
cell /sel/		n.	the smallest part of any living thing 细胞；单人房间；电池
wander /ˈwɔndə/		vi.	to walk slowly with no special plan 漫步；离题
structure /ˈstrʌktʃə/		n.	the way that something is made 结构；建筑物
		vt.	建筑，构成，组织
violent /ˈvaiələnt/		a.	very strong 猛烈的，剧烈的；暴力引起的
concern /kənˈsəːn/		vt.	使关心；涉及
		n.	关切的事；关心；关系；企业
concerned /kənˈsəːnd/		a.	worried 关心的
sole /səul/		a.	one and only, single 唯一的；独有的
		n.	鞋底
solely /ˈsəuli/		ad.	alone, only 只是
mechanics /miˈkæniks/		n.	working structure or functioning system (用作复数) 结构；技工；(-S)机械学、力学
milky /ˈmilki/		a.	牛奶的，乳状的，乳白色的
substance /ˈsʌbstəns/		n.	a solid or liquid material 物质；实质；大意
adjust /əˈdʒʌst/		vt.	to change sth. slightly 校准，调整，调节
		vi.	(*to*) 适应
readjust /riːəˈdʒʌst/		vt.	重新调整，再调整
▲ **defer** /diˈfəː/		vt.	to put off or hold back until a later date, delay 推迟，延期
		vi.	听从，服从

Part A
Intensive Reading

deferred	a.	延期的，缓召的
biological /baiə'lɔdʒikəl/	a.	生物学的
berry /'beri/	n.	浆果
cheerily /'tʃiərili/	ad.	快活地，兴高采烈地
★*stern* /stə:n/	a.	very serious and strict 严厉的，严格的
	n.	船尾
amaze /ə'meiz/	vt.	to surprise sb. very much 使吃惊
adjustment /ə'dʒʌstmənt/	n.	调整；调节器
amazement /ə'meizmənt/	n.	惊愕，惊异
dot /dɔt/	n.	a small, round mark 点，圆点
	vt.	点于；散布于
haste /heist/	n.	hurry, quickness of movement 急速，匆忙
★*hasty* /'heisti/	adj.	匆忙的，草率的
	a.	said, made, or done too quickly 急忙的，匆忙的
hastily /'heistili/	ad.	急速地；轻率地
▲*eyebrow* /'aibrau/	n.	眉毛
temper /'tempə/	n.	strong emotion, esp. anger 脾气；(钢等) 韧度
	v.	调和；回火
economics /ˌi:kə'nɔmiks, ˌekə-/	n.	the study of the way that countries spend money and make, buy and sell things 经济学
tackle /'tækl/	n.	（橄榄球比赛中）擒抱对方球员；用具；滑车；辘轳
	vt.	处理；交涉
outstanding /aut'stændiŋ/	a.	very good indeed 突出的，显著的；未解决的
qualify /'kwɔlifai/	v.	to provide with necessary skills and knowledge （使）具有资格，（使）合格
dumb /dʌm/	a.	unable to speak; cannot speak on a particular occasion for being angry, shocked or surprised 哑的，说不出话的；stupid 愚蠢的
▲*lenient* /'li:njənt/	a.	gentle, merciful in judgment 宽大的，仁慈的，慈悲为怀的
hint /hint/	n.	sth. that you say, but not in a direct way 暗示，提示，线索
	v.	暗示

Unit 2 Campus Life

distribution /ˌdistri'bjuːʃən/	n.	分配，分发；散布	
medium /'miːdjəm/	n.	means by which sth. is expressed 方法，手段；媒体；媒介	
	a.	中间的，中等的	
agency /'eidʒənsi/	n.	operation, means 作用，手段；代理行；专业行政部门	
electrical /i'lektrikəl/	a.	of or about electricity 电的，电气科学的	
electrically /i'lektrikəli/	ad.	电力地，与电有关地	
★ **propel** /prə'pel/	vt.	to drive forward 推进，驱使	
vehicle /'viːikl/	n.	anything that carries people or things from one place to another 交通工具，车辆；传播媒介，手段	
★ **profound** /prə'faund/	a.	deep, complete, very strongly felt 极深的，深厚的；渊博的；深奥的	
stir /stəː/	v.	to cause to move 搅动，移动；激起	
	n.	strong reaction of excitement 惊动，轰动	
uneasy /ʌn'iːzi/	a.	not comfortable or at rest 心神不安的，担心的	
uneasily /ʌn'iːzili/	ad.	不安地，担心地	
instantly /'instəntli/	ad.	immediately 立即地，即刻地	
appealingly /ə'piːliŋli/	ad.	上诉地，哀求地	
encouragingly /in'kʌridʒiŋli/	ad.	鼓励地	
★ **imitation** /imi'teiʃən/	n.	the act of copying sth. 模仿；仿制；赝品	
★ **locomotive** /ˌləukə'məutiv/	n.	railway engine 机车，火车头	
	a.	运动的	
hopeful /'həupful/	a.	having hope; giving hope 怀有希望的，有希望的	
hopefully	ad.	有希望地，有前途地	
allowance /ə'lauəns/	n.	sum of money given regularly 津贴，补助	
embarrass /im'bærəs/	vt.	to make sb. feel shy or worried about what other people think of them 使不好意思，使尴尬	

PHRASES

take away from	减损
or rather	more exactly 或者更准确地说

40

keep up with (sb.)	to remain level with (sb.) 与……的速度一样，跟上（某人）
let off (steam)	(of a railway engine) to allow (unwanted steam) to escape 排放（废蒸汽），放走，放过
round off	to end in a satisfactory way 完成，圆满结束
end up	to finish (esp. in a particular place or way) 结束，告终

EXERCISES

Reading Comprehension

Task 3

The following statements are the main ideas of some paragraphs of the text. Match each statement with its related paragraph number(s).

A. In the economics course, another student, an outstanding tackle on the university football team, had more difficulty than the writer. However, most of his professors helped him along.

B. In the end, he and the writer give an example of how the economics professor elicited an answer from the tackle on the subject of transportation and distribution by imitating various sounds made by a train.

C. The writer failed to pass his botany course, because he could never see through a microscope.

D. He finally took a deferred pass, but he was still not successful.

Task 4

Choose the right answer out of the four choices for each question and answer the questions raised.

1. What is the author's main idea?

    a. His personal experience as a university student.

    b. Two different types of teachers in his university.

    c. His conflict with the instructor of the botany class.

    d. The courses he enjoyed and hated to take as a student.

2. Which of the following words best describes the professor who teaches botany?

    a. Patient.   b. Skillful.

    c. Imaginative.   d. Enthusiastic.

Unit 2 Campus Life

3. Which of the following words best describes the professor who teaches economics?
   a. Worried.
   b. Encouraging.
   c. Anxious.
   d. Attractive.
4. Which course(s) did the author hate to take?
   a. Economics.
   b. Both botany and economics.
   c. Botany.
   d. Both botany and physics.
5. What does the sentence "No light came into the big tackle's eyes." imply?
   _____
6. What does the sentence "He glanced appealingly around the room" imply?
   _____
7. What is the basic tone of this passage?
   a. Humorous.
   b. Critical.
   c. Emotional.
   d. Annoying.

Vocabulary

Task 5

Match words with similar meanings. Some of them in Column B can be used more than once.

A	B
1. mechanics	a. distribution
2. allowance	b. method
3. dot	c. spot
4. agency	d. means
5. medium	e. technician
6. wander	f. payment
7. hint	g. indirect statement
	h. walk aimlessly
	i. economics

Task 6

Choose from among the words and expressions listed below to replace the underlined ones, making necessary changes.

pursue	substance	violent	in haste
lose one's temper	on reflection	keep up with	sole
be concerned about	glance at		

Part A
Intensive Reading

1. Henry <u>had a brief look at</u> the newspaper while he ate his breakfast.
2. The doctor <u>was worrying about</u> the patient's health.
3. I agreed to come <u>only</u> on account of your mother.
4. Bill got out of the taxi <u>in a hurry</u> and left his luggage behind.
5. The cloth is coated in a new waterproof <u>material</u>.
6. When the young man was stopped by the policeman, he <u>became angry</u> and shouted at him.
7. <u>After reconsidering</u>, he regretted his hasty decision.
8. Patrick had to work hard <u>not to fall behind</u> the other students in his class.
9. The criminal gave the boy a <u>powerful</u> blow on the head.
10. The policeman <u>searched for</u> the murderer through several cities.

Task 7

Using the proper form, choose the correct word to fit into each sentence.

1. to adjust, adjustable, adjustment
   a. Please _____ the table-lamp so that the light falls on the book.
   b. She will not be able to get along with them unless she _____ her way of thinking.
   c. The foreign student has made a most satisfactory _____ of his microscope.
   d. An _____ electric lamp can be placed in various positions.
2. to tackle, tackle
   a. The government must _____ the problem of rising unemployment.
   b. Secret Service agents _____ the gunman before he could escape.
   c. There are many ways of _____ the problem.
3. to qualify, qualification, qualified
   a. Anna was extraordinarily well _____ to run the business.
   b. George won his tennis match and _____ for the semifinals.
   c. Please list your _____ on your CV.
   d. Is there a height _____ for the police force?
   e. Mary accepted the proposal with only a few _____.
4. electric, electrical, electrically
   a. Tony switched on the _____ kettle.
   b. The story involves Michael Faraday, the inventor of the _____ generator.
   c. The atmosphere in the room was _____.
   d. Bill owned a factory that made _____ devices.
5. to amaze, amazement, amazing
   a. The teacher was _____ to find that a poor pupil had achieved a mark of 100 on an important test.

Unit 2 Campus Life

    b. It is _____ that the experiment was a complete success.

    c. I was simply _____ by the author's attitude toward life.

    d. This terrible news struck me dumb with _____.

6. to hope, hope, hopeful, hopefully

    a. Maggie never gave up _____ that a cure for the disease would be found.

    b. The ministers seem _____ that an agreement will be reached.

    c. I _____ that you feel better soon.

    d. _____, dad will get home before his supper gets cold.

7. embarrass, embarrassing, embarrassed, embarrassment

    a. A good teacher should always avoid _____ the students.

    b. The little girl glanced at me horribly _____.

    c. He suffers the _____ of not remembering the name of his guest.

    d. Seeing he was _____ with his luggage, I offered to help him.

    e. He should not have _____ her in front of their guests.

Task 8

The word "medium" may have different meanings in different sentences. Match the sentences with the proper Chinese equivalents of the word.

1. Tony tried to keep the story out of the media.	中等的
2. Olivia was of medium height and weight.	媒介物
3. Sound travels through the medium of air.	新闻媒体
4. Lucy chose the medium of print to make her ideas known to the public.	手段

Task 9

Translate the following sentences into English, using the words or phrases given in the brackets.

1. 他正致力于设计一种增强透镜放大率的新装置。有了这一新装置，人们能清楚地看到细胞的每个点。(work on, lens, dot)
2. 因为学校的津贴相当优厚，所以许多学生提出了申请。在宣布分配津贴的那天，每位申请人看起来都很焦急不安。(allowance, distribution)
3. 这位教授约45岁，中等身材。浓黑的眉毛和严厉的声音使他看上去很凶。(medium, stern, fierce)

Task 10

Complete the following passage with proper words, the first 1 or 2 letters of which

Part A

Intensive Reading

are given to help you. Be sure to use their proper forms.

The professor entered the classroom. The i-(1) he removed his overcoat he read what the previous class had left on the blackboard. He walked back and forth in front of the class, nervously a-(2) his glasses.

Finally, it was time to start. To b-(3) with, he gave an example: "To house a football team with 20 white and 20 black players, is it possible that all of the pairs of roommates will be of the s-(4) color?" "Of course," I said. No one re-(5). "Either everybody in this class is dead, or I am," I thought. I couldn't imagine why anyone would take a math course unless the topic a-(6) to him. No one could explain the blank stares and the p-(7) silence when the professor asked a question. Then he gave some h-(8), but still no one broke the silence. The room was too quiet and I felt em-(9). Then, everybody copied down the answer on the board in order to go back to their little c-(10) and memorize it. I was really p-(11). "Hey, what are you doing here?" I wanted to get up and shout a-(12) the class myself.

Grammar

Task 11

Rewrite the following sentences using your own words.

1. While he was not dumber than an ox, he was not any smarter.
_____

2. No light came into the big tackle's eye.
_____

3. Bolenciecwcz had the look of a man who is being led into a trap.
_____

4. Mr. Bassum himself rounded off the little show.
_____

5. None gave him more hints, in answering questions, or asked him simpler ones than the economics professor.
_____

Task 12

Combine each pair of the following sentences by using an appropriate connective adverb, paying attention to the use of punctuation.

1. A. There is a car parked right in front of our gate.
   B. I can't get out.

Unit 2 Campus Life

2. A. I have no objection to other people driving cars.
   B. I refuse to drive one myself.
3. A. Jane had understood nothing.
   B. She had not sought to understand.
4. A. The word is an uncountable noun and is used in a general sense.
   B. It takes no article.
5. A. Turn off the main road here.
   B. You will come to the lake.
6. A. Tom was only able to read very slowly in English.
   B. It took him a long time to finish reading the English textbook.
7. A. Some of the examination questions were very difficult.
   B. Susan managed to answer them satisfactorily.
8. A. It seemed likely that Tim would fail the test.
   B. To everyone's surprise, he passed it easily.
9. A. Helen finds languages quite easy.
   B. She has little difficulty in learning German.
10. A. There were a number of good reasons why Mary should not finish the experiment.
    B. She insisted on continuing and completing it.

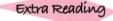

Extra Reading

Task 13

Read the following two advertisements and answer the following five questions about each one.

a.

b.

1. Who put up the poster? _____
2. Where is the company located? _____
3. Who will be interested in the advertisement? _____
4. What practical benefit might students get? _____
5. Where would you expect to see the poster? _____

描述法（二）(Description)

过程的描述

既然有过程就必然有次序，关键在于搞清楚全过程的每一个步骤，再利用表示列举的衔接短语，按照过程的前后次序描述每一个步骤。过程的描述往往按照时间顺序或过程的发展顺序进行描述。

1. 按照过程的发展顺序描述

如果某个描述涉及到多个步骤，应该按照过程的发展顺序把这些步骤交代清楚。既然完整的过程分为多个步骤，那么这些步骤的顺序则显得至关重要。成功地按过程描述实际上告诉了读者如何去完成具体任务。

描述过程常用的衔接词和短语：

1) Firstly ... Secondly ... Thirdly ... Finally ...

2) First, Then, Next, After this, Lastly

3) Afterward, Furthermore, Moreover, In addition to ...

2. 按照时间顺序描述

在讲述故事或描述事件的时候，最简单同时也最清楚的方法是按照时间的顺序描述，

Unit 2 Campus Life

也就是按照事情发生先后顺序，较早发生的事情在前面描述，较晚发生的事情在后面描述。时间作为一个主线条可以为读者提供非常清楚的思路。

常用衔接词和短语：

首环节： first, firstly, at first, first of all, in the first place, to begin with, one

中间环节：second, secondly, in the second place, next, afterwards, after that, then, later, another, third, thirdly, still another, in addition, besides, furthermore

末环节： lastly, at last, finally, eventually, in the end

Task 14

Rearrange the following sentences.

How a New Road is Built

___ (a) Though I had been on the train for more than thirty hours and spent a sleepless night, I didn't feel tired at all, and I believed my days in Beijing would be as sunny as the skies.

___ (b) Like other passengers, I began to collect my things, and put my mug, towel, atlas (地图册), apples, and other things into my bag.

___ (c) I walked out of the train and was carried forward by the stream of people into an underground passage and then into a big hall.

___ (d) My heart gave a leap when I heard the announcement that our train would soon arrive at its destination — Beijing.

___ (e) As I stepped out of the station, I was dazzled (眩目) by the bright autumn skies of Beijing.

___ (f) To the tune of a beautiful song the train pulled into the station and gently stopped by a platform.

Task 15

Please organize the following instructions into a coherent paragraph, and discuss the questions in the brackets.

How to Deal with Snakebites in the Field

1) Tie a handkerchief, necktie, or belt on your victim above the bite to prevent the blood from flowing to the heart.

2) Decide whether to take the victim to the doctor or call for a doctor (*How will you make a decision?*)

3) Remove the venom

   a. make cuts in a crisscross (十字) fashion on the bitten area, cutting about one fourth inch deep;

b. suck out the blood and spit it out [*Will you die if you swallow the blood?*]
4) Don't give whiskey [*Do you know why?*]; you can give coffee or some other beverage to the victim.
5) Reassure the victim

ranslation

拆合法 (Splitting and Combining) (2)

允许顺拆，自然也就应该允许倒拆。所谓倒拆法，顾名思义，就是把原文的句子按意群拆散，逆着原文的顺序逐片往前倒译，如：

- His delegation welcomed the fact that UNDP was prepared to respond to emergency needs as they rose, despite the basically long-term operations that characterized those programs.
  虽然以开展长线业务项目为主是联合国开发计划署的特点，但它也作了一些应急准备；对此，他的代表团持欢迎态度。

试比较：

他的代表团欢迎这样一个事实，那就是联合国开发计划署已经准备好应付一旦出现的紧急需要，尽管基本上长期业务活动是该机构的特点。

倒拆法也是由两种语言的结构差异和行文特点所决定的。有时候，不倒过来译，译文就会显得语无伦次或者根本不堪卒读。如：

- It is a truth universally acknowledged, that a single man in possession of a good fortune must be in want of a wife.
  凡是有钱的单身汉，总想娶位太太，这是一条举世公认的真理。

- 离开老家，转眼有年把了。
  A year or so has passed since I left my hometown.

Unit 2 Campus Life

有时候，我们还会采取部分倒拆法，即：将句子的主语保留不动，而把原文句尾部分移至主语之后，再安排原来的谓语部分，如：

- We often discover what will do, by finding out what will not do.

  我们往往通过弄清什么行不通，从而发现什么行得通。

- It was impossible for him to keep a secret when he was in drink.

  他一喝醉就管不住自己的嘴了。

- My own daughter, not yet 13, was one of only two girls in a class of 30 without a mobile phone.

  我自己的女儿，13岁还不到，他们30个人的一个班，只有两个女孩子没有手机，她就是其中的一个。

- 清华大学的前身是清华学堂，始建于1911年。

  Tsinghua University was established in 1911, originally as "Tsinghua Xuetang".

有时我们还会发现一句话得从半中腰的一个意群译起，顺着往下拆，然后再回过头来译前半截，这样的译法可以叫做半倒拆法。如：

- I put on my clothes by the light of a half-moon just setting, whose rays streamed through the narrow window near my crib.

  半轮晓月渐渐西坠，月光透过小床边的一个窄窄的窗户射了进来，我趁着月光穿上衣服。

Task 16

Translate the following sentences into idiomatic Chinese, using the method you've learned.

1) I went to that class straight from the botany class, which didn't help me any in understanding either subject.

2) But not as mixed up as another student in my economics class who came there direct from a physics laboratory.

3) None gave him more hints, in answering questions, or asked him simpler ones than the economics professor, a thin, kind-hearted man named Bassum.

4) I might suggest the one which we commonly take in making long journeys across land.

5) There was a profound silence in which everybody stirred uneasily, including Bolenciecwcz and Mr. Bassum.

Quotation

西洋语的结构好像连环,虽则环与环都联络起来,毕竟有联络的痕迹;中国语的结构好像无缝天衣,只是一块一块的硬凑,凑起来还不让它有痕迹。西洋语法是硬的,没有弹性的;中国语法是软的,富于弹性的。惟其是硬的,所以西洋语法有许多呆板的要求,如每一个 clause 里必须有一个主语;惟其是软的,所以中国语法只以达意为主,如初系的目的位可兼次系的主语,又如相关的两件事可以硬凑在一起,不用任何的 "connective word"。

——王力（1900—1986）

The structure of a western language is just like a chain of rings. Every ring is linked to each other, the traces of the linkage, however, are easy to be seen. The structure of Chinese is quite another thing. It seems a seamless heavenly robe — flawless and perfect. It is forcibly pieced together, yet hardly no trace of the stitches are to be seen. Therefore, we say the grammar of a western language is inflexible while the grammar of Chinese is flexible. Because of its inflexibility, one needs to follow a lot of strict grammar rules: a subject, for example, is a must for every clause. On the contrary, because of its flexibility, the primary request for a speaker of Chinese is to have himself understood: for example, he can have the object of the main clause function at the same time as the subject of the subordinate clause, and have two connected things combined by no connective word.

— *Wang Li (1900 — 1986)*

Part B — Extensive Reading

I. The Real Test

By Suzanne Chazin

I had no idea of what lay in store for me the first time I stepped into David Marain's advanced math class. It was a warm September day in 1981. Someone had opened one of the windows, but I was in a cold sweat. Math frightened me.

At exactly 8 a.m., a young man with glasses leaped into the room. "My name's Mr. Ma-rain, emphasis on the second syllable," he said brightly. I had heard from other students that Mr. Marain was just shy of a Ph.D. in mathematics. It didn't surprise me. He seemed to possess the wit and self-confidence of someone who, without trying, always ran ten steps ahead of the group. As he joked with the brightest kids, I sank deeper in despair.

At 16, I had no special talents, yet inside I was burning with desires. Already I had sworn that by age 30, I would become a novelist, songwriter and world traveler. Math never figured in my future. I was in Mr. Marain's class for another reason.

Advanced math was a precondition for calculus and the national Advanced Placement calculus test. Passing the AP exam could earn a student up to a year of college math credits — a big help in keeping down tuition costs. To my parents, this was an incredible bargain. I did not want to disappoint them.

Mr. Marain wrote a formula on the blackboard and asked us to prove it. Carefully, I copied the line of x's, y's and numbers into my notebook. But after a few steps, I was confused.

Mr. Marain moved swiftly around the room, looking over students' shoulders. I tried to cover the mostly blank sheet of paper with the loose sleeve of my blouse. Once Mr. Marain realized I wasn't a math whiz, I was certain he'd encourage me to drop out.

Suddenly, from the corner of my eye, I could see him standing next to me. This is it, I told myself. But, instead, he bent down and wrote an equation on the page.

"Try this," he said gently. I did, and from there the formula seemed to prove itself. "Very good," he said, smiling from behind his glasses, as though I'd arrived at the answer on my own.

He seemed kinder than any teacher I'd ever known, never looking down upon a student for falling behind in class and never scoffing at a question, no matter how obvious or irrelevant. Most surprising of all, Mr. Marain seemed to make no distinction between the top students and those who could only just pass examinations.

Nevertheless, it was clear I was one of the slowest in class. On our first major exam, I got a C minus. That afternoon, I went to see Mr. Marain. "I don't belong with the other students," I said, near tears.

I hoped he might find a way to minimize the importance of the grade. Instead, he leaned on his gray metal desk and fixed me in his gaze. "What do you want out of this class?" he asked.

"I don't want to fail," I muttered.

"You won't fail," he promised. "And I won't let you walk away, as long as you are willing to do your very best." He suggested coming in after school for reviews. Mr. Marain was demanding excellence from me.

Over the coming months, our after-school reviews took on the regularity of athletic training. "I know math is a struggle for you," Mr. Marain said once when I put down the chalk in disgust, unable to solve a problem. "But struggling against obstacles makes us stronger."

With Mr. Marain's help, I got a B in advanced math. But I knew that 12th-grade calculus would be an even greater struggle.

My fears were well-founded. First semester I got a C plus.

"Hang in there," Mr. Marain said. "A grade doesn't tell the whole story."

My skills were put to the test one Saturday morning in May 1983 when I took the Advanced Placement calculus exam. Weeks later, the results came in. On a scale of one to five, I'd received a four — high enough to get a year of college math credits and save my parents thousands of dollars in tuition.

I thanked Mr. Marain, even wrote a letter to the Board of Education about him. But I knew I would never touch another math book. And if I didn't, what reason would I have to think of him again?

Yet I did think of him. In my 20s, I became a magazine writer. Life seemed full of limitless opportunities. Then I turned 30, and suddenly I realized I had yet to write the novel or publish the song I had promised myself I would. I couldn't control a painful feeling that I'd stalled somewhere along the way.

It had been a long time since someone had demanded the best of me, and I longed for that again. So I went back to Mr. Marain, hoping he could help.

We talked for a long while, about former times, old friends, struggles and disappointments, mine and — surprisingly — his too.

"I was once in a position similar to the one you're in now." he said. Then he told me the defeats and failures he'd suffered in his school and university years, and how he had overcome them.

Unit 2 Campus Life

"If you can't overcome it," he said, "you must strike out in a new direction with everything you've got."

65 "You see," he added, "we all have failures and regrets. The question is what we do with them. No one can always be the best," he said. "But if you do your best — give everything you have got — you'll either overcome your obstacles or find a new, possibly better direction."

"That's where real success comes from — working hard at something with all your heart and soul."

70 A few days later, an envelope arrived. Inside was a poem Mr. Marain had written years ago, called "Ode to a Calculus Class". I remembered him handing it out at the end of senior year. Now I reread the final lines with new-found appreciation:

But the real test of whether
it was worth the pain
75 *will come in a decade or two,*
if a few return and say: "You know,
I've learned a lot since then,
but I still remember you." (1067 words)

NEW WORDS

sweat /swet/	n.		water that comes out of your skin when you are hot or afraid 汗
	v.		(使) 出汗
leap	vi.		(leapt/lept/ 或 leaped) to jump 跳，跃
	n.		sudden jump 跳跃；飞跃，跃进
emphasis /ˈemfəsis/	n.		special force given to certain words, ideas, or details, in speaking, writing, drawing, etc., to show that they are particularly important 强调，重点
▲syllable /ˈsiləbəl/	n.		a word or part of a word which contains a single vowel sound 音节
wit /wit/	n.		power of thought, intelligence 智力，才智
confidence /ˈkɔnfidəns/	n.		faith; full trust 信心；信任
self-confidence	n.		自信心
despair /disˈpɛə/	n.		loss of hope 绝望

Part B
Extensive Reading

talent /'tælənt/		n.	the natural ability to do sth. very well 天才，才干，才能
swear /swɛə/		v.	(swore, sworn) to promise seriously 发誓，宣誓；诅咒
novelist /'nɔvəlist/		n.	someone who writes novels 小说家
precondition /ˌpri:kən'diʃən/		n.	sth. that must happen or exist before sth. else can happen 前提，先决条件
placement /'pleismənt/		n.	放置，布置
incredible /in'kredəbl/		a.	surprising and very difficult to believe 难以置信的；不能相信的
formula /'fɔ:mjulə/		n.	(*pl.* formulas or formula) a series of numbers or letters that represent a mathematical or scientific rule 公式；原则；配方
notebook /'nəutbuk/		n.	a book made of plain paper on which you can write notes 笔记本
confuse /kən'fju:z/		vt.	mix sb.'s ideas, so that they cannot think clearly or understand 搞乱，使糊涂
confused /kən'fju:zd/		a.	not able to think clearly 困惑的，烦恼的
blank /blæŋk/		a.	without writing 空白的，空着的；茫然的，无表情的
		n.	empty space 空白；空白处；空白表格
loose /lu:s/		a.	宽松的；不精确的；自由的
sleeve /sli:v/		n.	袖，衣袖
blouse /blauz/		n.	a shirt for women (妇女的) 罩衫，宽大的短外套
whiz /wiz/		n.	someone who is very fast, intelligent or skilled in a particular activity 极出色的人，能手
equation /i'kweiʃən/		n.	formula expressing equality between two quantities 方程式，等式
▲**scoff** /skɔf/		v.	(*at*) 嘲笑，嘲弄
irrelevant /i'relivənt/		a.	不相关的
distinction /dis'tiŋkʃən/		n.	being, keeping things different or distinct 差别，不同；区分，辨别；优秀
nevertheless /ˌnevəðə'les/		conj.	but, however 然而，不过
		ad.	仍然，不过

55

Unit 2 Campus Life

★minimize	/ˈminimaiz/	vt.	to make sth. seem less serious or important than it really is 把……估计得最低；使减到最低程度
gaze	/geiz/	n.	a steady fixed look 凝视，注视
		v.	to look steadily for a long or short period of time 凝视，注视
★mutter	/ˈmʌtə/	v.	to speak quietly or in a low voice 轻声低语，咕哝
athletic	/æθˈletik/	a.	运动的
disgust	/disˈgʌst/	n.	a very strong feeling of dislike 厌恶
		v.	to cause disgust 使厌恶
obstacle	/ˈɔbstəkl/	n.	sth. which stands in the way and prevents action, movement, or success 障碍，阻碍，干扰
semester	/siˈmestə/	n.	学期
scale	/skeil/	n.	a series of numbers, amounts, etc. that are used for measuring or fixing the level of sth. 等级；大小；[pl.] 天平；刻度
		vt.	攀登
limitless	/ˈlimitlis/	a.	无限的，无界限的
painful	/ˈpeinfəl/	a.	causing pain 困难的，令人不快的；疼痛的，引起疼痛的
★stall	/stɔ:l/	v.	to fail to keep going; to avoid doing sth. until a later time 停止，停顿；拖延
disappointment	/ˌdisəˈpɔintmənt/	n.	失望
failure	/ˈfeiljə/	n.	lack of success 失败，不成功
overcome	/ˌəuvəˈkʌm/	vt.	find an answer to a difficult thing in your life 战胜，克服；（感情等）压倒
ode	/əud/	n.	a long poem addressed to a person or thing 颂歌
reread	/ˈri:ˈri:d/	vt.	重读，再读

PHRASES

in store	kept ready for future use 存储着；预备着
be shy of	be short of 缺少

Part B

Extensive Reading

ahead of	in front of 在前面，领先
keep down	to control sth. and prevent it from increasing 控制，限制，压缩
drop out	to give up, leave before sth. has finished 退出，放弃，退学
arrive at	to reach, come to 达到，达成
on one's own	alone; without anyone's help 独自地；独立地
look down upon	regard sb./sth. with contempt 蔑视，瞧不起
fall behind	to fail to keep level with, lag 落后
make no distinction	to treat in the same way 同等对待
as long as	on condition that 只要
do one's best	do all one can 尽其全力，尽量
take on	to put on (a quality, appearance); charge oneself with, to be responsible for 具有，呈现；承担
count on	expect with confidence, depend on 指望，依赖
put sth. to the test	to find out how useful or effective sth. is by using it 使某物受检验，受考验
on a scale of	在……等级
long for	want sth. very much 渴望
strike out	to begin to do sth. different 独立闯新路，开辟（道路等）
hand out	to give sth. to each member or a group of people 分发

EXERCISES

Reading Comprehension

Task 1

Find answers from the text to the following questions.

1. Why was Ms. Chazin in a cold sweat on such a warm September day?
2. What does the sentence "He always ran ten steps ahead of the group" mean?
3. What was the reason for her taking an advanced math class?
4. Did she finally pass it? Why or why not?
5. Why did she go back to Mr. Marain long after her graduation?

Unit 2 Campus Life

6. What kind of person is Mr. Marain?
7. What is the "real test"?
8. What advice from Mr. Marain is valuable/useful to you?

Vocabulary

Task 2

Which words match the following definitions?

1. _____ : importance
2. _____ : intelligence
3. _____ : the natural ability to do something very well
4. _____ : sth. in the way that stops progress or makes it difficult
5. _____ : not able to think clearly
6. _____ : with nothing written on it; empty
7. _____ : jump
8. _____ : belief in oneself or others
9. _____ : find an answer to a difficult thing in your life
10. _____ : the state of having lost all hope
11. _____ : difference
12. _____ : quick or fast
13. _____ : look at somebody or something for a long time
14. _____ : a strong feeling of dislike

II. Students Learn to Cheat

Cheating is on the rise in US schools, with attitudes on the part of students changing and the Internet serving as a primary.

In a recent survey of high school students in the United States, 74 percent admitted that they had copied, used forbidden notes or helped someone else cheat on a test. 72 per cent acknowledged at least one incident of serious cheating on a written assignment.

In a survey of 2,200 students at 21 colleges conducted two years ago, one third of the students admitted to an incident of serious test cheating; about half admitted to cheating on written assignments. Research shows that the number of students engaging in the most serious forms of test cheating has doubled since the 1960s in high schools and college.

Students place the blame for this phenomenon on society and people in positions of authority. Consider the view of this high school junior from Massachusetts: "To be successful in the world today people must cut corners, cheat, and backstab...Everybody cheats. Just not everybody gets caught."

The view of a student at one of America's most prestigious universities is even more telling. "In the real world, there are few rules and people cheat all of the time. It is a very competitive world, and when you are in a competitive environment, you do what it takes to win, whether it be cheating or whatever."

While students have cheated for generations, the ease with which they are able to justify their behaviour by blaming it on others is a more recent and worrisome phenomenon. It's even easier when they see teachers and administrators themselves accused of cheating, for example those charged with improperly administering standardized math and reading tests in order to boost scores.

Adding to the confusion, what students and teachers view as cheating often differs. Nowhere is this more confusing than with the use of the Internet. Some students view anything on the Internet as public information and feel free to save text from a website and "paste" it into an assignment without citing the source. Even when they know this is inappropriate, students believe they are well ahead of teachers when it comes to understanding the Internet, and they see little risk in plagiarizing.

Students also receive mixed messages at home. For example, in a recent survey, one in five high school students acknowledged that they had submitted for credit work that had been done primarily by their parents. While such assistance might be appropriate in elementary school, parents who are doing assignments for children in high school are sending a message that grades are the most important and how you achieve them doesn't matter.

Of course, many of these attitudes are not new. Cheating has always been a part of school. What is worrisome is that increasingly students view education as just a hurdle that needs to be crossed to get to the next level, whether that's earning a diploma, gaining admission to college or graduate school or getting a job interview. When education is viewed as simply a means to an end, it is not surprising that so many students cheat. And for many, there's a sense of entitlement that they deserve to be at that next level. If they have to cheat a bit to get there, so be it.

But the future is not all bleak. In high schools and on college campuses, an increasing number of students and faculty are taking action. Students who are willing to work hard and be honest are becoming frustrated with the lack of response to high levels of cheating. So are teachers who truly care about what their students learn. In some cases, a cheating scandal has gotten

Unit 2 Campus Life

45 things moving.

In others, someone has heard about the successful efforts of another school.

The most effective first step a teacher or parent can take to reduce cheating is to simply talk to students. Let them know the issue is important, outline expectations and work to convince them of the relevance and learning value of tests and assignments. (683 words)

NEW WORDS

cheat	/tʃiːt/	v.	to do sth. that is not honest or fair 欺骗，骗取，作弊
		n.	欺骗，骗子
primary	/'praiməri/	a.	most important 主要的，首要的；最初的
forbid	/fə'bid/	vt.	to say that sb. must not do sth. 禁止，不许
seventy	/'sevənti/	num.	七十
acknowledge	/ək'nɔlidʒ/	vt.	to agree that sth. is true 承认；确认；报偿
conduct	/'kɔndʌkt, -dəkt/	v.	manage 进行，管理；引导
		n.	行为，举止；管理
engage	/in'geidʒ/	vt.	(in) to take part in 使从事于，使参加；雇佣
		vi.	(in) 从事于
phenomenon	/fi'nɔminən/	n.	sth. that happens or exists 现象
view	/vjuː/	vt.	consider sth. in the mind 看待；观察，观看
		n.	观点，见解；观察；景色
junior	/'dʒuːnjə/	n.	(美国大学或中学) 三年级学生；年少者；晚辈
		a.	年少的，下级的
backstab	/'bækstæb/	v.	以卑鄙的手段陷害
prestigious	/ˌpres'tiːdʒəs/	a.	享有声望的，声望很高的
ease	/iːz/	n.	with ease (with no difficulty) 容易，悠闲
		v.	缓和
worrisome	/'wʌrisəm/	a.	令人不安的
administrator	/əd'ministreitə/	n.	管理人，行政官
improperly	/ˌim'prɔpəli/	ad.	不正确地，不适当地
accuse	/ə'kjuːz/	vt.	to say that sb. has done sth. wrong 控告，谴责，非难
★administer	/əd'ministə/	v.	to control or manage sth. 管理；给予；执行
standardized	/'stændəˌdaizd/	a.	标准的，定型的

Part B
Extensive Reading

nowhere /ˈnəuhwɛə/	ad.	not anywhere 无处，到处都无	
paste /peist/	vt.	to stick sth. to sth. else 粘，贴	
	n.	糊，浆糊	
cite /sait/	vt.	to mention sth. as an example to support what you are saying 引用；传唤；表彰	
inappropriate /ˌinəˈprəupriit/	a.	not suitable 不适当的，不相称的	
plagiarize /ˈpreidʒiəraiz/	v.	剽窃，抄袭	
submit /səbˈmit/	vt.	to give sth. so that it may be considered 提交；主张	
	vi.	(*to*) 服从，顺从	
primarily /ˈpraimərili/	ad.	more than anything else 首先，起初，主要地，根本上	
appropriate /əˈprəupriit/	a.	suitable or right 适当的	
elementary /ˌeliˈmentəri/	a.	for beginners 初级的；基本的	
increasingly /inˈkriːsiŋli/	ad.	more and more 日益，愈加	
▲**hurdle** /ˈhəːdl/	n.	a problem or difficulty that you must overcome 障碍；跨栏	
	v.	跳过（栏栅）；克服（障碍）	
diploma /diˈpləumə/	n.	a piece of paper that shows you have passed an examination or finished special studies 毕业证书，毕业文凭	
admission /ədˈmiʃən/	n.	letting sb. go into a place 允许进入；入场费；供认	
entitlement /inˈtaitlmənt/	n.	权利	
deserve /diˈzəːv/	vt.	to be good or bad enough to have sth. 应受，值得	
★**bleak** /bliːk/	a.	not encouraging or hopeful 凄凉的，黯淡的	
campus /ˈkæmpəs/	n.	the area of land where the main buildings of all schools are 校园	
frustrate /frʌsˈtreit/	v.	to cause a person to feel angry or dissatisfied because things are not happening as he/she wants 使感到灰心；挫败，阻挠	
response /risˈpɔns/	n.	an answer or reaction to sth./sb. 回答，响应，反应	
scandal /ˈskændl/	n.	sth. that makes a lot of people talk about it, perhaps in an angry way 丑行，丑闻；流言蜚语；反感	
outline /ˈautlain/	vt.	to give a general description of sth. 略述；描画轮廓	
	n.	要点，概要；轮廓，外形	

Unit 2 Campus Life

convince /kən'vins/   *vt.*   make sb. believe sth. 使确信，使信服

PHRASES

on the part of sb.	就某人而言
cut corners	to do sth. in the easiest and quickest way, often by ignoring rules, being careless. etc. （做事）走捷径
be ahead of	to be in the lead over (sb./sth.) 领先
a means to an end	thing or action not important in itself but as a way of achieving sth. 用以达到目的的方法、事物或行动（其本身并不重要）

EXERCISES

Reading Comprehension

Task 1

Complete the following summary by using words from the box below, using the proper form. There are more words than you will need.

acknowledge	accuse	admit	assignment	authority	blame
cheat	competitive	effective	Internet	justify	mix
matter	percent	reduce	succeed	survey	value

    A national survey of high school students released recently found that they are (1)_____ more than ever and are less concerned about it than in the past.

    The survey found that 74 (2)_____ of students admitted cheating on an exam. A (3)_____ of 2,200 college students also found that one third of them (4)_____ to cheating on a test. Many students (5)_____ their behaviour by citing the pressure to achieve. They (6)_____ the phenomenon on society and people in (7)_____. They believe that in a (8)_____ world a person sometimes has to lie or cheat to (9)_____.

    The use of the (10)_____ is adding to the confusion. Students and teachers view cheating differently, especially when it comes to the use of the Internet. High school students also receive (11)_____ messages at home when their parents are doing assignments for them.

But an increasing number of students and teachers are taking actions to (12) _____ cheating. The message that a teacher or parent can send is that it (13) _____ very much if a student cheats. Students should know the learning (14) _____ of tests and assignments.

Task 2

Give words that are close in meaning to the underlined part in each of the following sentences.

1. Mike was caught <u>copying from his neighbour</u> in the exam.
2. Smoking is one of the <u>main</u> causes of lung cancer.
3. Tony <u>admitted</u> that he had been wrong.
4. Jane told us about a funny <u>thing that happened</u> at school, when her teacher fell in the pond.
5. All the students in the class <u>took part in</u> a heated discussion.
6. Mark was <u>charged with</u> failing to pay his taxes.
7. Scientists <u>mention</u> this experiment as their main support for this theory.
8. Is this <u>a suitable</u> time to have a word with you?
9. <u>The number of students entering</u> Chinese universities <u>has</u> increased by 15% this year.
10. These charities <u>are worthy of</u> your support.
11. She applied for admission and is still waiting for a <u>reply</u> from the school.
12. I <u>succeeded in making him feel</u> the need to go back.
13. Smoking is <u>not allowed</u> inside the building.
14. The experiments were <u>carried out</u> by leading scientists.
15. He was <u>charged with</u> failing to pay his taxes.
16. Companies are required to <u>give</u> monthly financial statements to the board.

Part C — Reading Skill

Reading for the Main Idea

The main idea is the most important message put forward by the author; it takes into account all the details, but does not introduce any new ones. In a well-written paragraph, most of

Unit 2 Campus Life

the sentences support, describe, or explain the main idea of that paragraph.

The main idea of a paragraph is often clearly stated in a topic sentence, which, in most cases, is at the beginning of the paragraph. But sometimes it is at the end of the paragraph, or in the middle of the paragraph. Notice there are cases when you find no topic sentence in a paragraph. Then you must infer from the detail or organization what its main idea is.

Finding the main idea in your reading is an essential skill. This skill is the key to improving comprehension and increasing speed, because once you have the main idea in mind, everything that follows seems to fall into place. You can see the parts (details, less important points, inferences) related to the whole (main idea).

EXERCISES

Below are some paragraphs. Read them carefully and underline the topic sentence in each paragraph. Then in a few words, or even one word, write down the topic of each paragraph. Remember the topic is the subject being discussed.

Task 1

Aside from all its other problems, London's weather is very strange. It can rain several times a day; rain may come suddenly after the sun was shining brightly. The air is damp and cold right through July. On one March afternoon on Hampton Heath last year it rained three times, there was one hailstorm (雹暴), during which the sun shone splendidly — all this within two hours time! It is not surprising to see men and women walking down the street on a sunny morning with umbrellas on their arms. No one knows what the next few moments will bring.

What is the topic of the paragraph? _____.

What is the main idea of this topic? (State the main idea in a complete sentence.)

_____.

Task 2

Did you know a change in the weather can affect your behavior? For example, a Japanese scientist studied the number of packages (包裹) and umbrellas left behind on buses and streetcars in Tokyo. He found that passengers were most forgetful on days when the air pressure was low. After studying patterns of car accidents in Ontario, the Canadians found that most accidents took place when there was low air pressure. Other studies show that a sudden rise in temperature within a low pressure area can lead to strange acts, including suicide (自杀).

What is the topic of the paragraph? _____.
What is the main idea of this topic? (State the main idea in a complete sentence.)

_____.

Task 3

It's easy to remember to turn off a light if it's not in use. People can use buses or streetcars (有轨电车) or even walk instead of each driving their own car. So there are many steps to take in order to ease the fuel crisis (危机). Not too many people are unhappy with house temperatures of 20℃. Anybody with a dishwasher or a washing machine can learn to use these machines less often. Of course watching less television could save large amounts of fuel too.

What is the topic of the paragraph? _____.
What is the main idea of this topic? (State the main idea in a complete sentence.)

_____.

Task 4

Americans might be embarrassed because their Japanese friends are so formal with them. Japanese might feel insulted (受侮辱) because their American business associates greet them casually (随便). Still, the forms of greeting in both countries only show respect for others. It just happens that Americans and Japanese have a different way of looking at human relationships and thus have a different way of showing respect.

What is the topic for the paragraph? _____.
What is the main idea of this topic? (State the main idea in a complete sentence.)

_____.

Unit 3

Cultural Differences

Aims and Objectives

In this unit you will learn:
1. Genre/Style: Exposition/Argumentation
2. Word Power: "To" Used as a Preposition
3. Grammar Focus: Prepositions/Adverbs
4. Writing Skill: Exemplification
5. Translation Skill: Splitting and Combing (3)
6. Reading Skill: Reading for the Implied Main Idea

Brief Introductions to the Texts

The first passage is about the diverse cultural influences upon the use of space. The second and third passages talk about the cultural differences in the world.

Unit 3 Cultural Differences

Part A — Intensive Reading

eading

Pre-Reading

Task 1

Use your common sense to decide whether the following practices are adopted in China or in the US. Put a check in the appropriate box. Then discuss in groups or in pairs about the advantages and disadvantages of these practices.

Practice\country	China	USA
1. Good fences make good neighbors.		
2. Going around examining things in a friend's room is quite all right.		
3. Using space as a refuge from others is the only way to achieve privacy.		
4. Asking people personal questions shows your concern for them.		
5. Withdrawing into oneself is a way of achieving privacy.		
6. "Knock before you enter" is a rule followed even by parents.		
7. Don't be curious about the private affairs of others.		
8. Respecting personal privacy is required of everyone.		

Task 2

Below are ten statements, 4 of which are true according to the text. Read the statements carefully. Choose the ones that you think are correct and discuss them with your partner(s).

1. What impresses a tourist immediately in a foreign country is its architectural features.
2. It is man who shapes his environment, but the environment doesn't influence him.
3. Functions of rooms determine the way space is used inside homes in America.
4. From the context, space means room or airspace.
5. Privacy is only a Western concept.
6. Privacy is different in different cultures.
7. The Japanese and Russians don't have privacy because they don't have a word for it.

8. If British people want to achieve privacy, they will lock the door and make themselves physically separated from others.
9. From the passage, we can see that the development of the sense of privacy depends on how large a room an individual lives in.
10. In America, one room usually serves only one function, while in Japan, one room may serve several functions.

Reading and Thinking

Space[1]

"We shape our buildings and they shape us."[2]
By **Winston Churchill**

How do you understand Winston Churchill's words?

Architectural Differences

When we travel abroad we are immediately impressed by the many ways buildings, homes, and cities are designed. The division and organization of space lend character and uniqueness to villages, towns, and cities. Yet, architectural differences may also cause confusion or

---

1. **Space:** This article is taken from *Beyond Language: Intercultural Communication for English as a Second Language* by Deena R. Levine and Mara B. Adelman, Prentice-Hall, Inc.
2. **We shape our buildings and they shape us:** People make their buildings according to their cultural patterns, and conversely, these buildings greatly affect their cultural patterns, because buildings have a close relationship with human behavior patterns, social forms, and institutions.

Unit 3 Cultural Differences

discomfort for the traveler. In the following example, a group of Americans living in a country in South America reacted emotionally to the architectural differences they observed.

What does this example show?

The Latin house is often built around a patio that is next to the sidewalk but hidden from outsiders behind a wall. It is not easy to describe the degree to which small architectural differences such as this affect outsiders. American... technicians living in Latin America used to complain that they felt "left out" of things, that they were "shut off". Others kept wondering what was going on "behind those walls."

What does "this" here refer to?

The separation of space inside homes may also vary from culture to culture. In most American homes the layout of rooms reveals the separateness and labeling of space according to function—bedroom, living room, dining room, playroom, and so on. This system is in sharp contrast to other cultures where one room in a house may serve several functions. In Japan, homes with sliding walls can change a large room into two small rooms so that a living room can also serve as a bedroom.

What does "this system" refer to?

When a home or a city's design is influenced by another culture, the "native" architecture can be lost or disguised. For example, a French architect was asked to design Chandigarh[1], the capital city in Punjab[2], India. He decided to plan the city with centralized shopping centers which required public transportation and movement away from the village centers. Eventually the Indians stopped

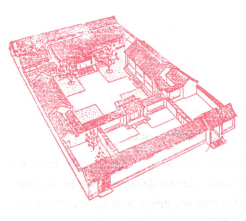

---

1. **Chandigarh** /ˈtʃʌndigə/: capital of Punjab State in NW India. It's a new administrative city, designed by the famous French architect and painter Le Corbusier (1887 — 1965) and built in the 1950s. 昌迪加

2. **Punjab** /ˈpʌndʒɑːb/: a state of India, a rich agricultural area 旁遮普邦

meeting each other socially in their small neighborhoods. Apparently, the introduction of a non-Indian style of architecture affected some of the cultural and social patterns of those living in the city.

> What does a non-Indian style of architecture refer to?

Privacy and the Use of Space

Architectural design influences how privacy is achieved as well as how social contact is made in public places. The concept of privacy is not unique to a particular culture but what it means is culturally determined. For example,

> ... according to Donald Keene, author of "Living Japan," there is no Japanese word for privacy. Yet one cannot say that concept of privacy does not exist among the Japanese but only that it is very different from the Western conception.

Similarly, there is no word in the Russian language that means exactly the same as the English word "privacy".

People in the United States tend to achieve privacy by physically separating themselves from others. The expression "good fences make good neighbors" indicates a preference for privacy from neighbors' homes. If a family can afford it, each child has his or her own bedroom. When privacy is needed, family members may lock their bedroom doors.

> When the American wants to be alone he goes into a room and shuts the door — he depends on architectural features for screening. The English, on the other hand, lacking rooms of their own since childhood, never developed the practice of using space as a refuge from others.

> Can you guess the meaning of "refuge" from the context?

In some cultures when individuals desire privacy, it is acceptable for them simply to withdraw into themselves. That is, they do not need to remove themselves physically from a group in order to achieve privacy.

> What is the function of this last sentence in the paragraph?

Young American children learn the rule "knock before you enter" which teaches them to respect others' privacy. Parents, too, often follow this rule prior to entering their children's rooms. When a

Unit 3 Cultural Differences

70 bedroom door is closed, it may be a sign to others saying, "I need privacy," "I'm angry," or "Do not disturb ... I'm busy." For Americans, the physical division of space and the use of architectural features permit a sense of privacy.

The way space is used to enable the individual to achieve privacy, 75 to build homes or to design cities is culturally influenced. Dr. Hall summarizes the relationship between individuals and their physical surroundings:

Man and his extension constitute one interrelated system. It is a mistake ... to act as though man were one thing and his house or 80 *his cities, ... or his language ... were something else.* (711 words)

What is discussed here?

NEW WORDS

architectural /ˌɑːkɪˈtektʃərəl/	a.	connected with the design of buildings 建筑上的，建筑学的	
impress /ɪmˈpres/	vt.	to make sb. have good feelings or thoughts about sb. else or sth. 留下印象；印，盖印	
division /dɪˈvɪʒən/	n.	something that divides or separates 分，分开；分配，分担，除（法），部门	
organization /ˌɔːɡənaɪˈzeɪʃən/	n.	planning or arranging sth. 组织；机构，团体	
character /ˈkærɪktə/	n.	the qualities which make a person different from another 性格，品质，特性，特征，人物，角色，符号；（汉）字	
confusion /kənˈfjuːʒən/	n.	mix-up 混乱，模糊	
discomfort /dɪsˈkʌmfət/	n.	不便之处，不适	
patio /ˈpɑːtiəʊ, ˈpætiəʊ/	n.	an open paved area joined with a house, on which people sit, eat, etc. 院子，天井	
sidewalk /ˈsaɪdwɔːk/	n.	[AmE.] footpath 人行道	
outsider /aʊtˈsaɪdə/	n.	外来者，外人	
technician /tekˈnɪʃən/	n.	person who has been trained to do sth. that involves some skill 技师，技术员	
complain /kəmˈpleɪn/	v.	to say that you don't like sth. 抱怨；控告	

Part A
Intensive Reading

layout /'leiaut/	n.	way in which sth. is arranged, planned, designed, etc. 布局，安排，设计
reveal /ri'viːl/	vt.	to allow sth. to be seen that was previously hidden 展现，显示；揭示，暴露
disguise /dis'gaiz/	vt.	to hide the identity (of sb. or sth.) by changing his/its appearance 佯装；隐藏
apparent /ə'pærənt/	a.	easy to see or understand 显然的，外观上的
apparently /ə'pærəntli/	ad.	显然地
★ privacy /'praivəsi/	n.	state of being alone and undisturbed 独处；隐私，私秘
concept /'kɔnsept/	n.	an idea 观念，概念
★ conception /kən'sepʃən/	n.	the act of forming an idea, plan, etc.; idea 构想，设想；思想，观念，概念
screen /skriːn/	n.	a movable or fixed device that provides shelter 屏风，遮帘；屏幕
	vt.	to shelter, hide, protect from view 遮蔽，隐蔽，掩护
childhood /'tʃaildhud/	n.	the time when you were a child 孩童时期
★ refuge /'refjuːdʒ/	n.	shelter from danger or trouble; a safe place 庇护，避难；避难所
withdraw /wið'drɔː/	vi.	to move back or away 缩回，退出
	vt.	remove or take sth. away 收回，撤销
prior /'praiə/	a.	earlier, coming or planned before 在前的，预先的；优先的；较重要的
prior to		在……之前
surrounding /sə'raundiŋ/	n.	environment 环境，周围的事物
constitute /'kɔnstitjuːt/	vt.	to make up or form 建成，组成；设立
interrelated /intə'rileitid/	a.	having a relationship with common and shared interest 互相联系的

PHRASES

lend to	to add sth. to sth. else 增添
leave out	not to include or put in; pay no attention to 省去；漏掉；冷落，忽视

Unit 3 Cultural Differences

shut off	to keep away (from); to separate (from) 阻断，排除；拒之门外，与世隔绝
in contrast to /with	as compared with 与……形成对比，和……对照
serve as	to fulfill the purpose of 充当，用作，当作
make contact (with)	to get in touch, esp. after much effort; to complete an electrical circuit 与……接触；通电(流)
prior to	prep. [fml] before (time or event) 在……之前

EXERCISES

Reading Comprehension

Task 3

The following statements are the main ideas of some paragraphs of the text. Match each statement with its related paragraph number.

A. Americans are taught from childhood to respect others' privacy.

B. The separation of space inside homes varies with different cultures.

C. Architectural differences, which are determined by the division and organization of space, always cause people to react emotionally.

D. Peoples' cultures shape their surroundings, that is, the way space is used, which in turn has a very great influence upon their cultures.

E. The concept of privacy and ways to achieve it also vary with different cultures.

F. The traditional social life of Indians in the city of Chandigrah has been affected by a foreign style of city design.

G. When desiring privacy, Americans prefer architectural features for screening, while people of other cultures simply withdraw into themselves, instead of using space as a refuge from others.

Task 4

Find answers to the following questions in the text.

1. What does the subtitle "We shape our buildings and they shape us" suggest?

2. What impresses us first in a foreign country?

3. How did the Americans living in a country in South America feel?

4. What does the design of most American homes show?

5. Why did the Indians finally stop meeting each other in their village communities?

6. What determines the concept of privacy?

7. What does the expression "good fences make good neighbors" imply?

8. How do Americans achieve privacy?

9. What may people of some cultures do when they withdraw into themselves?

10. What do members of an American family do when they need privacy?

11. Which rule teaches young American children to respect other's privacy?

12. What do American parents generally do before they enter their children's rooms?

Vocabulary

Task 5

Give words or phrases that are close in meaning to the underlined part in each of the following sentences.

1. Only one engine was still <u>working</u>.
2. You don't see animals in their natural <u>environment</u> at a zoo.
3. The computer error was <u>clearly</u> caused by a programming error.
4. Steven <u>hid</u> the fact from his mother.
5. Such influence can change one's <u>nature</u> for the better.
6. We objected to the <u>arrangement</u> of the house.
7. My father had showed no signs of being in pain <u>before</u> suffering a heart attack.
8. Each baby has its own <u>individual</u> personality.
9. We're still trying to <u>get in touch with</u> the person who wrote the original letter.
10. It is difficult to believe that the different groups living within their borders <u>make up</u> a single society.

Unit 3 Cultural Differences

11. Bob is a well-known <u>writer</u> of five detective novels.
12. Helen <u>was angry about</u> the fact that she had too much work to do.
13. Some competitors <u>dropped out</u> at the last minute.
14. Barbara is busy with the <u>arrangement</u> of her daughter's wedding.

Task 6

Using the proper form, choose the correct word to fit each sentence.

1. to divide, divide, division
    a. We should make a fair _____ of the profits.
    b. This big house has been _____ into apartments.
    c. The _____ between rich and poor countries is continually growing.
2. to confuse, confusion
    a. The road signs _____ me.
    b. She was in a state of mental _____.
    c. The meeting broke up in great _____.
    d. The little girl felt _____, even frightened.
    e. "Character" is a _____ word because it has many meanings.
3. technical, technically, technician, technique
    a. You'll have to improve your driving _____ if you want to pass your test.
    b. There have been a number of _____ problems with the production.
    c. _____, you aren't allowed to do that.
    d. One of our _____ will repair the broken machine.
    e. You should employ a variety of _____ in the test.
4. concept, conception
    a. He introduced the _____ of selling books via the Internet.
    b. We have no _____ of what people suffered during the war.
    c. Most children have no _____ of time.
    d. The basic _____ of physics can be quite difficult to understand.
5. summary, to summarize
    a. A brief _____ of the experiment is given at the beginning of the report.
    b. Could you _____ the story so far?
    c. Before each episode, the narrator _____ earlier events in the story.
    d. The assignment was to write a _____ of the news.
6. private, privacy
    a. In such matters _____ is impossible.
    b. Mrs. Ross asked for a _____ conversation.

c. I wish to speak to you in _____.
d. It's very impolite to intrude on another person's _____.
e. The Oscar-winning actress lived in absolute _____.

7. to extend, extension, extent
   a. They have built an _____ to the hospital.
   b. The _____ of a judge's power is limited by law.
   c. Can't you _____ your visit for a few more days?
   d. The new _____ to the old school will make room for more students.
   e. We _____ a warm welcome to our guest.

8. to relate, relation, related, relative, relatively
   a. He _____ his adventures to his children.
   b. The two things are said to be _____.
   c. The traveler used the map to discover where he was in _____ to his surroundings.
   d. Happiness is a _____ concept.
   e. It is _____ cold today.
   f. It is difficult to _____ these results with any known cause.

9. to impress, impression, impressive, impressively
   a. What's your _____ of our new teacher?
   b. Paul made a good _____ on his first day at work.
   c. Simon was so _____ by Clare's singing that he asked her to sing on the radio.
   d. All our warnings made little _____ on James.
   e. Mark always _____ on us the need to do our best.
   f. Your work is very _____.

Task 7

Explain the meanings of the italicized words in the following sentences in Chinese.

1. She *revealed* that she had serious money problems.
2. In a moment, the curtains will open to *reveal* tonight's star prize.
3. He felt he was on a downward *slide* in which nothing was going right in his life.
4. The history professor showed us *slides* of the Forbidden City.
5. I *slid* out of the room when nobody was looking.
6. Sheila's ambition is to write for the *screen*.
7. All applicants for the teaching jobs have to be *screened* to see whether they have a criminal record.
8. The house was hidden by a *screen* of tall trees.
9. The programme was too violent to be *screened* before 9 o'clock.

Unit 3 Cultural Differences

10. She raised her hand to *screen* her eyes from the sun.

Further Practice

Task 8

Put the following phrases into English.

1. 平均分配
2. 独特的经历
3. 揭露真相
4. 截止时间的延迟
5. 构成直接威胁
6. 果断的性格

Task 9

Translate the following sentences into English, using the words or phrases given in the parentheses.

1. 虽然人们都需要隐私，但人们获得隐私的方法却因文化而异。在一些人口密集的大城市，人们只能靠回避周围人的活动来达到获得隐私的目的。(achieve, withdraw into oneself)
2. 各个国家的建筑风格是由其特定文化决定的，而且由于建筑空间的划分和组织方式的不同，我们能在不同的地方欣赏到不同的建筑风格。(architectural, division)
3. 一般来说，各城市、乡村都有其独特的风俗习惯，但外国文化的引入却常常会影响当地人民的生活方式和社会交往。(introduction, affect)

Task 10

Write a summary of the text from the following four aspects.

1. Architectural differences
2. The influence of architectural design on people
3. The different ways to achieve privacy
4. The relationship between man and his surroundings

Grammar

Task 11

Complete the following sentences with the connectors given in the box below.

because	even if	for fear that	in order that	on condition
or	since	until	while	

1. Alice has been pursuing a career in architecture _____ she graduated in June.

Part A
Intensive Reading

2. Heat can be conducted from a hot body to a colder one _____ both are at the same temperature.
3. The people at the party were worried about John _____ no one was aware of where he had gone.
4. _____ air is made up of different substances, it is not a pure substance.
5. You can go there, _____ you are on good terms with all the neighbors.
6. _____ I admit that the situation is critical, I don't agree that there is no way out.
7. Any living thing, however small _____ simple it may seem, is far more complex than anything that has no life.
8. There is a lot for us to do _____ our industry can develop at a still higher speed.
9. We all seemed afraid to say what was in our minds, _____ it might start trouble.
10. We should go on with the work _____ we meet with all sorts of difficulties.

Extra Reading

Task 12

Read the following two introductions and answer the five questions that follow regarding each one.

a.
Intercultural Communicatio

An Advanced Resource Book

Adrian Holliday, Martin Hyde and **John Kullman**, all at Canterbury Christ Church University College, UK

'A novel and interesting approach ... educationally useful across many disciplines.'
– Brian Tomlinson, Leeds Metropolitan University

Intercultural Communication is a comprehensive resource book which provides students and researchers with support for advanced study of the topic. It introduces the key theories of intercultural communication and explores ways in which people communicate within and across social groups. The book is built around three themes

b.
Shortlisted for the BAAL Book Prize 2003
Communicating
The Multiple Modes of Human Interconnection

Ruth Finnegan, The Open University, UK

'It's an ideal work for student ... but would also be of interest to anyone who wants an insight into how human beings work with each other, and how far we have come in achieving this.'
– The Independent

In Communicating, the anthropologist Ruth Finnegan considers the many and varied modes through which we humans communicate and the multisensory resources we draw on. The book uncovers the amazing array of sounds, sights, smells, gestures, looks, movements, touches and material objects which humans use so creatively to interconnect both nearby and across space and time

Unit 3 Cultural Differences

– identity, otherization and representation – which are followed and developed over the book's three sections.

The book brings together influential articles, sets them in context and discusses their contribution to the field. These core readings are all fully annotated. *Intercultural Communication* includes readings by James Paul Gee, James P. Lantolf, Les Back, Richard Dyer, Jacques Derrida and Alastair Pennycook.

Section C of this volume builds on knowledge gained in the first two sections, setting thoughtful tasks around further illustrative material. This enables readers to engage more actively with the subject matter and encourages them to develop their own responses.

June 2004(UK)/August 2004(US): 246x174: 320pp: illus. 10 tables
Hb: 0-415-27060-X: **£55.00**
Pb: 0-415-27061-8: **£16.99**

– resources consistently underestimated in those Western ideologies that prioritize 'rationality' and referential language.

With examples from many cultures and historical periods, Finnegan draws together recent research in anthropology, sociolinguistics, cultural studies, cultural history and animal communication, to highlight the multidimensional character of human communicating.

2002: 234x156: 336pp: illus. 44 b+w photos
Hb: 0-415-24117-0: **£60.00**
Pb: 0-415-24118-9: **£17.99**

1. Who gives his high praise for the book? _____
2. What is the sub-title of the book? _____
3. When was the book published? _____
4. What is the size of the book? _____
5. What is the ISBN (International Standard Book Number) of the paperback? _____

riting

举例法 (Exemplification)

　　一般来讲，概括性太宽泛的句子不具有太强的说服力，往往需要一点具体内容加以支持。这个时候我们就要求助于例子了。本单元课文反复使用举例法，使原先抽象的概念（如"space"，"privacy"）变得具体，如果没有这些例子，读者很难理解什么是空间，什么是隐私。

　　对处于英文写作基础阶段的学习者来讲，一般要借助衔接词来引导例子，举例法中常用的衔接词有：

　　1) 介词短语：for example, for instance, in illustration of, by way of examples

2) 形容词短语：such as, such... as ...

3) 副词：as

4) 动词短语：be an example of , be a case in point, take an example, provide an example, use an example, bring forward a case, draw an example

Task 13

Read the following two paragraphs, and find the examples cited and the sign post (引导词) used for the example.

1) Mexico has long been a popular country for tourists from all over the world. It offers many unique educational and entertainment opportunities. The Museum of Anthropology（人类学）in Mexico City is world famous. Other smaller museums can be found in the capital, in provincial cities and on university campuses. A further attraction is provided by the many pre-Colombian archeological sites（哥伦布之前的考古场所）. Additional insights into the country's culture, past and present, can be found in the many splendid murals（壁画）that adorn（装点）theaters, universities and other public buildings.

2) Some people will do the strangest things to gain fame. For example, there are those who go in for various kinds of marathons, dancing or blowing bubbles gum for days at a time, to get their names in the paper or in record books of some kind. Then there are people who sit on flagpoles for a week or more, apparently enjoying the attention they receive from the crowd below. There are people who hope to impress others because they ate the most cream pies or because they collected the most bottle tops. And there are even people who seek public notice by way of setting a record for the number of articles of clothing they can put on at one time or the number they can take off. Of course, there are a few mentally twisted individuals who seek fame at the expense of other people's property or even lives, but fortunately the great majority of people satisfy their urge to be remembered in ways that produce little more damage than a bad case of indigestion.

Task 14

Read the following passage, and fill in the blanks with a word or phrase from the table.

What Is Language?

A language is a signaling system which operates with symbolic（符号化）vocal sounds（嗓音）, and which is used by a group of people for purposes of communication.

Let us look at this definition in more detail because it is language, more than anything else, that distinguishes man from the rest of the animal world.

Other animals, it is true, communicate with one another by means of cries. For example,

Unit 3 Cultural Differences

many birds utter warning calls at the approach of danger; apes（猿）utter different cries, such as expressions of anger, fear and pleasure. But these various means of communication differ in important ways from human language. For instance, animals' cries are not articulate（发音清晰的）. This means, basically, that they lack structure. They lack, for example, the kind of structure given by the contrast between vowels（元音）and consonants（辅音）. They also lack the kind of structure that enables us to divide a human utterance（发音）into words.

We can change an utterance by replacing one word by another: a good illustration of this is a soldier who can say, e.g. "tanks approaching from the north", or he can change one word and say "aircraft approaching from the north" or "tanks approaching from the west"; but a bird has a single alarm cry, which means "danger!"

This is why the number of signals that an animal can make is very limited: the famous gorilla, the *Great Tit* is a case in point; it has about twenty different calls, whereas in human language the number of possible utterances is infinite. It also explains why animal cries are very general in meaning.

| illustration | for example | a case in point | an example | for instance | such as |

1) At the approach of danger many birds utter warning calls: this is _____ of animals' communication with each other.
2) Cries, _____ those of danger, fear and pleasure, are uttered by apes.
3) There are important differences between human language and animal communication: _____, animals' cries are not articulate.
4) Animals' cries lack, _____, the kind of structure that enables us to divide a human utterance into words.
5) A good _____ of changing an utterance by substituting one word for another is a soldier who can say "tanks approaching from the north" or "tanks approaching from the west."
6) The number of signals that an animal can make is very limited: the *Great Tit* is _____.

Task 15

How do you summarize the relationship of space, privacy and culture according to the second part of the text? Please write a passage to summarize the relationship, and further discuss it in your own situation.

Translation

拆合法 (Splitting and Combining) (3)

这一单元里我们将介绍拆合法中的抽拆法。

有些句子并不长，结构也不怎么复杂，但译起来总觉得不甚理想，甚至不通顺，比如下面的一句：

- Flying from Australia to Hong Kong, the tourist group then traveled thousands of *interest-filled miles* through China by train.

弄不好，就会译成下面这个样子：

旅行团从澳大利亚乘飞机到香港，然后坐火车在中国旅行了非常有趣的几千里（或：然后坐火车在中国各地作了几千里非常有趣的旅行）。

这句话所以难译就因为一个词：interest-filled，没有这个词，谁都能轻而易举地译成中文。然而，这个词明摆在那儿，回避是不行的。解决办法就是将它抽出来，连同 miles 一起放到后面去：

旅行团从澳大利亚飞到香港，然后坐火车到中国各地旅游，**这个趣味盎然的旅程长达数千里。**

下面这句话中的 "which is the common name for man-made materials" 也是一个很棘手的地方，同样也宜采用抽拆法，不过，这一次我们是将它提前了：

- Many man-made substances are replacing certain natural materials because either the quality of the natural product cannot meet our ever-increasing requirement, or, more often, because the physical properties of the synthetic substance, *which is the common name for man-made materials*, have been chosen, and even emphasized, so that it would be of the greatest use in the fields in which it is to be applied.

人造材料通称合成材料，许多人造材料正在取代某些天然材料，一是因为天然物产的数量有限，满足不了我们日益增长的需求，更多的是因为偏好而且强调

Unit 3 Cultural Differences

合成材料的物理特性。因而，在那些拟应用人造材料的领域，人造材料将会派上极大的用场。

英译汉常会用到各种拆译法，汉译英则更多地会用到合译法。如前所述，英语句子结构比较紧凑，主次分明，汉语则比较松散，主次从形式上看不是十分分明。所以汉译英时，最主要的一点就是要进行语义分析，找出句子的主次，确定主谓，然后对其他部分按照其在句中的功能进行合理安排，如：

- 最后，他又加了几句，自认为是点睛之笔，没想到，到了老师眼里却成了画蛇添足。
  And finally he added a few more sentences, which his teacher thought quite unnecessary, as finishing touches.

- 我有一个朋友，天底下像他那么毛的怕是再也找不出第二个了。
  I have a friend who must be the sloppiest person in the world.

- 有一种人我最不喜欢和他下棋，那便是太有涵养的人。
    这个句子比上面两个句子要复杂一些，初学翻译的人往往一开始便把精力放在了考虑"有"究竟用"have"还是用"there be"句型上，而不是从全句着眼，分析这句话的核心意思。其实这句话换一种说法就是：我最不喜欢与之下棋的人就是太有涵养的人。这样一来，句子的主语就确定下来了，即"人"，其他问题也就迎刃而解了：
The last man I would like to play chess with is a man with too much self-control.

- 杀死他一大块，或是抽了他一个车，他神色自若，不动火，不生气，好像是无关痛痒，使得你觉得索然寡味。
  When he sees a huge piece of his position taken (besieged) by his opponent (as in *Go*), or a chariot lost to his opponent through an erroneous move (as in Chinese chess), he remains calm and unruffled, as if nothing whatever has happened. And that air of his will surely make you feel flat and insipid.

- 说他大手大脚，多数情况下是他活该，但也有冤枉他的时候。

    He has often, not always justly, been criticized for his extravagance.

Task 16

Translate the following sentences into idiomatic Chinese or English, using the method you've learned.

1) In Japan, homes with sliding walls can change a large room into two small rooms so that a living room can also serve as a bedroom.
2) He decided to plan the city with centralized shopping centers which required public transportation and movement away from the village centers.
3) 其实进来的是一个黑瘦的先生，八字须，戴着眼镜，挟着一摞大大小小的书。
4) 她被清华大学录取的消息不胫而走，没出几个小时，全村就尽人皆知了。
5) 他浓眉大眼，很帅。
6) 有下象棋者，久而无声响，排闼视之阒不见人，原来他们是在门后角里扭做一团，一个人骑在另一个人的身上，在他的口里挖车呢。

Quotation

Translation is a process that involves looking for similarities between languages and cultures ... because it is constantly confronting dissimilarities.

— *Lawrence Venuti*

翻译是一个在不同的语言和文化中求同的过程……因为整个翻译过程都要不断地面临差异。

——劳伦斯·韦努蒂

Unit 3 Cultural Differences

Part B ▶Extensive Reading

I. US-French Bickering: Tradition, Not News

Toronto — If you were to believe what you read about France these days, you might think there was something new about Franco-American bickering. But nothing could be further from the truth. While the French ambassador to Washington took the latest spat to a new level last week, alleging a White House-inspired "disinformation campaign" against France, it was really all a part of a long tradition.

Americans and the French spent the second half of the 20th century quarreling on the international stage. And they will continue to spat in the century to come.

Why? It's not that they actually disagree about the fundamental aspects of running a country. Both embrace democratic values, liberty, women's rights, and the primacy of law. Both oppose terrorism. But after 2 years studying the French as fellows of an American institute, we realized that the real difference between the French and Americans is subtler, and more fundamental than these values.

The real difference is in their concept of privacy. By privacy, we don't mean the issue of legally protecting personal information. We're not talking about ideas of personal space. By privacy, we mean each culture's intuitive sense of what's intimate and what's public.

The reasons the French come across to Americans as "rude," "aloof," or "arrogant" have less to do with their attitude, than with their different idea of what you talk about, and what you don't, or what you show, and what you hide.

Almost all Americans traveling in France are stunned at how rude the service is in stores. Many tourists fail to realize that the French, whether they are shop owners, waiters, or clerks, expect to hear two simple words from any outsider on their premises: "*bonjour*"[1] when you enter, and "*au revoir*"[2] when you leave. The reason is simple: The French consider a store an extension of the home of the owner, not a public space. If you don't greet them properly, you can be sure the service will be rude.

---

1. **bonjour**: (法语) 你好
2. **au revoir**: (法语) 再见

On the other hand, behavior that seems rude might not be what you think it is. French ideas about what's private and public also affect the way they make conversation. It's considered rude in France to ask a stranger his name or what he does for a living — information Americans typically use as a polite way to start a conversation.

The French will never ask you about your job right off the bat. To them, it sounds like a way of trying to find out how much you earn. And guess what? Money is an extremely private matter in France. The French may think about money all the time, but they don't like talking about it. If you broach the topic of money with an acquaintance, brace yourself for a rude reaction. It's like an American starting off a conversation by asking your religion.

So how do you start a conversation in France? Even though the French want to know who you are and what you do, they won't ask you. To start a conversation, they'll express an opinion about something — it could be the weather or the national education system for all you know. Your job is to return the favor and give them your opinion back—or at least to display some wit if you have no opinion.

French conversation is like a tennis game. One party serves, and the other returns. To an American, this feels uncomfortably competitive, as if their conversation partners are trying to beat them with arguments. True enough. French conversation is something like a competitive sport. Except that the real goal is to keep the ball in the air as long as possible, not to win.

The French love good conversation. To this end, they are happy to resort to the odd hard shot. Americans are typically taken aback by this. They feel like they are being "attacked" and take it personally. Yet that's because they instinctively believe that arguing is something you do in private.

For the French, expressing disagreement in public is not only acceptable, it's a sign that a relationship is strong. We observed this over and over at dinner parties where there were both North American and French guests. North American couples typically project an image of harmony, supporting and reinforcing each other. Meanwhile, the French couples argued openly in front of the room of guests, even about domestic matters.

To the French, it's normal for couples to argue. So why hide it? The French are actually suspicious of couples that seem too harmonious.

For anyone following international news these days (and who isn't?), the couples theory should ring a bell. What enraged Americans about France's refusal to join the coalition was not so much that the French disagreed about how to disarm Iraq, but that the French refused to show solidarity with Americans at the international dinner table. (819 words)

Unit 3 Cultural Differences

NEW WORDS

bicker	/'bikə/	vi.	斗嘴
		n.	口角
tradition	/trə'diʃən/	n.	sth. that people in a certain place have done or believed for a long time 传统，惯例
ambassador	/æm'bæsədə/	n.	an important person who goes to another country and work there for the government of his/her own country 大使
spat	/spæt/	vi./n.	争吵
★allege	/ə'ledʒ/	vt.	to state that sth. bad is a fact without giving proof 宣称，断言
disinformation	/dis,infə'meiʃən/	n.	故意的假情报
campaign	/kæm'pein/	n.	a plan to do a number of things in order to achieve a special aim 运动；战役
		vi.	参加活动
disagree	/,disə'gri:/	vi.	不一致，不适宜
aspect	/'æspekt/	n.	one part of a problem, idea, etc. (问题等的)方面；方向；面貌
embrace	/im'breis/	v.	to accept sth. eagerly 信奉，拥抱；包含；包围
		n.	拥抱
democratic	/,demə'krætik/	a.	民主的，有民主精神的
primacy	/'praiməsi/	n.	首位
oppose	/ə'pəuz/	vt.	to try to stop or change sth. because you do not like it 反对，反抗
terrorism	/'terəriz(ə)m/	n.	恐怖主义
institute	/'institju:t/	n.	a group of people who meet to study or talk about a special thing 学会，学院，协会
		vt.	建立，设立
subtle	/'sʌtl/	a.	not very noticeable 微妙的；狡猾的；隐约的
legal	/'li:gəl/	a.	allowed by law 法律的；合法的
legally	/'li:gəli/	ad.	法律上，合法地
intuitive	/in'tju(:)itiv/	a.	直觉的
intimate	/'intimit/	a.	having a close, personal relationship 亲密的，隐私的

Part B
Extensive Reading

		vt.	暗示
		n.	密友
rude /ruːd/		a.	not polite 粗鲁的，无礼的；粗糙的
aloof /ə'luːf/		a.	冷淡的
★arrogant /'ærəgənt/		a.	thinking that you are better and more important than other people and not caring about their feelings 傲慢的，自大的
★stun /stʌn/		vt.	to surprise a person by giving him/her some unexpected news 使晕倒，使惊吓；打晕
		n.	晕眩，打昏，惊倒
owner /'əunə/		n.	a person who has sth. 所有者，业主
★premise /'premis/		n.	[pl.] 经营场所；前提
		v.	立前提
bat /bæt, bɑːt/		n.	球棒；蝙蝠
		v.	用球棒击球
extremely /iks'triːmli/		ad.	very 极端地，非常地
broach /brəutʃ/		vt.	开始讨论，提出
topic /'tɔpik/		n.	a subject that you talk, write or learn about 话题，主题
acquaintance /ə'kweintəns/		n.	a person that you know but who is not a close friend 相识，熟人
★brace /breis/		vt.	支住，撑牢
		n.	支柱
reaction /ri(ː)'ækʃən/		n.	sth. that you do or say because of sth. that has happened or been said 反应，反作用，反动（力）
religion /ri'lidʒən/		n.	the belief in a god or gods who made the world and who can control what happens in it 宗教，信仰
display /di'splei/		vt.	to show sth. 显示，表现；陈列，展览
wit /wit/		n.	saying things in a clever and funny way 风趣；智慧
competitive /kəm'petitiv/		a.	竞争的
partner /'pɑːtnə/		n.	one of two people who do sth. together or are closely involved in some way 伙伴，合伙人；配偶
resort /ri'zɔːt/		vi.	(to) to do or use sth. not because you prefer it but because there is no other choice available 求助，诉诸
		n.	凭借；手段；常去之地,胜地

89

Unit 3 Cultural Differences

odd /ɔd/	*a.*	strange or unusual 奇特的；临时的；单数的
aback /ə'bæk/	*ad.*	向后地
harmony /'hɑːməni/	*n.*	having the same ideas, etc., with no arguments 协调，融洽
reinforce /ˌriːin'fɔːs/	*vt.*	to make sth. stronger 加强, 增援
domestic /də'mestik/	*a.*	of or about the home or family 家庭的；国内的；驯服的
★ **suspicious** /səs'piʃəs/	*a.*	(*of*) not believing 可疑的, 怀疑的
harmonious /hɑː'məunjəs/	*a.*	和谐的，协调的
theory /'θiəri/	*n.*	an idea that tries to explain sth. 理论；学说；意见
enrage /in'reidʒ/	*vt.*	激怒
refusal /ri'fjuːzəl/	*n.*	saying "no" when sb. asks you to do sth. or have sth. 拒绝，推却
★ *coalition* /ˌkəuə'liʃn/	*n.*	同盟；结合
disarm /dis'ɑːm, diz-/	*vt.*	解除武装
★ *solidarity* /ˌsɔli'dæriti/	*n.*	团结

PHRASES

come across	make an impression of the specified type 使人产生某种印象
on one's premises	in one's house or other building and the land on which it is built 在某人的经营场所
right off the bat	[*AmE.*] immediately 立即
start off	to begin to move 开始活动
for all sb. knows	do not know anything about it 亦未可知，谁知道呢
keep the ball in the air	让球尽可能滞空
to this end	for this purpose 为达此目的
resort to sth.	to do or use sth. bad or unpleasant because you feel you have no choice 求助于
be taken aback	to shock or surprise sb. 使某人震惊或惊奇
ring a bell	to sound familiar or to remind you, not very clearly, of sth. 听起来耳熟，模糊地记得

Part B

Extensive Reading

EXERCISES

Reading Comprehension

Task 1

Decide whether the following statements are true or false according to the text.

1. The argument between the U.S. and France on international issues will go on for ages.
2. The French and Americans have little in common with regard to fundamental values.
3. In the article, the concept of privacy means freedom from public attention.
4. Americans and the French have a different understanding of the concept of privacy.
5. To Americans, a store is certainly a public space.
6. What is considered rude in France is not common practice in the U.S. either.
7. A polite way to start a conversation in France is to express an opinion about something.
8. In the article, the idea of "keeping the ball in the air as long as possible" implies that you can talk with a stranger about something as long as possible.
9. Expressing disagreement in public is something that American couples typically do.
10. What made Americans angry at the French was that the French refused to show solidarity with them on the international stage.

Vocabulary

Task 2

Complete the following sentences with words given in the box below, change forms if necessary.

ambassador	campaign	aspect	institute	legal	owner	private
typical	bat	topic	acquaintance	reaction	religion	display
partner	argument	competitive	resort	domestic	refusal	

1. _____ it is the girls who offer to help, not the boys.
2. He is the British _____ to Germany.
3. It's a _____ to play tricks on people on April 1.
4. Simon has a wide circle of _____.
5. They organized a _____ to stop people smoking.
6. Posters for the concert were _____ throughout the city.
7. Spelling is one of the most difficult _____ of learning English.
8. Children, hold your _____ hand when you cross the street.

Unit 3 Cultural Differences

9. I shook him to try to wake him up but there was no _____.
10. His _____ to contribute money angered the organizers.
11. The National _____ of Health funds medical research in many areas.
12. I hear the crack of a _____ and the voices of children.
13. I never discuss politics or _____ with strangers.
14. Sue accepted the decision without _____.
15. If we have to lower our prices to remain _____, we will.
16. There is hope the countries will reach a settlement without _____ to armed conflict.

Task 3

Choose words from Column B that are opposite in meaning to those in Column A. Note there are some extra items in Column B.

Column A
1. democratic
2. intimate
3. rude
4. extreme
5. wit
6. odd
7. reinforce
8. oppose
9. harmony
10. display

Column B
a. polite
b. slowness
c. unrepresentative
d. competitive
e. hide
f. disagreement
g. normal
h. weaken
i. support
j. public
k. harmony
l. regular
m. refusal

II. Getting Along Verbally and Nonverbally

When you are in another country, it is important to know the language, but it is equally important to know how to communicate nonverbally. Before saying anything, people communicate nonverbally or by making gestures. According to a pioneer in nonverbal communication, only 30 to 35 percent of our communication is verbal. The rest is nonverbal. When people don't know the language, the most common way to communicate is through gestures. However, many gestures have different meanings, or no meaning at all, in different parts of the world.

10 In the United States, for example, nodding your head up and down means "yes". In some parts of Greece[1] and Turkey[2], however, this motion can mean "no". In Southeast Asia, nodding your head is a polite way of saying "I heard you."

In ancient Rome, when the emperor wanted to spare someone's life, he would put his thumb up. Today in the United States, when someone puts his/her thumb up, it means "Everything is all 15 right." However, in Sardinia[3] and Greece, the gesture is insulting and should not be used there.

In the United States, raising your clasped hands above your head means "I'm the champion" or "I'm the winner." It is the sign prizefighters make when they win a fight. When a leading Russian statesman made this gesture after a White House[4] meeting, Americans misunderstood and thought he meant he was a winner. In the Soviet Union, however, it is a sign of friendship.

20 In the United States, holding your hand up with the thumb and index finger in a circle and the other three fingers spread out means "Everything is O.K." and is frequently used by astronauts and politicians. In France and Belgium[5], it can mean "You're worth nothing."

There are other nonverbal signals that people should be aware of when they go to another country, such as the distance to maintain between speakers. Americans usually feel comfortable 25 when speaking with someone if the distance between them is about eighteen inches to arm's length. Anything closer makes them feel uncomfortable.

When talking to Americans, it is also important to make eye contact. If you look down when talking to an American, he/she may feel that you are embarrassed, afraid, or trying to hide something.

30 In addition to knowing how to communicate nonverbally in a country, it is important to know what you can and cannot discuss. In the United States, there are certain topics to avoid when you first meet someone. For example, don't ask people their age, weight, religion, marital status, how much money they earn, or how much something costs. You can talk about work, the weather, traffic problems, sports, food, news of the day, where one lives, consumer subjects 35 (computers, car repairs, and so forth), and travel or vacation plans.

---

1. **Greece:** 希腊
2. **Turkey:** 土耳其
3. **Sardinia:** 撒丁岛
4. **White House:** 白宫
5. **Belgium:** 比利时

Unit 3 Cultural Differences

These few examples illustrate that your actions can speak louder than your words. In a particular cultural context, what you say and what you don't say are equally important. (498 words)

NEW WORDS

★verbal /ˈvɜːbl/		a.	of or using words; spoken 言辞的；口头的
verbally /ˈvɜːbli/		ad.	in spoken words 口头上
motion /ˈməʊʃn/		n.	movement or a way of moving 运动，动作；手势；提议
		v.	示意
southeast /ˌsaʊθˈiːst/		n./a./ad.	midway between south and east 东南，东南的，向东南
emperor /ˈempərə/		n.	head of an empire 皇帝
insult /ɪnˈsʌlt/		v.	to do sth. to offend by speech or act 侮辱，辱骂，对人无理
/ˈɪnsʌlt/		n.	words or action that insults 侮辱，凌辱
clasp /klɑːsp/		v.	to hold sb./sth. tightly 紧握，搂抱
		n.	扣子，钩；握，抱住
champion /ˈtʃæmpjən/		n.	person or team taking the first place in a competition 冠军，捍卫者，拥护者
prizefighter /ˈpraɪzˌfaɪtə(r)/		n.	职业拳击手
★statesman /ˈsteɪtsmən/		n.	a person taking an important part in the management of state affairs 政治家
index /ˈɪndeks/		n.	a list or words from A to Z at the end of a book 索引；标志，[数学]指数
		vt.	编入索引中
▲astronaut /ˈæstrənɔːt/		n.	a person who travels in space 宇航员，太空人
politician /ˌpɒlɪˈtɪʃn/		n.	a person who works (wants to work) in the government 政治家，政客
signal /ˈsɪgnl/		n.	a light, sound or movement that tells you sth. without words 信号
		a.	显著的；重大的；信号的
		v.	发信号

Part B
Extensive Reading

aware /ə'wɛə/	a.	(*of sth.*) knowing about sth. 知道的，明白的，意识到的
▲marital /'mærɪtl/	a.	of marriage 婚姻的
status /'steɪtəs/	n.	position in society 地位，身份；状态，情形
consumer /kən'sjuːmə/	n.	a person who uses (manufactured) goods 消费者，用户
illustrate /'iləstreit/	vt.	to explain or make sth. clear by using examples, pictures or diagrams 说明，阐明；图解，加插图于
action /'ækʃən/	n.	sth. that you do 行为；行动；作用；情节
context /'kɔntekst/	n.	conditions in which an event, action, etc. takes place 背景，环境；语境，上下文

PHRASES

get along	to make progress; to manage 进展；过活，生活
be aware of	知道，觉察到，明白
in addition to	as well 除……外（还），加于……之上
and so forth	and so on 等等

EXERCISES

Reading Comprehension

Task 1

Find answers to the following questions.

1. How much of our communication is nonverbal?
2. What is the most common way to communicate with people speaking an unfamiliar language?
3. How many kinds of nonverbal communication signals are mentioned in the passage?
4. How do you understand the phrase "your actions can speak louder than your words" in paragraph 9?
5. What is the main idea of the passage?

Unit 3 Cultural Differences

Task 2

Give words or phrases that are close in meaning to the underlined parts in each of the following sentences.

1. The rocking <u>movement</u> of the ship upset her stomach.
2. Doctors have high social <u>positions</u> in most countries.
3. Store managers should protect the rights of <u>customers</u>.
4. He could get fifty dollars extra income every month <u>as well as</u> his salary.
5. Bill was <u>offended</u> that he hadn't been invited to the party.
6. The <u>winner</u> of the race will receive a prize of $500.
7. Some people believe that face is an <u>indication of</u> character.
8. I am <u>familiar with</u> the difficulties you face.
9. To <u>explain</u> her point, she told a story about how her family felt when they moved here.
10. We should see the matter in its historical <u>background</u>.
11. I <u>signed</u> that I was turning left.
12. David is regretting his <u>deed</u>.

Part C — Reading Skill

Reading for the Implied Main Idea

When a main idea is not stated clearly, or when the writer suggests the idea to you through the information given in the paragraph, the idea is implied. An implied main idea is one that is suggested.

The first boring task is to prepare breakfast. Tommy and Mary need juice and eggs before a day at school; my husband, Bill, coffee and bread before he speeds off to the office, when everyone is finally away, doing something he or she enjoys, I clean the table and wash the dishes. Then I have to make beds, wash the kitchen floor, and clean the living room. I also have to do washing, prepare lunch and supper, and do all kinds of things, all along thinking of the exciting things my *children are learning in school while their housewife mother watches the house in the suburbs; and Bill, the people he meets, the things he sees on the streets every day — these are things I'll never know. I sweep floors, sew buttons, wash dishes. That's my work in the world.*

One way to state the main idea of the paragraph is "My life as a housewife is full of dull, boring tasks".

No one sentence makes that point, and the writer never tells us exactly that her life is filled with dull, boring jobs. Instead, we add up the details she gives us in order to state the main idea in our own words. She finds making breakfast dull, washing dishes boring, cleaning the house lonely and tiresome. She wishes that she could see the exciting things her husband finds in his work. Putting all that information together, we conclude that the writer is trying to show us that as a housewife she leads a dull life.

Read the following paragraphs carefully to find out whether the main idea is stated or implied. If it is stated, write down the number of the sentence that conveys the main idea in the blank provided beneath each paragraph. If the main idea is not clearly stated, write a complete sentence that conveys the main idea of the paragraph.

Task 1

(1) Dishes have to be washed. There are floors to sweep and clothes to wash, fold, and put away. (2) Windows need to be washed, and furniture needs to be dusted and polished. (3) Besides these small jobs, houses need constant organization too.

1. Is the main idea stated in a topic sentence? _____
   If so, what is the number of the sentence? _____
2. In your own words, what is the main idea of this paragraph? (Write a complete sentence.)

_____

Task 2

(1) College classrooms are no longer full of only eager, young faces fresh out of high school. (2) The eighteen-year-old is still there, of course, (3) but next to him may sit someone just as eager — and old enough to be his grandmother. (4) Grandmother may have always wanted to learn French, and now at last her chance has come. (5) Across the room is a thirty-year-old man who may have just spent four years in the Army. (6) He postponed his studies, but has now found a chance to go to school. (7) Right in front of him sits a housewife who found out there is just enough time for a class or two while her children are at school. (8) Then there is the middle-aged

Unit 3 Cultural Differences

driver who is back in school because he wants a new career. (9) This variety on the college campus shows our nation-wide trend to "life-long learning."

1. Is the main idea stated in a topic sentence? _____

   If so, what is the number of the sentence? _____

2. In your own words, what is the main idea about this topic? (State the idea in a complete sentence.) _____

Task 3

(1) Body temperature determines whether you are a morning person or an evening person. (2) During the course of a day, our body temperature rises and falls at regular times. (3) Although we don't notice the change, it does affect our sleeping patterns. (4) When body temperature is up, we are awake. (5) As it falls, we grow tired and, finally, we sleep. (6) As a result, anyone who has a fast-rising temperature cycle is a "morning person" and can immediately jump out of bed. (7) An "evening person", on the other hand, has a body temperature that rises slowly. (8) It doesn't reach its high point until mid-afternoon when this person feels best.

1. Is the main idea stated in a topic sentence? _____

   If so, w hat is the number of the sentence? _____

2. In your own words, what is the main idea about this topic? (State the idea in a complete sentence.) _____

Unit 4

On Relations

Aims and Objectives

In this unit you will learn:
1. Genre/Style: Exposition
2. Word Power: Antonyms
3. Grammar Focus: The Word "While" and Parallelism
4. Translation Skill: Shift/Conversion (2)
5. Writing Skill: Comparison and Contrast
6. Reading Skill: The Organization of a Discourse

Brief Introductions to the Texts

The passage "Thanksgiving" focuses on two concepts, individualism and family. Americans place high value on individualism. Each person stands on his/her own merits. One person rather than a committee or group is responsible for the business or some part of it. If the business he/she is in charge of does not do well, it is the leader who takes responsibility. This is often true even when some subordinates might be the cause of any problems. Americans also value belonging to a family. The passage attempts to explain the interplay of these two ideals.

"Why I Want a Wife" uses sarcastic humor to make a point about the burdens some wives suffer. Since the author is a woman, the humor of saying that she wants a wife is obvious. In explaining why she wants a wife, she illustrates the many benefits a wife provides to her husband.

The last passage in this unit is an adaptation of O'Henry's "October and June." He wrote mostly about ordinary people and gained notoriety for the surprise endings to his stories.

Unit 4 On Relations

Part A — Intensive Reading

eading

Pre-Reading

Task 1

Please tell one another how much you know about Thanksgiving?
Time: _____
Traditional food: _____

Task 2

Answer the following questions briefly.
1. Why are young people so eager to move out of home?
2. When will the Chinese show gratitude and best wishes?

Reading and Thinking

Thanksgiving

By Ellen Goodman[1]

     Soon they will be together again, all the people who travel between their own lives and each other's. The package tour[2] of the season will
5 tempt them this week to the

---

1. **Ellen Goodman:** 爱伦·古德曼 a journalist who won the Pulitzer Prize in 1980 for distinguished commentary. This piece was first published in the Boston Globe in 1980.
2. **package tour** 或 **package holiday:** holiday tour with many details arranged in advance by travel agents and sold at a fixed price（由旅行社）代办的（包价）旅行

family table. By Thursday, feast day, family day, Thanksgiving day, Americans who value individualism like no other people will collect around a million tables in a ritual of belonging.

    They will assemble their families the way they assemble dinner:
10 each one bearing a personality as different as cranberry sauce[1] and pumpkin pie. For one dinner they will cook for each other, fuss for each other, feed each other and argue with each other. They will nod at their common heritage, the craziness and caring of other generations. They will measure their common legacy — the children.

15   All these complex cells, these men and women, old and young, with different dreams and disappointments will give honour again to the group they are a part of and apart from: their family. Families and individuals. The "we" and the "I". As good Americans we all travel between these two ideals. We take value trips from the great American
20 notion of individualism to the great American vision of family. We wear out our tires driving back and forth, using speed to shorten the distance between these two principles.

    There has always been some pavement between a person and a family. From the first moment we recognize that we are separate we
25 begin to struggle with aloneness and togetherness. Here and now these conflicts are especially sharp. We are, after all, raised in families...to be individuals. This double message follows us through life. We are taught about the freedom of the "I" and the safety of the "we". The loneliness of the "I" and the intrusiveness of the "we". The selfishness
30 of the "I" and the burdens of the "we".

    We are taught what Andre Malraux[2] said: "Without a family, man, alone in the world, trembles with the cold." And taught what he said another day: "The denial of the supreme importance of the mind's development accounts for many revolts against the family." In theory,
35 the world rewards "the supreme importance" of the individual, the ego. We think alone, inside our heads. We write music and literature with an enlarged sense of self. We are graded and paid, hired and

---

1. **cranberry** /ˈkrænˌbəri/ **sauce and pumpkin pie:** 酸果蔓酱和南瓜馅饼
2. **Andre Malraux:** 安迪·马罗克斯

Sidebar questions:
- What does "a ritual" refer to?
- Can you replace "bearing" with another word?
- What do "these complex cells" mean?
- What are "these two ideals?"
- Are the principles the same as those "ideals"?
- What does "this double message" refer to?
- Does he catch a cold?

Unit 4 On Relations

fired, on our own merit[1]. The rank of individualism is both exciting and cruel. Here is where the fittest survive.

The family, on the other hand, at its best, works very differently. We don't have to achieve to be accepted by our families. We just have to be. Our membership is not based on certificates but on birth. As Malraux put it, "A friend loves you for your intelligence, a lover for your charm, but your family's love is unreasoning: you were born into it and of its flesh and blood[2]."

The family is formed not for the survival of the fittest but for the weakest. It is not an economic unit but an emotional one. This is not the place where people fiercely compete with each other but where they work for each other. Its business is taking care, and when it works, it is not indifferent but kind.

<mark>Whose business?</mark>

There are fewer heroes, fewer stars in family life. While the world may glorify the self, the family asks us, at one time or another, to submerge it. While the world may abandon us, the family promises, at one time or another, to protect us. So we commute daily, weekly, yearly between one world and another. Between a life as a family member that can be nurturing or smothering. Between life as an individual that can free us or flatten us. We hesitate between two separate sets of demands and possibilities.

The people who will gather around this table Thursday live in both of these worlds, a part of and apart from each other. With any luck the territory they travel from one to another can be a fertile one, rich with care and space. It can be a place where the "I" and the "we" interact. On this day at least, they will bring to each other something both special and something to be shared: these separate selves. (703 words)

<mark>Which word does "one" refer to?</mark>

---

1. **on one' own merit:** deserving approval due to one's own behavior or value 凭自己的价值，功绩
2. **its flesh and blood:** one's own relatives 肉体，这里指自己的骨肉和亲人

Part A
Intensive Reading

NEW WORDS

★ tempt /tempt/		vt.	to attract (sb.) to have or do sth., to persuade (sb.) to do sth. wrong or foolish 引诱，诱惑；说服，劝诱
★ feast /ˈfiːst/		n.	religious anniversary or festival splendid meal 宗教节日；盛宴
		v.	to take part in a party or pass time in party 参加宴会；款宴
individualism /ˌindiˈvidjuəlizəm/		n.	the idea that freedom of thought and action for each person is the most important quality of a society, rather than shared effort and responsibility 个人主义，利己主义
cranberry /ˈkrænbəri; ˈkrænberi/		n.	a small round red fruit with a sour taste 酸果蔓的果实
sauce /sɔːs; sɔs/		n.	liquid or semi liquid dressing 调味料
		vt.	to season or flavor with sauce 给……加味，调味
★ pumpkin /ˈpʌmpkin/		n.	a large round vegetable with hard yellow or orange flesh 南瓜
fuss /fʌs/		n.	unnecessarily nervous, excitement, esp. about unimportant things 大惊小怪，忙乱，小题大做
		vi.	to pay too much attention to small, unimportant details; to worry a lot about unimportant things 小题大做；(为琐事) 烦恼，过于忧虑
▲ legacy /ˈleɡəsi/		n.	money, etc. received by a person under the will of and at the death of another person; sth. handed down from ancestors 遗产；遗留下来的东西
apart /əˈpɑːt/		ad.	separated by a certain distance, distant; in parts 相间隔；分离，分开
		a.	分离的，分隔的
ideal /aiˈdiəl/		a.	satisfying one's idea of what is perfect 理想的，完美的
		n.	idea, example, looked upon as perfect 理想
idealistic /ˌaidiuˈlistik/		a.	理想主义的，唯心主义的
notion /ˈnəuʃən/		n.	idea, opinion 观念，意见

103

Unit 4 On Relations

pave /peiv/	vt.	to cover with a hard, smooth surface 铺砌
pavement /ˌpeivmənt/	n.	sidewalk [BrE.] 人行道
alone /əˈləun/	a.	only or without any others 单独的，独一无二的，孤独的，独自的
aloneness /əˈləunis/	n.	孤独
togetherness /təˈgeðənis/	n.	the pleasant feeling of being united with other people in friendship and understanding 团结精神；归属感
conflict /ˈkɔnflikt/	n.	quarrel, struggle, fight, argument between two or more groups of people or countries 冲突，争论，抵触
/kənˈflikt/	vt.	(beliefs, needs, or facts, etc.) to be very different and cannot easily exist together or both be true; to fight or disagree actively 相反，抵触，冲突
▲intrude /inˈtruːd/	vi.	(into, on, upon) to bring in unnecessarily; to come in when not wanted 侵入，侵扰；打扰
intrusive /inˈtruːsiv/	a.	intruding or tending to intrude 入侵的，闯入的
intrusiveness	n.	侵入；打扰
burden /ˈbəːdən/	n.	a heavy load that you carry；something difficult or unpleasant that you have to deal with or worry about 担子；负担
tremble /ˈtrembəl/	vi.	to shake uncontrollably as from fear, coldness, excitement, etc. 颤抖，哆嗦
	n.	shaking 颤抖，哆嗦
denial /diˈnaiəl/	n.	statement that sth. is not true; a rejection 否认，否定；拒绝
supreme /sjuːˈpriːm;suˈpriːm/	a.	highest in degree or rank or authority; most important, greatest 最高的，至上的，最重要的，极度的
revolt /riˈvəult/	vi.	rise in rebellion 起义，造反，反叛
	vt.	to make someone feel unpleasantly shocked or disgusted 使厌恶，使反感
	n.	rebellion, rising 起义，造反，反叛；厌恶，反感
theory /ˈθiəri/	n.	(explanation of the) general principles of an art or science 理论，原理，学说；意见，看法，见解
ego /ˈiːgəu/	n.	self, self-love 自我，自我意识
enlarge /inˈlɑːdʒ/	vt.	to make larger 扩大，扩展
	vi.	to become larger, grow; to speak or write at greater

Part A
Intensive Reading

			length or in greater detail 扩大；(*on, upon*) 详述
membership	/'membəʃip/	*n.*	the state of being a member; number of members 会员身份；会员数
certificate	/sə'tifikit/	*n.*	written or printed statement, issued by an authority 证（明）书
charm	/tʃɑːm/	*n.*	attractiveness; power to give pleasure 吸引力；给人快感之能力
unreasoning	/ʌn'riːzəniŋ/	*a.*	describes feelings or beliefs that are not based on reason or judgment 不用理智的，盲目冲动的，未加思量的
survival	/sə'vaivəl/	*n.*	state of continuing to live or exist 生存，幸存
economic	/iːkə'nɔmik/	*a.*	connected with trade, industry, and wealth; of or concerning economics 经济的；经济学的
fierce	/'fiəs/	*a.*	having a savage and violent nature; extremely severe or violent; terrible 凶猛的，残忍的；可怕的；强烈的，猛烈的
fiercely	/'fiəsli/	*ad.*	猛烈地，厉害地
compete	/kəm'piːt/	*vi.*	to take part in a race, contest, examination, etc. 比赛，竞争
indifferent	/in'difrənt/	*a.*	not caring about or interested in someone or something 无关紧要的
glory	/'glɔːri/	*n.*	great honor, praise 光荣，荣誉
glorify	/'glɔrifai/	*vt.*	to give honor or high praise to; to cause to be or seem excellent than is actually the case 颂扬；美化，使增光
glorious	/'glɔːriəs/	*a.*	famous, having or deserving glory 光荣的
submerge	/sʌb'məːdʒ/	*vt.*	to place or plunge under water; to cover with water 浸没，淹没
		vi.	to go under or as if under water 潜入水中
abandon	/ə'bændən/	*vt.*	to leave completely and forever, to leave (a relation or friend) in a cruel way; to give up 丢弃，离弃，抛弃；放弃
commute	/kə'mjuːt/	*vi.*	(*between, from ... to*) to compensate; to travel frequently between one's work and one's home 补偿；经常乘公交车上下班（尤指在市区与郊区之间）

Unit 4 On Relations

▲smother /ˈsmʌðə/	vt.	to hold back 抑制
flatten /ˈflætən/	vt.	to make or become flat 变平；变单调
possibility /ˌpɔsiˈbiliti/	n.	state of being possible; sth. that is possible 可能(性)；可能的事
territory /ˈteritəri/	n.	the land a country controls；an area of knowledge or experience 领土，版图；(行为、知识等)领域，范围
fertile /ˈfəːtail/	a.	(of land) producing good crops 肥沃的，丰产的，丰富的
interact /ˌintərˈækt/	vi.	(the two things) to act on each other 互相作用，互相影响

PHRASES

apart from	besides, with the exception of 除……之外，且莫说……
wear out	(for one thing) to become useless or break down because of over-use or wear 穿破，用坏
back and forth	backwards and forwards 来回
after all	anyway 毕竟，到底
account for	to be the explanation or cause of 说明，解释；(指数量)占
be at its/one's best	in the best of health 身心俱佳，处于最好的状态
at one time or another	有时，又有时

EXERCISES

Reading Comprehension

Task 3

Answer the following questions briefly.

1. The first paragraph mainly talks about _____.
2. How does the typical American family treat its family members?
3. Why do Americans travel between two ideals?

Part A
Intensive Reading

4. Are the conflicts between the "I" and the "we" avoidable?
5. Why do many people revolt against the family?
6. How can one gain membership to a family?
7. There are few heroes or stars in family life. Why?
8. What special meaning does the author give to Thanksgiving?

Task 4

Paraphrase the italicized part in each sentence.

1. (Par. 1) ...Americans who value individualism *like no other people* will *collect around a million tables* in a ritual of belonging.
2. (Par. 4) There has always been some *pavement* between a person and a family.
3. (Par. 9) It can be a place where the *"I" and the "we"* interact.

Task 5

Complete the following passage by using words or phrases from the box.

| pick up | thanks | held | move | stuff | home | traditional |

Thanksgiving, (1) _____ on the fourth Thursday in November, is time for far-flung families to join around a common table. Grown children brave the busiest travel season of the year to return to their ancestral nest, where they eat too much, drink too much, and (2) _____ year-old arguments as though they had never left (3) _____.

The traditional meal centers around a roast turkey (4) _____ with breadcrumbs and sage, supplemented by a generous assortment of candied yams topped with baby marshmallows, baked potatoes, creamed onions, dinner rolls, cranberry relish, pumpkin pie, apple pie, Indian pudding and ice cream. The goal is to eat so much that nobody can (5) _____, and then watch football on television. On this day it is (6) _____ to bow one's head and give for life's many blessings. However, most celebrants are actually silently giving (7) _____ that they only see their families once a year.

Vocabulary

Task 6

Complete the following sentences by choosing a word from the box below, using the proper form.

| notion | tempt | feast | fuss | apart from |
| abandon | alone | conflict | burden | tremble |

Unit 4 On Relations

1. Don't make so much _____ over losing a penny.
2. The warm sun _____ us to go swimming.
3. Christmas is an important _____ for American people.
4. The children hardly see anyone, _____ their parents.
5. They have no _____ of time.
6. I don't think that John would _____ his friends if they were in trouble.
7. I am anxious about leaving Jimmy _____ in the house.
8. He was faced with the severe financial _____ of caring for a wife and five children.
9. His voice began to _____ and tears came to his eyes.
10. This is a serious dispute and could lead to armed _____.

Task 7

A. Guess the meaning of the following italicized words according to the context.

1. Among the parcels was a *package* for Kevin.
2. It was an interesting round-the-world *package* tour.
3. Kevin *tempted* his friends into stealing the money.
4. I was greatly *tempted* to telephone her, but I didn't.
5. The pupils *assembled* in the school hall.
6. We need skilled workers who can *assemble* cars very quickly.
7. The president's political ideas were too *complex* to get support from ordinary people.
8. This industrial *complex* consists of ten manufacturing plants.
9. A bicycle and a motorbike are built on the same *principle*, though the force that moves them is different.
10. My father was a man of *principle* who would never do anything dishonest or fair.
11. This meeting is to be held on neutral *territory*.
12. All this is familiar *territory* to readers of her recent novels.

B. Fill in the blanks with appropriate words.

In America, each person is expected to make decisions for himself or herself about all aspects of life—education, career and home. The family usually has much (1) _____ influence on the behavior of any member than is generally true in China. Children are encouraged from an early age to be self-reliant—taking (2) _____ of their clothes and bedrooms—and to begin (3) _____ for themselves and even learning to manage their own money.

It is another American (4)_____ to place great importance on privacy. Many Americans believe that everyone needs some private time to be (5) _____ and think one's private thoughts. This account (6) _____ the fact that everyone will defend their own (7) _____ at one time or another. To show their respect for the (8) _____ of a child, parents usually will not be (9) _____ on a child's private matters. This (10) _____ applies to all aspects of life, including the family and social relations.

Grammar

Task 8

Put together the beginnings (#1~6) and endings (#7~12) of sentences by using "while".

Model: Man dreams of fame while woman wakes to love.

1. While I understand your point of view, ...
2. Change is absolute, ...
3. Some house plants grow well if placed near a window with plenty of sunlight, ...
4. In an American's home, the living room is considered "public space", ...
5. While teachers do not want the students to become overly dependent on them, ...
6. As a child grows up, he tells less and less to his parents ...
7. ... he hides more and more in his heart.
8. ... others prefer to be in a more shaded spot.
9. ... I don't share it.
10. ... they will not reject anyone who needs help.
11. ... other rooms are rather private.
12. ... remaining the same is relative.

Further Practice

Task 9

A. Put the following phrases into English.

1. 个性坚强的人
2. 陶冶你的情操
3. 以读书来增长见识
4. 建立一种理论
5. 理论和实践的结合
6. 按照原则行事

Unit 4 On Relations

B. Put the following sentences into English.

1. 在理论上，适者生存的观点使得我们不再以某人的年龄和经历，而是根据其本身的才干提升他。因此，我们必须不断用知识充实我们的头脑，以便能适应新社会的需要。
2. 我们都有自己不同的梦想和遗憾。生活也因此才变得如此丰富多彩。

Extra Reading

Task 10

Look at the following pictures carefully and match the instruction with the right picture.

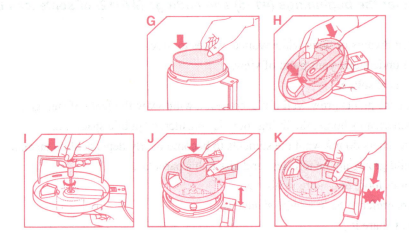

Assembling the Ice-Cream Maker

1. Insert the spindle of the stirrer into the hole at the underside of the motor unit. If necessary, turn the stirrer to ensure the spindle is fully located into the motor unit.
2. Turn the top clockwise into the direction of the arrow until it locks ("click"). The Ice-Cream Maker is now ready for use.
3. Insert the front edge of the motor unit under the lip in the center of the lid. The narrow part of the motor unit should be lowered downwards to the lid until it locks ("click!")
4. Place the deep-frozen cooling container inside the bowl.
5. Place the top of the Ice-Cream Maker with the stirrer in position onto the top of the bowl. Ensure the two indication marks meet.

比较对比法 (Comparison and Contrast)

通常，当我们要侧重说明两个事物的相同点时，我们会运用比较法（Comparison）；而当我们要侧重说明两个事物的不同点时，我们就运用对比法（Contrast）。在进行比较对比的时候，我们往往可以使用下面这两种方式：

1) First A then B

先集中说明一个事物，再集中说明另一个事物，这样读者就可以清晰地发现两者间的异同。

2) Item by Item

按照比较对比特征的顺序，先讨论两个事物的某一特征的异同，再讨论两个事物另一特征的异同，依此类推。

Example 1:

The domestic hen has short wings which it rarely uses because it has a very heavy body and lives on the ground. It is clumsy in flight and can cover only short distances. Its feet are designed for scratching the ground to find seeds and worms. It has a short beak adapted for eating this kind of food although it will also eat almost any other kind of food. Hens nest on the ground. They have been bred for egg production and can lay up to 300 eggs a year.

A duck has webbed feet so that it can swim easily and walk on soft ground. It has a long, flat beak which it uses to search for food in river and pond mud. It has powerful wings which enable it to fly long distances. A duck lays 5 to 12 eggs at a time and may lay twice a year.

Example 2:

Different Roommates

I am amazed at how little trouble it is living with and liking two such different roommates. Their physical appearances differ greatly. With small brown eyes and straight black hair to her shoulders, Julie is tall and lean. Pat, on the other hand, is tiny. Under five feet tall, she keeps her

Unit 4 On Relations

hair short and fluffy（蓬松）. These two girls also have different kinds of interests. Julie likes reading or relaxing quietly in front of the television set. But for Pat the outdoor life holds more interest than books or screens. The most interesting difference between them is their approach to schoolwork. Julie grows tense before an exam. Pat, on the contrary, takes everything easy, and exams are no exception. Since I can live in harmony with my two roommates in spite of their differences, I am confident that I will be able to get along with most people anywhere.

Task 11

Try to analyze which method the following paragraph adopts, and fill in the blank with appropriate words.

   In college and university courses, the objective test and the essay exam are two _____ methods of evaluation commonly used to measure a student's grasp of subject matters. The objective exam usually consists of a large number of unrelated questions; _____ , the essay exam requires the student to organize his response in the essay form and to demonstrate analytical and compositional skill. Although the objective test and the essay exam have _____ goals — the assessment of a student's academic achievement — the techniques of the two types of examination _____ significantly.

Task 12

Below are two examples of Chinese students' attempt at the exercise.
1) **Make improvements on the samples.**
2) **Compare the two samples, and try to find their differences in language use and structure.**
3) **Decide which sample you like best, and state your reasons.**

   Sample 1:
   Living in the dormitory and at home are two very different ways.
   Firstly, you are taken care of at home by your families, but should take care of yourself in the dormitory. For example, when you living at home, your mother will wake you up, cook for you, wash clothes of yours and so on. But in the dormitory, you must do all of this by yourself, you use a clock to wake you up, you went to the canteen to have your meals, and you wash you clothes. Then, at home you can do whatever you want to do, for your parents will stand you, however, if you want to be a welcomed member of the dormitory, you have to be polite and tolerant. In the dormitory, everyone is equal, and you must treat others just like the way you want others to treat you. Finally, living in the dormitory is more free than at home. If you living at home, your parents will pay careful attention to you in every minute, they don't allow you do many things that they thought bad for you, while in the dormitory no one will forbid you any

more, so you must learn to restrain yourself when you are enjoying your freedom.

Sample 2:
Which Is Better, in the Dormitory or at Home?

If you ask some persons this question, maybe most of them will choose "at home" with no thinking. Sure, it is more satisfied to live at home. You can get a big room of your own, in which you can do anything you like to. There's no people but yourself. No one will disturb you or make you stop. And all the people in your family would give you their love and help. They will do anything to make you free. You needn't do washing or cooking, but often have nothing to do, just watching TV or sleeping.

However, if you have lived in the dormitory for a long time, you will find the advantage. Of course, you can't get a big room but share it with some other ones. Sometimes, there is lots of noise when you want to do something important. And you must wash your clothes by yourself. It seems much worse that living at home. But everyone will be away from your family. You must learn to live alone. And in the dormitory, you can learn how to communicate with others. You can do many things by yourself to get more ability. Then you'll be better after graduation.

比较对比中常用的句型：

1) A and B are similar (or alike) in ... aspects
2) A is similar to B in that ...
3) A and B both have the characteristic of ...
4) A is the same as B in that ...
5) A bears some similarities to B in that ...
6) There is a similarity of A to B in ...
7) A is dissimilar to B in that ...
8) The differences between A and B are that ...

比较对比中常用的衔接词：

however, while, whereas, but, nevertheless, (on the one hand, ...) on the other hand, in (sharp) contrast to

Task 13

With reference to the structure and unity of the text, write a paragraph of about 50 words, describing the most distinct feature of your city.

Unit 4 On Relations

Translation

转换法 (Shift/Conversion) (2)

第一册中我们从总体上介绍了这一方法，这里我们将着重介绍英汉互译实践中的主被动转换问题。

首先要说明一点，英语由"be + v-ed"结构构成的被动语态，译成汉语时不能一概译为汉语的"被字式"，这是许多初学者极易犯的一个错误。造成这种"被被不绝"的原因在于大家对汉语表达被动意义的方式缺乏必要的认识。应该承认，汉语从结构上一眼便可以看出的被动句的确不如英语的被动句多，但这并不等于说汉语被动句不如英语多。需要指出的是，被动句有结构被动句（Syntactic Passive）和意义被动句（Notional Passive）之分。英汉两种语言中都存在着结构被动句和意义被动句，具有明显的结构特征的被动句，即英语中的"be + v-ed"和汉语中的"被字式"都属于结构被动句，没有明显的结构特征，但意义上被动的句子叫做意义被动句，如英语中的 Your hair needs cutting；汉语中的"他吓得魂飞魄散"。

可以这样说，英语表达被动的形式比较单一，主要靠"be + v-ed"这种形式，虽然也存在为数不多的几种意义被动句，但远不能与汉语相比；而汉语虽然结构被动句远比英语少，但其意义被动句却相当丰富，因而我们说汉语表达被动的形式远非英语所能及。下面我们提供了一些英文例句，请大家试着用地道的汉语译出来，并借此归纳一下汉语表达被动意义的方式或手段：

1. Once the matter is confirmed, it should be dealt with promptly.
2. The area was devastated by a typhoon.
3. The hut was washed away by the flood.
4. What I sent to her was stealthily changed.
5. Kissinger was alarmed by China's first atomic blast in October, 1964.
6. They were deeply moved by his deed.
7. The handling of the accident remains to be decided upon by the higher authorities.
8. The correctness of the argument has yet to be proved.
9. It is said that the two countries are having secret negotiations.

10. She was received by a secretary of the CEO.
11. A nation is sure to get into trouble if virtue is not rewarded and vice not punished.
12. It must be dealt with at the appropriate time with appropriate means.
13. as is mentioned above, ...
14. Care should be taken to see that the letter is properly addressed.

下面我们再看几个英语被动句的翻译：

- Love and a cough cannot be hidden.

    爱情如同咳嗽，有了藏不住。

- What we were offered was a big fat zero.

    我们得到的是一个大零蛋。

- Are parents meant to love all their children equally?

    莫非/是不是说做父母的一定要一视同仁地爱自己的每一个孩子？

- Science consists in grouping facts so that general laws or conclusions may be drawn from them.

    科学的要义就在于搜集整理事实，以便从中引出普遍性的规律或结论来。

- The garden party was washed away by rain.

    游园会因下雨取消了。

Task 14

Translate the following sentences into Chinese, using the method you've learned.

1) We are taught about the freedom of the "I" and the safety of the "we". The loneliness of the "I" and the intrusiveness of the "we". The selfishness of the "I" and the burdens of the "we".
2) We are taught what Andre Malraux said: "Without a family, man, alone in the world, trembles with the cold." And taught what he said another day: "The denial of the supreme importance of the mind's development accounts for many revolts against the family."
3) We are graded and paid, hired and fired, on our own merit.
4) We don't have to achieve to be accepted by our families.
5) Our membership is not based on certificates but on birth.
6) The family is formed not for the survival of the fittest but for the weakest.

Unit 4 On Relations

Quotation

I do not hesitate to read all good books in translations. What is really best in any book is translatable — any real insight or broad human sentiment.

— *Ralph Waldo Emerson* (1803 — 1882)

所有优秀的译著我都愿意读。随便哪本书，其中货真价实的东西，真知灼见也好，人类情操也好，都是可译的。

——拉尔夫·沃尔多·爱默生 (1803 — 1882)

Part B Extensive Reading

I. Why I Want a Wife

By **Judy Syfers**[1]

I belong to that classification of people known as wives. I am a wife. And, not altogether incidentally, I am a mother.

Not too long ago a male friend of mine appeared on the scene fresh from a recent divorce. He had one child, who is, of course, with his ex-wife. He is obviously looking for another wife. As I thought about him while I was ironing one evening, it suddenly occurred to me that I, too, would like to have a wife. Why do I want a wife?

I would like to go back to school so that I can become economically independent, support myself, and, if need be, support those dependent on me. I want a wife who will work and send me to school. And while I am going to school I want a wife to take care of my children. I want a wife

---

1. **Judy Syfers:** a free-lance writer (自由写作家). She was born in 1937 in San Francisco, educated at the University of Iowa. This essay first appeared in a magazine in 1971 and has become a classic of feminist satire.

to make sure that my children eat properly and are kept clean. I want a wife who will wash the children's clothes and keep them mended. I want a wife who is a good nurturant attendant to my children, who arranges for their schooling, makes sure they have an adequate social life with their equals[1], takes them to the park, the zoo, etc. I want a wife who takes care of the children when they are sick, a wife who arranges to be around[2] when the children need special care, because, of course, I cannot miss classes at school. My wife must arrange to lose time at work and not lose the job. It may mean a small cut in my wife's income[3] from time to time, but I guess I can tolerate that. Needless to say, my wife will arrange and pay for the care of the children while my wife is working.

I want a wife who will take care of my physical needs. I want a wife who will keep the house clean. A wife who will pick up after my children[4], a wife who will pick up after me. I want a wife who will keep my clothes clean, ironed, mended, replaced when need be, and who will see to it that my personal things are kept in their proper place so that I can find what I need the minute I need it. I want a wife who cooks the meals, a wife who is a good cook. I want a wife who will plan the menus, do the necessary shopping, prepare the meals, serve them pleasantly, and then do the cleaning up while I do my studying.

I want a wife who will not bother me with rambling complaints about a wife's duties. But I want a wife who will listen to me when I feel the need to explain a rather difficult point I have come across in my course of studies. And I want a wife who will type my papers for me when I have written them.

I want a wife who will take care of the details of my social life. When I meet people at school that I like and want to entertain, I want a wife who will have the house clean, prepare a special meal, serve it to me and my friends, and not interrupt when I talk about the things that interest me and my friends.

And I want a wife who knows that sometimes I need a night out by myself. I want a wife who assumes the complete responsibility for birth control, because I do not want more children. I want a wife who will remain faithful to me so that I do not have to disturb my intellectual life with jealousies.

If, by chance, I find another person more suitable as a wife than the wife I already have, I want the liberty to replace my present wife with another one. Naturally, I will expect a fresh, new

---

1. **their equals:** children of their age
2. **arrange to be around:** to manage to be available, or manage to be with the children when they need special care
3. **a small cut in one's income:** lose a small amount of money from one's income
4. **pick up after sb.:** to clean up the house after sb. has made it dirty

Unit 4　On Relations

life; my wife will take the children and be solely responsible for them so that I am left free.

When I am through with school and have a job, I want my wife to quit working and remain at home so that my wife can more fully and completely take care of a wife's duties.

My God, who wouldn't want a wife? (714 words)

NEW WORDS

classification /ˌklæsifiˈkeiʃən/	n.	group, division, or class into which sth. is placed 分类，分级
★ *incidentally* /ˌinsiˈdentli; insəˈdentli/	a.	accompanying but not forming a necessary part; small and comparatively unimportant 附属的，随带的，微不足道的
economical /ˌiːkəˈnɔmikəl/	a.	not wasteful; using money, time, goods, etc. carefully 节俭的，节约的
economically /ˌiːkəˈnɔmikəli/	ad.	节俭地
dependent /diˈpendənt/	a.	varying according to; (*on/upon*) supported by 取决于；依靠的，依赖的
nurture /ˈnəːtʃə/	vt.	to bring up; to give care, training, or education to 养育；教养
nurturant /ˈnəːtʃərənt/	a.	滋养的，养育的
adequate /ˈædikwət/	a.	enough for the purpose; only just enough, having the necessary ability or quality 充足的，足够的；适当的，胜任的
tolerate /ˈtɔləreit/	vt.	to allow without protest 忍受，容忍
ramble /ˈræmbl/	vt.	to walk for pleasure, with no special destination; to wander in one's talk, not keeping to the subject 漫步；漫谈
rambling /ˈræmbliŋ/	a.	漫步的；散漫的，杂乱无章的
complaint /kəmˈpleint/	n.	statement expressing annoyance, unhappiness, pain, etc.; formal statement about a person or thing causing trouble or annoyance 抱怨，怨言；控告，申诉
entertain /ˌentəˈtein/	v.	to give a party (for), to provide food and drink in one's house; to amuse and interest 招待，款待；使娱乐
interrupt /ˌintəˈrʌpt/	vi.	to break sb.'s speech by saying sth. 打断，打扰

	vt.	to break the flow of sth. continuous 打断，打扰；中止，阻碍
faithful /ˈfeiθful/	a.	full of or showing loyalty; true to the facts or to an original 忠诚的，忠实的；如实的
jealous /ˈdʒeləs/	a.	anxiously looking after what one has; wanting to get what sb. else has; envious 唯恐失去的；嫉妒的；羡慕的
jealousy /ˈdʒeləsi/	n.	the feeling of hating the lucky person who has received sth. that one wishes one had those things 妒忌，嫉妒
quit /kwit/	v.	to go away from; to leave (a job) 停止，放弃；辞（职）

PHRASES

to serve as	作为，用作
if need be	if it is necessary 如果有必要
make sure that/ of sth.	to feel sure; to do what is necessary in order to feel sure to get sth. 确信，使有把握；查明
needless to say	of course, as was to be expected 不用说
see to sb. or sth. that	to take care of sb. or sth. 照料
come across	to find sb. or sth. by accident 偶然遇见，偶然发现
serve meals to sb.	to give (food, etc.) to people at a meal 招待某人，帮助上菜
by chance	by accident; unexpectedly 偶然地；碰巧

EXERCISES

Reading Comprehension

Task 1

A. The following statements describe the actions and attitudes of a perfect wife. Decide whether they are true or false according to the passage.

1. She becomes the family breadwinner so that her husband can go to school.

Unit 4 On Relations

2. She loses time at her job so that she can give more attention to the children when they are sick. If necessary, she will even pay for the care of the children.
3. She takes up any career she wants and hires someone to clean the house, iron and mend clothes.
4. She shares with her husband the responsibility for cooking good meals and bringing up children.
5. She listens to her husband when he wants to talk about his problems and keeps quiet about her own problems and does not make complaints about her duties.
6. She entertains her husband's friends at home and sees to it that the children do not bother them.
7. She gives up her career when her husband gets a job and wants her to stay at home.
8. She allows her husband to leave in order to marry a younger woman if he wants to but she refuses to take the responsibility for raising the children alone.

B. Find short answers in the text to the following questions.

1. The tone of the passage is _____.
   a. formal   b. informal
   c. playful   d. ironic
2. According to this passage, a wife should, above all, _____.
   a. pay more attention to keeping the house rather than keeping up her appearances
   b. accept the fact that a woman's place is in the home
   c. try her best to please her husband and friends
   d. respect her husband's wishes in most cases
3. With which of the following statements would the author most likely disagree?
   a. A wife should take a more active part both at home and at work.
   b. A husband's career and interests are as important as that of his wife.
   c. A wife should be equal in all things to her husband.
   d. A wife's main task is to complement, not compete with her husband.
4. In this passage, the author chose to repeat "I want a wife who ..." rather than use "she" or "her" to refer to a wife in the family. It probably suggests that _____.
   a. it mainly deals with women's issues
   b. a wife is defined as a voiceless and formless servant
   c. a person of either sex should be able to do a wife's job
   d. any husband would like to have this type of ideal wife
5. The purpose of the author seems to be _____.
   a. to make clear some misunderstanding concerning a wife's duty
   b. to complain about all the responsibilities she and other women assume

c. to explain why she herself would like to have a wife
d. to define a wife's economic, physical, social responsibilities

vocabulary

Task 2

A. Choose from Column B the definitions of words in Column A. Note there are more items in Column B.

Column A	Column B
1. economical	a. to show hospitality to guests
2. bother	b. without waste
3. complaint	c. remaining true, constant and loyal
4. entertain	d. relation to finance
5. faithful	e. showing great mental ability
6. intellectual	f. to disturb
	g. expression of displeasure or resentment
	h. feed and support sb.

B. Then choose the words in Column A to complete the following sentences.

1. Even though he was often cruel to this dog, it remained _____ to him.
2. If you don't have time, don't _____ to reply.
3. She _____ ten people at dinner.
4. Philosophy is an _____ exercise.
5. Although she hates to stay at home for her husband and children, she nerver makes any _____.
6. A small car is more _____ to drive than a big one, because it uses less petrol.
7. Bertrand Russel appealed to all sorts of people, not just _____.

C. Complete the following sentences by putting the Chinese into English.

1. adequate
   a. Their earnings _____ （足够了）.
   b. Your work is _____ （做得不错）, but I'm sure you could do better.
   c. She is working hard to prove _____ （胜任这项工作）.
2. jealous
   a. You should be more _____ （珍惜）all that you possess at the moment.
   b. A lot of people are _____ （嫉妒）your success.

Unit 4 On Relations

3. quit
   a. He has _____ （戒烟）.
   b. It hasn't _____ （雨还没有停）yet.
   c. He _____ （辞去了工作）because the salary was too low.

4. interrupt
   a. Stop _____ （打断）me when I'm talking.
   b. He will be upset if you _____ （打扰）him at this moment.
   c. Do not _____ （插嘴）. Let him finish, please.

II. October and June

(Adapted)

By **O' Henry**[1]

The captain gazed gloomily at his sword that hung upon the wall. In the closet nearby was stored his faded uniform, stained and worn by weather and service. What a long, long time it seemed since those old days of war's alarms!

And now, veteran that he was of his country's hard times, he had been reduced to resigned
5 surrender by a woman's soft eyes and smiling lips. As he sat in his quiet room he held in his hand the letter he had just received from her — the letter that had caused him to wear that look of gloom. He reread the fatal paragraph that had destroyed his hope.

In declining the honor you have done me in asking me to be your wife, I feel that I ought to speak frankly. The reason I have for so doing is the great difference between our ages. I like you
10 *very, very much, but I am sure that our marriage would not be a happy one. I am sorry to have to refer to this, but I believe that you will appreciate my honesty in giving you the true reason.*

The Captain sighed, and leaned his head upon his hand. Yes, there were many years between their ages. But he was strong and tough, he had position and wealth. Would not his love, his tender
15 care, and the advantages he could give her make her forget the question of age? Besides, he was almost sure that she cared for him.

The Captain was a man of prompt action. In the field he had been distinguished for his decisiveness and energy. He would see

---

1. **O' Henry:** (1862 — 1910) 欧·亨利，美国 20 世纪初著名的短篇小说家

20 her and plead his cause again in person. Age! What was it to come between him and the one he loved?

In two hours he stood ready, in light marching order, for his greatest battle. He took the train for the town where she lived.

Theodora Deming was on the steps of the handsome old mansion, enjoying the summer 25 dusk, when the Captain came up the gravel walk. She met him with a smile that was free from embarrassment. As the Captain stood on the step below her, the difference in their ages did not appear so great. He was tall and straight and clear-eyed and browned. She was in the bloom of lovely womanhood.

"I wasn't expecting you," said Theodora. "Didn't you get my letter?"

30 "I did," said the Captain, "and that's why I came. I say, now, Theo[1], reconsider your answer, won't you?"

Theodora smiled softly upon him. He carried his years well. She was really fond of his strength, his wholesome looks, his manliness — perhaps if...

"No, no," she said, shaking her head, positively. "It's out of the question. My age and yours 35 are — but don't make me say it again — I told you in my letter."

The Captain flushed a little through the bronze on his face. He was silent for a while, gazing sadly into the dusk. Beyond a line of woods that he could see was a field where the troops had once camped on their march toward the sea. How long ago it seemed now! Truly, Fate and Father Time[2] had tricked him bitterly. Just a few years came in between himself and happiness!

40 Theodora's hand crept down and rested in the clasp of his firm brown one. She felt, at least, that affection that is like love.

"Don't take it so hard, please," she said, gently, "Someday you'll be glad I didn't marry you. It would be very nice and lovely for a while—but, just think! In only a few short years what different tastes we would have. One of us would want to sit by the fireside and read, and maybe 45 nurse this or that disease of evenings, while the other would be crazy for balls and theaters and later suppers. No, my dear friend. While it isn't exactly January and May, it's a clear case of October and pretty early in June."

"I'd always do what you wanted me to do. Theo. If you wanted to — "

"No. You think now that you would, but you wouldn't. Please don't ask me any more."

50 The captain had lost his battle. But he was a tough fighter, and when he rose to say good-bye his mouth was grimly set and his shoulders were squared.

---

1. **Theo:** a pet name, Theodora 的昵称
2. **Father Time:** 时间老人

Unit 4 On Relations

He took the train that night. On the next evening he was back in his room, where his sword was hanging against the wall. He was dressing for dinner, tying his white tie into a very careful bow. And at the same time he was talking to himself.

55 "Upon my honor, I believe Theo was right, after all. Nobody can deny that she's a peach, but she must be 28, at the very kindest calculation."

For, you see, the Captain was only 19. And his sword had never been drawn except on the parade ground, which was as near as he ever got to war. (832 words)

NEW WORDS

gaze /geiz/	v.	to look steadily for a long or short period of time 凝视，注视
	n.	a steady fixed look 凝视，注视
★ **gloom** /gluːm/	n.	darkness; a feeling of deep sadness 黑暗
gloomy /ˈgluːmi/	a.	almost dark; having or giving little hope or cheerfulness 黑暗的，昏暗的；沮丧的，愁容满面的
gloomily /ˈgluːmili/	ad.	黑暗地
sword /sɔːd/	n.	a weapon with a long blade and a handle 剑，刀
closet /ˈklɔzit/	n.	small room for storing things （壁）橱
fade /feid/	vi.	to lose colour; to disappear or die gradually 褪色；逐渐消失，变弱
veteran /ˈvetərən/	n.	a person who has had much or long experience, esp. as a soldier 老手，老兵
resign /riˈzain/	v.	to give up a job or position 辞职，放弃，辞去；(to) be ready to accept uncomplainingly 使顺从
surrender /səˈrendə/	vi.	to give oneself up, esp. as a prisoner; (to) to give way to 投降；屈服于，让步
	vt.	to give sth. up; to abandon 交出；放弃
fatal /ˈfeitl/	a.	causing or resulting in death 致命的，毁灭性的
decline /diˈklain/	v.	to become smaller, weaker, or worse; to refuse, usu. politely 下降，减少，衰落；谢绝
	n.	gradual and continued loss of strength 下降，减少，衰落

Part B
Extensive Reading

frank /fræŋk/		*a.*	showing clearly the thoughts and feelings, open 坦白的，直率的
frankly /ˌfræŋkli/		*ad.*	坦白地，直率地
honesty /ˈɔnisti/		*n.*	the quality of being trustworthy 诚实，正直
tender /ˈtendə/		*a.*	gentle and loving; not hard or difficult to bite through; painful, quickly feeling pain 温柔的；嫩的；疼痛的，一触即痛的
action /ˈækʃən/		*n.*	doing sth.; an effect of heat, light, matter, etc. 行动，行动过程；作用
distinguish /diˈstiŋgwiʃ/		*v.*	(*between, from*) to see, hear, recognize, understand well, the difference 区别，辨别，分清
distinguished /diˈstiŋgwiʃt/		*a.*	(*for*) marked by excellent quality or deserved fame 卓越，杰出
decisive /diˈsaisiv/		*a.*	having a decided result; showing determination or firmness 决定性的；坚定的，果断的
decisiveness /diˈsaisivnis/		*n.*	决定性；坚定
★ **plead** /pli:d/		*v.*	to ask earnestly; to argue in favour of; to advance reasons for (a cause, etc.) 恳求，请求；为……辩护；提出……为理由(或借口)
★ **mansion** /ˈmænʃən/		*n.*	a large house 大厦
dusk /dʌsk/		*n.*	time just before it gets quite dark 薄暮，黄昏
▲ **gravel** /ˈgrævəl/		*n.*	a mixture of small stones with sand, used on the surface of roads or paths 碎石
embarrass /imˈbærəs/		*vt.*	to cause to feel uneasy or socially uncomfortable 使尴尬，使不好意思
embarrassment /imˈbærəsmənt/		*n.*	the act of embarrassing 尴尬
womanhood /ˈwumənhud/		*n.*	the condition or period of being a woman 女人，女人气质
reconsider /ˈri:kənˈsidə/		*vt.*	to think again and change one's mind about (a subject) 重新考虑，重新审议
▲ **wholesome** /ˈhəulsəm/		*a.*	healthy 健康的
manly /ˈmænli/		*a.*	having the strong qualities expected of a man 有男人刚强气质
manliness /ˈmænlinis/		*n.*	刚毅

Unit 4 On Relations

★ **flush** /flʌʃ/	vi.	(of a person, his skin, or face) to turn red as a result of a sudden flow of blood to the skin 脸红
★ **bronze** /brɔnz/	n.	reddish brown 青铜色
troop /truːp/	n.	[pl.] soldiers; a group of persons or animals, esp. when moving 军队，部队；一群，一队，一大批
fate /feit/	n.	imaginary cause beyond human control that is believed to decide events 命运
creep /kriːp/	vt.	[crept, crept] to move quietly and carefully 悄悄地或小心地移动
affection /əˈfekʃən/	n.	gentle, lasting love, as a parent for its child, fondness 爱，感情
fireside /ˈfaiəsaid/	n.	the area around the fireplace, often thought of as representing the pleasures of home life 炉边，家庭
★ **grim** /grim/	a.	讨厌的，糟糕的；严厉的；严酷的，无情的
grimly /ˈgrimli/	ad.	unpleasant, not cheerful 不愉快的
bow /bau/	vi./n.	a bending forward of the upper part of the body to show respect or yielding 鞠躬，低头
	vt.	to bend or curve 低下（头），欠身；压弯
/bəu/	n.	弓，弓形物
deny /diˈnai/	vt.	to say that sth. is not true 否定
peach /piːtʃ/	n.	a round fruit with soft yellowish-red skin and sweet juicy flesh; a pretty young girl that is greatly admired 桃；年轻貌美的女子
calculate /ˈkælkjuleit/	v.	to find out by working with numbers; to work out by using one's judgment; to plan 计算，核算；估计，推测；计划，打算
calculation /ˌkælkjuˈleiʃən/	n.	计算；估计
parade /pəˈreid/	n.	a line of people or vehicles moving somewhere together; an occasion on which soldiers march together in front of important people or the public 游行；检阅
	v.	to (cause to) walk together in a formal group, so that other people can see them （使）列队行进，（在……）游行

Phrases

care for	like 喜欢
in person	physically present 亲自
be free from	without 没有……的
out of the question	impossible 不可能的
after all	in spite of everything 毕竟,终究

EXERCISES

Reading Comprehension

Task 1

Answer the following questions according to the information given in the text.

1. What caused the Captain to be so unhappy?
2. What was the true reason for the woman's refusal?
3. What does the sentence "Age! What was it to come between him and the one he loved" imply?
4. What does "his greatest battle" mean?
5. What does the sentence "While it isn't exactly January and May, it's a clear case of October and pretty early in June" imply?
6. What is the surprising end of the story?

Task 2

Paraphrase the following sentences or put them into Chinese.

1. He had been reduced to resigned surrender by a woman's soft eyes and smiling lips.
2. In two hours he stood ready, in light marching order, for his greatest battle.
3. He carried his years well.
4. The Captain flushed a little through the bronze on his face.
5. Just a few years came in between himself and happiness.
6. Don't take it so hard, please.
7. In only a few short years what different tastes we would have.

Unit 4 On Relations

Vocabulary

Task 3

Match the words in column A with their synonyms in Column B:

Column A	Column B
1. embarrass	a. healthy
2. fade	b. love
3. decline	c. feel uneasy or uncomfortable
4. frank	d. open
5. wholesome	e. say that sth. is not true
6. affection	f. lose colour
7. deny	g. refuse politely

Task 4

Replace the underlined parts of the following sentences with words or phrases given below, making changes where necessary.

| distinguish | fond | resign |
| in full bloom | calculate | decline |

1. Henry is color-blind and he can hardly <u>recognize the difference</u> between red and green easily.
2. The apple trees are <u>producing all their flowers</u> at the moment.
3. My younger brother was very <u>keen on</u> music.
4. My grandfather became very forgetful in his <u>last years</u> of life.
5. The cost of maintaining an old car is <u>estimated</u> at $500 a year.
6. Mrs. Oates <u>abandoned</u> her job so she could spend more time with her children.

Part C ▶ Reading Skill

The Organization of a Discourse

lmost every good communication of ideas has two simple parts — a point is made, and evidence is given to explain or support the point. Textbooks and technical writing try to communicate ideas, and they usually do so in pretty much the same way—by putting forward a point and then supporting it with reasons, details, and facts. You can become a better reader if you can learn to recognize this simple form of discourse organization.

Not only paragraphs but also essays are often made up of the same two parts. Just as a paragraph has a main idea sentence, so an essay will often have a main idea paragraph, or even more than one. The other paragraphs in the essay contain details or ideas that develop and support the main idea of the essay. Learning to recognize these two parts quickly at any level of discourse is sure to increase your reading comprehension.

Finding the main idea is the key to understanding a discourse. Once you understand the main idea that a writer is trying to make, everything else in the discourse should fall easily into place. You will know what point is being made, and what evidence is being given to support the point. You will see the parts (*the supporting paragraphs*) in their relationship to the whole (*the main idea*).

The main idea of a discourse is often written near the beginning, in the very first paragraph. So you should read the start of a discourse carefully, to see if you can decide what it is going to be about, and whether you need to know more about this subject or not. The very end of a discourse is also a good place to look for its main idea. Many writers feel that it is best to explain the main idea of an essay (or speech) twice - once at the beginning, to let the reader know what it is that he is going to be reading; and once again in the last part, or conclusion, in which the writer explains exactly what it is that he has just proved or said, and what it means for the reader.

Sometimes the main idea of a discourse will not be written down at all, but will be shown by all of the paragraphs acting together.

Read the passage below and work out how the discourse is organized.

The Coconut Tree

One night, I stood in a group of great coconut trees with an old man who had spent his life taking care of them.

"If you could count those stars," he told me, pointing to the sky, "then you could count all the ways that coconuts help us."

Many people call it the tree of life, and in fact this strange tree is more useful than any other kind of tree. What other tree is there that gives us not only everything that we need to make a house, but most of the things that go inside one: beds, cups, and even soap? That not only heats a house with fire and cools it with air, but also lights it with burning coconut oil in a coconut lamp?

Unit 4 On Relations

The coconut tree gives clothes to the whole family. It gives a man who catches fish the things he needs to make a boat and to make the nets to catch the fish. It not only cooks food but is food—as well as many kinds of drinks. A single good nut is as good for you as a large steak. You could live forever on things made from the coconut tree. In developed countries, people use coconut tree products every day—in factories, cars, and the making of cigarettes—and new uses are always being found. Nearly 45,000 square kilometers now grow these trees and twenty-five billion nuts are used every year.

What is the main idea of the passage? In which paragraph is it located? Can you name the details that support the main idea?

Main idea: _____
Details: _____

Now read the two discourses below. You should:

1. Write down the main idea for each discourse. Note the main idea may be expressed in more than one sentence.
2. Write down the details that support or explain the main idea.
3. Write a concluding paragraph for each discourse.

A. Food

When we speak of a human need, we mean something which is necessary to life, something we can not live without. Food is a human need. Without it we would starve to death; but even if we have plenty of food, but of the wrong kind, our bodies will have problems from lack of the right food. This is known as malnutrition.

In countries which are not developed, man's food needs are the same as in the most advanced societies. We all need food and could live a good life on very few types of food. People in very undeveloped countries eat only the kinds of food which can be grown near their homes, whereas people in developed countries eat foods which are often grown many thousands of miles away from their homes. People in undeveloped countries are happy with fewer different kinds of foods than people in very developed ones are, so we can say that though the needs of the two kinds of people are the same, their wants are different. People in the developed countries eat many different types of meat—they could live on only one, but they would be very unhappy because what they ate every time was the same. Even special foods such as chicken would be less fun to eat if you had them every day. But we can't live just on meat—we need other kinds of food like bread, rice, and vegetables to keep up our health.

B. Buses

Nobody, except maybe little children, thinks that a trip on a bus is exciting. Although there are thousands of cars on the roads, more people travel by bus than by car. Workers hurrying to their offices or factories, children going to school, people going out to buy things, all use buses. If all the buses were to stop running for a day, work would stop in all the offices and factories and most classrooms would be empty. So we see the importance of buses in a big city.

Buses today are large and have good seats, mostly facing the front. To get the driver to stop at a place, you just push a button which rings a bell near the driver. And usually you don't have to wait very long to catch a bus. You can go from almost any part of the city to any other by bus.

Of course, there are problems with bus travel. Often the buses are very full, especially in the morning right before work and in the evening right after, and then you may have to wait for a long time before a bus comes that has room for more people. If you get into a crowded bus, you will have to stand up for the whole trip and hold onto a handle. This can be dangerous because it is easy to fall down if the bus stops or starts very suddenly.

Reading for Pleasure

All happy families resemble one another, but each unhappy family is unhappy in its own way.
From *Anne Karenina* written by Leo Tolstoy (1828 — 1910)

"Home is the place where,
when you have to go there,
They have to take you in."
"I should have called it
Something you somehow haven't to deserve."
From *The Death of the Hired Man* written by Robert Frost (1874 — 1963)

Unit 5

Living a Full Life

Aims and Objectives

In this unit you will learn:
1. Genre/Style: Exposition/Argumentation
2. Word Power: Antonyms
3. Grammar Focus: Subjunctive Mood
4. Writing Skill: Definitions
5. Translation Skill: Shift/Conversion
6. Reading Skill: Transition Words (1)

Brief Introductions to the Texts

The first passage is about dreaming and its many advantages.

The second talks about Japanese businessmen's admiration of an essay on youth by an American author and the meaning of youth clarified by the American author.

The third passage is about what happened to a disabled French veteran of the First World War at a reunion dinner, who was suspected of stealing a large gold coin.

Unit 5 Living a Full Life

Part A — Intensive Reading

Pre-Reading

Task 1

First, read the following passage carefully and then discuss it with the other students in the group.

Dreams are generally accepted to be illusions, having much in common with day-dreams—the fantasies of our waking life. When dreaming, one tends to believe fully in the reality of the dream world, however inconsistent, illogical and odd it may be.

People differ greatly in how much they claim to be dreaming. Some say they dream every night, others only occasionally. Individual differences probably exist, but some people immediately forget dreams and others have good recall.

In our dreams our thinking becomes concrete, pictorial and nonlogical, and expresses ideas and wishes we are not conscious of. Dreams are absurd and unaccountable because our conscious mind, not willing to acknowledge our subconscious ideas, disguises them. There is almost certainly some truth in Freud's view that dreams express the subconscious mind.

Task 2

Discuss with your partner how to express the italicized part in each sentence using different words.

1. *Now and again* I have had horrible dreams.
2. *To begin with*, I like the idea of *wandering into another kind of existence*.
3. *As a child* I could never understand *why grownups took dreaming so calmly*.
4. This dream life is often *overshadowed by huge mysterious anxieties*.
5. There are *moments of sorrow or terror* in the dream world that are *worse than anything we have known under the sun*.
6. This dream life is *like glimpses of another form of existence altogether*.
7. This dream life is *a further helping of experience*.

8. This dream life is *another slice of life cut differently for which*, it seems to me, we are never *sufficiently grateful*.
9. I cannot say *offhand*, but certainly *rather more than I could afford*.

Reading and Thinking

Dreams
By J.B. Priestley[1]

Now and again I have had horrible dreams, but not enough of them to make me lose my delight in dreams. To begin with, I like the idea of dreaming, of going to bed and lying still and then, by some queer magic, wandering into another kind of existence. As a child I could never understand why grownups took dreaming so calmly when they could make such a fuss about any holiday. This still puzzles me. I am mystified by people who say they never dream and appear to have no interest in the subject. It is much more astonishing than if they said they never went out for a walk. Most people—or at least most Western Europeans—do not seem to accept dreaming as part of their lives. They appear to see it as an annoying little habit, like sneezing or yawning.

I have never understood this. My dream life does not seem as important as my waking life, if only because there is far less of it, but to me it is important. As if there were at least two extra continents added to the world, and lightning excursions running to them at any moment between midnight and breakfast. Then again, the dream life, though queer and confusing and unsatisfactory in many respects, has its own advantages. The dead are there, smiling and talking. The past

What does the word "them" refer to?

How do most people feel toward dreams?

What does the sentence imply?

What is described here?

---

1. **Priestley, John Boynton** (1894—1984): He was the son of a schoolmaster. After serving in the British army during the First World War, he went to Cambridge, where he got his M.A. His literary career began with the publication of two books in 1922. He was also one of the most prolific writers of our age. The Good Companions (1929) won him great fame. His direct, idiomatic style appeals to the general reader.

Unit 5 Living a Full Life

is there, sometimes all broken and confused but occasionally as fresh as a daisy. And perhaps, the future is there too, waving at us. This dream life is often overshadowed by huge mysterious anxieties, with luggage that cannot be packed and trains that refuse to be caught; and both persons and scenes there are not as dependable and solid as they are in waking life, so that Brown and Smith merge into one person while Robinson splits into two, and there are thick woods outside the bathroom door and the dining-room is somehow part of a theater balcony; and there are moments of sorrow or terror in the dream world that are worse than anything we have known under the sun. Yet this other life has its interests, its enjoyments, its satisfactions, and, at certain rare intervals, a peaceful glow or a sudden excitement, like glimpses of another form of existence altogether, that we cannot match with open eyes. Silly or wise, terrible or delightful, it is a further helping of experience, an additional joy after dark, another slice of life cut differently for which, it seems to me, we are never sufficiently grateful. Only a dream! Why only? It was there, and you had it.

"If there were dreams to sell," Beddoes[1] inquires, "what would you buy?" I cannot say offhand, but certainly rather more than I could afford. (458 words)

NEW WORDS

horrible /ˈhɔrəbl/	a.	making you very afraid, very sad, or shocked 可怕的, 恐怖的；讨厌的
★ **queer** /kwiə/	a.	strange, unusual 奇怪的, 异常的
existence /igˈzistəns/	n.	being real 存在, 实在, 生活, 存在物, 实在物
puzzle /ˈpʌzl/	v.	to make you think a lot because you cannot understand or explain it （使）迷惑，（使）为难, 迷惑不解
	n.	sth. that is difficult to understand or explain 难题, 谜
mystify /ˈmistifai/	vt.	to make sb. wonder; to confuse sb. completely 使迷惑；使困惑

---

1. **Beddoes, Thomas Lovell:** (1803—1849) English writer 贝多斯

Part A

Intensive Reading

astonish /əsˈtɒnɪʃ/		vt.	to surprise sb. very much 使惊讶
▲sneeze /sniːz/		vi.	to have a sudden uncontrolled burst of air out of the nose and mouth 打喷嚏
		n.	an act, sound, etc. of sneezing 喷嚏（声）；打喷嚏
yawn /jɔːn/		v.	to open the mouth wide and breathe in deeply, as when tired or uninterested 打呵欠
		n.	an act of yawning 呵欠
lightning /ˈlaɪtnɪŋ/		n.	a powerful and sudden burst of light in the sky passing from one cloud to another or to the earth 闪电
		a.	very quick, short, or sudden 闪电似的
excursion /ɪkˈskɜːʃən/		n.	a short journey made for pleasure, usually by several people together 远足，短途旅行，（集体）游览
confuse /kənˈfjuːz/		vt.	mix sb.'s ideas, so that they cannot think clearly or understand 使困惑，使糊涂；搞乱
daisy /ˈdeɪzi/		n.	雏菊
overshadow /ˌəʊvəˈʃædəʊ/		vt.	to throw a shadow over 遮蔽，使蒙上阴影
anxiety /æŋˈzaɪəti/		n.	fear an uncertainty about the future 焦虑，挂念；渴望，热望
dependable /dɪˈpendəbl/		a.	可靠的
★merge /mɜːdʒ/		v.	(into) to become lost in or part of sth. else or each other 合并；结合
split /splɪt/		v.	to break sth. into two parts （使）分裂；劈开；分享
		n.	裂口；分裂
sorrow /ˈsɒrəʊ/		n.	sadness 悲哀；悲痛
terror /ˈterə/		n.	very great fear 恐怖；引起恐怖的人或事物
rare /reə/		a.	that you don't often see, hear, etc. 稀罕的；杰出的；（空气等）稀薄的；（肉类）半熟的
interval /ˈɪntəvəl/		n.	a space between things 间隔，间距；幕间休息
glow /gləʊ/		n.	warm feeling 激情，兴高采烈；光辉；光亮
		vi.	to give out light without flames or smoke 发光，激情，兴高采烈
glimpse /glɪmps/		vt.	to have a quick view of 一瞥，一看
delightful /dɪˈlaɪtfʊl/		a.	令人愉快的，可喜的
slice /slaɪs/		n.	share or part 一份，部分，薄片，切片
		vt.	to cut into thin flat pieces 切(片)

Unit 5 Living a Full Life

sufficient /sə'fiʃənt/	a.	enough 足够的，充分的	
sufficiently /sə'fiʃəntli/	ad.	足够地，充分地	
grateful /'greitfəl/	a.	feeling or showing thanks to another person 感激的，感谢的	
inquire /in'kwaiə/	v.	to ask 打听，询问；调查，查问	
offhand /'ɔːf'hænd/	ad.	at once 立即	
	a.	careless 随便的	

PHRASES

now and again/then	sometimes 时而，不时
to begin with	as the first reason, in the first place 首先，第一
make a fuss about	to express unreasonable fear or excitement about (sb., sth., or doing sth.) 大惊小怪，小题大做
add to	to put together with sth. else; increase 增添；增加
in (many) respects	在(许多)方面
merge into	to (cause to) mix with, so as to become part of sth. 合并，结合
split into	to (cause to) separate into (smaller parts) (使)分裂
under the sun	anywhere 天下，世界上
at intervals	happening regularly after equal periods of time or appearing at equal distances 不时，相隔一定的距离

EXERCISES

Reading Comprehension

Task 3

Decide whether the following statements in the table are dreams, facts, or opinions. Put a tick in the appropriate box. Note that some may fit into more than one category.

Part A

Intensive Reading

	Dream	Fact	Opinion
1. I have had dreams at times.			
2. I like the idea of dreaming.			
3. Grownups took dreaming calmly.			
4. Grownups made such a fuss about any holiday.			
5. I am mystified by people who say they never dream.			
6. The dead are there, smiling and talking.			
7. There's luggage that cannot be packed.			
8. There're trains that refuse to be caught.			
9. Persons and scenes there are not very dependable and solid.			
10. Brown and Smith merge into one person.			
11. The dining room is part of a theatre balcony.			
12. This other life has its interests.			
13. Dream life is an additional joy after dark.			

Task 4

Find answers to the following questions in the text.

1. What does the phrase "by some queer magic" imply?

2. How many people have the same attitude as the author towards dream life?

3. What does the third sentence in Par. 2 suggest?

4. Who are Brown, Smith and Robinson?

5. What do we experience in our dreams?

6. Which two words in the passage describe the two extremes of feelings that one can experience toward dreams?

7. What do you think is the author's attitude toward dreams?

8. What has made the reading of the passage enjoyable?

Unit 5 Living a Full Life

vocabulary

Task 5

Give words that are close in meaning to the underlined part in each of the following sentences.

1. My class is going on a <u>trip</u> to the Summer Palace.
2. I am <u>confused</u> as to why she said that.
3. It is late and they are waiting with <u>worry</u> for your return.
4. Susan took <u>pleasure</u> in winning the chess match.
5. We are <u>thankful</u> to you for all this help.
6. I'd like to express my <u>sadness</u> at the death of your father.
7. The large crowd <u>separated</u> into groups going in different directions.
8. Tina <u>took a glance</u> at her boss.
9. Tim accidentally <u>cut</u> his fingers when cutting vegetables.
10. Our boss took a large <u>share</u> of the profits.
11. This young man has <u>adequate</u> knowledge for the work.
12. I'd like to <u>ask</u> about the trains for Shanghai.
13. I've got a <u>terrible</u> feeling that I've forgotten something.
14. We were <u>shocked</u> at how much she had aged.
15. The children have been <u>divided</u> into five groups according to their ability.
16. It's very <u>uncommon</u> to have hot weather like this in April.

Task 6

Choose the right word to fit into each sentence, using the proper form.

1. horror, horrible, horribly, to horrify
   a. My younger sister was _____ by the sight of the horseman.
   b. I've never had such a _____ meal.
   c. The man had begun to scream _____.
   d. The sight increased his _____.
   e. I found to my _____ that the man was mad.
2. to satisfy, satisfactory, satisfaction, satisfactorily
   a. We hope everything will turn out _____ in the end.
   b. The workers found it difficult to _____ him, as Jimmy required _____ work from everyone.
   c. Ted feels great _____ at having his ability recognized.
   d. The two parties have _____ settled the matter.
   e. Terry will not be _____ with such a small salary.

3. anxiety, anxious, anxiously
   a. Your behavior will cause _____ for your father.
   b. Patty was _____ about her daughter being out so late at night.
   c. "How long am I going to stay?" she whispered _____.
   d. It is late and they are waiting with _____ for your return.
4. sorrow, sorrowful
   a. It was a _____ day in that town when the orders came to close down the mine.
   b. The old lady came to express her _____ at the death of their son.
   c. Diana finds it difficult to get over the very natural _____ at leaving home.
5. terror, terrible, to terrify, terrorism
   a. Being lost in a strange place after dark was a _____ experience.
   b. The criminal was the _____ of the neighborhood.
   c. The courts and the police made much progress in the struggle against _____.
   d. The thought of flying _____ Klaus so much that he decided to go by boat.
   e. The old lady's _____ was so great that she could do nothing.
6. sufficient, sufficiently, sufficiency
   a. The table is not _____ wide for our purpose.
   b. My father earns _____ money to provide for us.
7. to add, addition, additional
   a. Sam is the newest _____ to our office.
   b. Factors beyond their control _____ to their success.
   c. There's no _____ charge for children under twelve.
   d. _____ your name to the list.
8. to astonish. astonished, astonishing. astonishingly, astonishment
   a. A look of _____ crossed Emma's face.
   b. The Prime Minister was said to be _____ by the decision.
   c. To my absolute _____ the scheme was a huge success.
   d. It was _____ to see the size of the crowds.
   e. Lynn _____ everybody by announcing her engagement.

Task 7

Fill in the blanks with appropriate words.

The strange behavior of sleepwalkers has puzzled the police and scientists for centuries. There is a __1__ supply of stories about sleepwalkers, who have been said to __2__ mathematical problems, do shopping and take a swim. In rare cases, sleepwalking is used as an excuse __3__

Unit 5 Living a Full Life

some radical behaviour.

Is the sleepwalker actually __4__ or asleep? Scientists have decided that he is half-and-half. A sleepwalker can walk in his sleep, __5__ around, and do other things, but he does not think __6__ what he is doing.

The only way to cure sleepwalking is to remove the worries and __7__ that cause it. So far, no __8__ explanations have ever been found. The simplest one is that it is the acting out of a dream. The dream usually comes from anxiety, __9__ , guilt, __10__ or nervousness.

Although sleepwalking itself is nothing to become alarmed about, the problems that cause the sleepwalking may be very serious.

Task 8

The word "glow" may mean different things in different sentences. Match the sentences with the proper Chinese equivalents of the phrase.

1. A cigarette *glowed* in the dark.	光亮
2. The *glow* of romance seemed to have worn off.	（脸）红
3. Her face has a natural, healthy *glow*.	激情
4. His cheeks *glowed* after the workout.	发光

Further Practice

Task 9

Translate the following sentences into English, using the words or phrases given in the parentheses.

1. 我们吵吵嚷嚷地争论着谁会获胜。他看上去却对这个话题没有兴趣。(to make a fuss about, have no interest in)
2. 虽然朴素的乡村生活在许多方面不令人满意，但却有着它自己的许多益处。今天许多人都喜欢宁静的乡村生活。(unsatisfactory in many respects, take pleasure in)
3. 我们对他为我们所做的一切没有表现出足够的感激之情。我们应该为此感到惭愧。(sufficiently grateful for, feel ashamed of)

Task 10

According to the text, match each of the phrases in Column A with an appropriate expression in Column B.

Part A
Intensive Reading

Column A	Column B
1. to like the idea of	a. so calmly
2. to have no interest	b. a walk
3. to go out for	c. luggage
4. to pack	d. part of one's life
5. to catch	e. in the subject
6. to take dreaming	f. as a little habit
7. to accept dreaming	g. trains
8. to see dreaming	h. dreaming

Grammar

Task 11

Fill in the blanks in the following sentences with appropriate connectors.

1. Jet planes usually fly very fast; _____, they have made the world a much smaller place in which to live.
2. Travel in space can be very exciting; _____, it can also be boring and lonely at times.
3. A foreign student who reads only 200 words a minute is reading at about half the speed of a native speaker of English; _____, he takes about twice as long to read the same assignment.
4. They have been trying to develop a car that is powered by electricity, _____, they haven't succeeded yet.
5. George knew how he could improve his test scores, _____ he did not have enough time to study.
6. Jane had not realized how long the magazine was _____ how difficult it was to read.
7. You may do anything you like _____ it is not against the law.
8. Certain materials whose resistivity is not high enough to classify them as good insulators, _____ is still high compared with the resistivity of common metals, are known as semi-conductors.

Unit 5 Living a Full Life

定义法 (Definitions)

定义法即通过给出定义使被说明的事物有明确的界定。常用的定义法有两种，简单定义和扩展定义。

1. 简单定义

简单定义（Simple Definitions）即通过一句话，给出被说明事物的定义，如果定义在文中不需要着重强调，就通常使用简单定义法。第一单元和本单元的课文都采用了这种方法，例如：

1) The environment is everything that surrounds us: plants, animals, buildings, country, air, water — literally everything that can affect us in any way.

2) Ecology is the science of how living creatures and plants exist together and depend on each other and on the local environment.

3) A speech community is any group of people who speak the same language no matter where they happen to live.

通过上述例子我们可以看出，简单定义有着非常规范的框架结构，你能总结出来吗？

2. 扩展定义

顾名思义，扩展定义（Extended Definition）即在简单定义基础上的扩展。扩展定义的落脚点不再是某个东西是什么，而是某个东西怎么样，在简单定义的基础上增加了补充信息。请见下面的例子：

1) A door is a movable structure contained within a framework which separates two areas by covering an opening and whose principle purpose is to facilitate entrances and exits. There are all kinds of doors. There are hanging doors, swinging doors, overhead doors, trap doors, and sliding doors. Doors come in all sizes and shapes and are customarily made of wood, steel, aluminum, or glass. Without doors, our living would not be nearly as comfortable or secure as it is.

2) Induction is the kind of reasoning by which we examine a number of specific instances and

on the basis of them, arrive at a conclusion. Every cat we encounter has claws; we conclude all cats have claws. Every rose we smell is fragrant; we conclude all roses are fragrant. Every Saturday morning for six weeks the newspaper boy is late delivering the paper; we conclude that he sleeps in on Saturday mornings, and we no longer look for the paper before nine o'clock. In each case we have reasoned inductively from a number of instances; we have moved from an observation of some things to a generalization about all things in the same category.

Task 12

Try to summarize the basic structure of simple definition, and write a simple definition for the following words:

1) Hospital (institution, doctor, medical services)
   A hospital is _____.
2) Boomerang (飞去来器)(a curved piece of wood, return to, thrower)
   A boomerang is _____.
3) Journalism (新闻业)(profession, inform, events)
   Journalism is _____.
4) Book (pages, bind, edge, open)
   A book is _____.

Task 13

Please write extended definitions of the following words or phrases with reference to the information provided in the brackets.

1) Protein: [one of the main classes of food, essential to animals, obtain from what they eat, be high in protein contents, cheese, eggs, meat, fish, milk, make up a large part of, build, maintain, repair, tissue, bone, muscles]

   _____
   _____

2) Telescope: [an instrument, magnify, see, study, photograph, consists of, a long tube, at one end, at the other end, eyepiece, two lenses, a large and convex lens, objective lens]

   _____
   _____

Unit 5　Living a Full Life

Task 14

Read the text, and write a paragraph of about 100 words on Dreams which includes the following points:

1) Your own definition of dream instead of the definition cited in dictionaries
2) Your own attitude on dreams

转换法 (Shift/Conversion) (3)

　　在第 1 册第 4 单元中，我们提到过语言单位的平移、升格及降格问题，语言单位的推移问题实际上也属于转换的范畴。

　　英语结构严谨，注重句子成分之间的一致问题，颇有"牵一发而动全身"的特点，汉语相对而言，结构松散，没有很多形式方面的要求，可有可无的词语，只要不影响理解则可省去，具有"点到为止"的特点，因而汉译英往往要采用增译法，英译汉则正好相反。由于这个原因，大家可能会以为汉译英时语言单位一般都会升格，英译汉时语言单位都会降格。实际情况正好与之相反。虽然英语的抽象词汇似乎多于汉语，但英语行文中往往是有一说一，有二说二，如"grain"就是"grain"，"fruit"就是"fruit"，不像汉语，"粮食"还有许多别称或代称，如"五谷杂粮"。汉语行文中如果前面"粮食"不说"粮食"而说"五谷杂粮"，后面的"水果"则也不会说成"水果"，而会找一个与之相对应的说法，以求对称和平稳，如："天津卫这地方，大马路不种五谷杂粮，小胡同里不长瓜果梨桃"。这个例句里还有两个地方值得注意："大马路"和"小胡同"。哪儿的大马路上又何曾种过五谷杂粮？哪儿的小胡同里又何曾长过瓜果梨桃？这不废话吗？然而，这就是汉语，这就是汉语的修辞习惯！其实，"大马路"和"小胡同"只是变相地重提"天津卫这地方"。如果说白了，这句话无非是说：天津卫这地方不产粮食和水果。而照此译成英文则是恰到好处：The city of Tianjin produces neither grain nor fruit. 据此我们说，英文相对于汉语而言，语言比较平实，英译汉若不对某些语言单位进行适当升格，恐怕译文在读者看来就会过于平实，缺乏文采了，如：

- Proverbs are the popular sayings that brighten so much Latin American talk, the boiled-down wisdom that you are as apt to hear from professors as from peasants, from beggars as from élégantes. Brief and colorful, they more often than not carry a sting.

  谚语是流行的俗话，为拉美人言谈增色不少；谚语是智慧的结晶，随处可闻：从大学教授到乡村农夫，从市井乞丐到窈窕淑女。谚语简洁明快，绚丽多彩，但往往也无不带刺。

- When some people discharge an obligation you can hear the report for miles round.

  有的人做了屁大一点儿该做的事儿，方圆几里地都听得见响声。

- They never confine themselves to one science, but are inevitably masters of several. The big book of Nature they know by heart. Only the other day I was reading an account of a great novelist, a most sophisticated and subtle person, and was told that he knew the name and habits and history of every wild flower and plant and tree and bird in the country. Nor is that all. There is not one of these big-wigs who is not (I quote the customary phrases) a sensitive and accomplished musician, or an extraordinarily fine amateur water-colourist, or the possessor of a magnificent prose style. We are always told that, had circumstance been different, their talents were such that they need only have given their serious attention to one or other of these arts to have procured for themselves lasting and perhaps world-wide reputations.

  他们从不只死钻一门学问，而是广涉博猎，最终个个都不可避免地成了若干领域的大师。连大自然这本大书他们也是烂熟于胸，了若指掌。就在前不多时，我还在拜读一文坛巨擘的传记来着，此公阅历超群，学问精深，据称对本土花草树鸟的名字、习性和来龙去脉，他是如数家珍，无一不知，无一不晓。而且这还算不上什么。这些大腕儿级的人物，套用一句俗语，没有哪一个不是造诣匪浅乐感敏锐的音乐大师、卓尔不群挥毫泼墨的水彩高手、风格隽永文如锦绣的散文名家。书上还常常这样写道：纵然是身处别样的环境，凭他们的天赋，在这些方面稍稍钻研一下，也足以使他们留名丹青，说不定还会名扬天下。

- Kant, seated behind a little desk, spoke in a conversational tone, in a low voice, and very rarely indulged in gesture, but he enlivened his discourse with humour and abundant

Unit 5 Living a Full Life

illustrations. His aim was to teach his students to think for themselves and he did not like it when they busied themselves with their quills to write down his every word. "Gentlemen, do not scratch so," he said once. "I am not oracle."

康德坐在一张小课桌后讲课，声音不大，娓娓道来。他很少比划，但是旁征博引，妙语连珠，课讲得生动有趣。康德注重培养学生独立思考的能力，不喜欢他们埋头一字不落地在那儿记笔记。有一次，他对学生们说："诸位，用不着这么玩命记，我又不是什么圣人。"

Task 15

Translate the following sentences into Chinese, using the method you've learned.

1) As a child I could never understand why grownups took dreaming so calmly when they could make such a fuss about any holiday. This still puzzles me. I am mystified by people who say they never dream and appear to have no interest in the subject. It is much more astonishing than if they said they never went out for a walk. Most people — or at least most Western Europeans — do not seem to accept dreaming as part of their lives.

2) My dream life does not seem as important as my waking life, if only because there is far less of it, but to me it is important... Then again, the dream life, though queer and confusing and unsatisfactory in many respects, has its own advantages. The dead are there, smiling and talking. The past is there, sometimes all broken and confused but occasionally as fresh as a daisy. And perhaps, the future is there too, waving at us.

Quotation

'Tis much like dancing on ropes with fettered legs: a man may shun a fall by using caution; but the gracefulness of motion is not to be expected.
— *John Dryden* (1631 — 1700)

[逐字翻译]与戴着脚镣在绳索上跳舞十分相似：小心翼翼，不摔倒或许还可以，但动作的优雅就指望不上了。

——约翰·德莱顿 (1631 — 1700)

Part B

Extensive Reading

I. How to Live Beautifully

By **Margaret Mason**

In my newspaper column some time ago, I reprinted a short essay on youth by Samuel Ullman, an author unknown to me.

General Douglas MacArthur, I learned, often quoted Ullman's "Youth" essay and kept a framed copy over his desk throughout the Pacific campaign[1]. It's believed that the Japanese picked up the work from his Tokyo[2] headquarters.

Unlikely as it may sound, this essay, written more than 70 years ago, is the basis of many Japanese businessmen's life philosophies. Many carry creased copies in their pockets.

"Anyone worthy of respect in Japanese business knows and uses this essay," says one longtime Japan observer. When one of Ullman's grandsons, Jonas Rosenfield, Jr., was having dinner in Japan a few years ago, "Youth" came up in conversation. Rosenfield told his dinner companion, a Japanese business leader, that the author was his grandfather. The news was shocking.

"'You are the grandson of Samuel Ullman?' he kept repeating," says Rosenfield, head of the American Film Marketing Association[3]. "He couldn't get over it."

Then the executive pulled a copy of "Youth" from his pocket and told Rosenfield, "I carry it with me always."

Several years ago, several hundred top businessmen and government leaders gathered in Tokyo and Osaka[4] to celebrate their admiration of Ullman's essay. Konosuke Matsushita[5], founder of the Panasonic Company, said "Youth" had been his motto for 20 years.

Someone asked, "Why don't Americans love the essay as much as we do? It sends a message about how to live beautifully to men and women, old and young alike."

---

1. **the Pacific campaign:** a series of military actions in the Pacific in 1944—1945 in which the Americans defeated the Japanese 太平洋战役
2. **Tokyo:** the capital and financial and commercial center of Japan 东京
3. **American Film Marketing Association:** 美国影片销售协会
4. **Osaka:** the second largest city of Japan 大阪
5. **Konosuke Matsushita:** 松下幸之助,日本松下电器公司创始人

Unit 5 Living a Full Life

Samuel Ullman was born in 1840 in Germany and came to America as a boy. He fought in the U.S. Civil War[1] and settled in Birmingham[2], Alabama[3]. He was a hardware merchant with a great enthusiasm for public service that continues even now, 67 years after his death. In the last few years more than $36,000 from Japanese royalties on a book and a cassette reading of his work has gone to a University of Alabama at Birmingham scholarship fund. Not bad for a man who started writing in his 70s.

Youth

By **Samuel Ullman**

Youth is not a time of life; it is a state of mind; it is not a matter of rosy cheeks, red lips and supple knees; it is a matter of the will, a quality of the imagination, a vigor of the emotions; it is the freshness of the deep springs of life.

Youth means a temperamental predominance of courage over timidity, of the appetite for adventure over the love of ease. This often exists in a man of 60 more than a boy of 20. Nobody grows old merely by a number of years. We grow old by deserting our ideals.

Years may wrinkle the skin, but to give up enthusiasm wrinkles the soul. Worry, fear, self-distrust bows the heart and turns the spirit back to dust.

Whether 60 or 16, there is in every human being's heart the lure of wonder, the unfailing childlike appetite of what's next and the joy of the game of living. In the center of your heart and my heart there is a wireless station: so long as it receives messages of beauty, hope, cheer, courage and power from men and from the Infinite, so long are you young.

When the aerials are down, and your spirit is covered with snows of cynicism and the ice of pessimism, then you are grown old, even at 20, but as long as your aerials are up, to catch waves of optimism, there is hope you may die young at 80. (604 words)

NEW WORDS

| column /ˈkɔləm/ | n. | that regularly appears in a newspaper or magazine 专栏（文章）；柱，圆柱；直行 |

---

1. **the U.S. Civil War:** （美）南北战争 (1861 — 1865)
2. **Birmingham:** a city in Alabama, U.S., the leading industrial center of the South 伯明翰市
3. **Alabama:** a Southern state of the U.S. 亚拉巴马州

Part B
Extensive Reading

reprint /ˌriːˈprint/	v.	再版
frame /freim/	vt.	to put a border around sth. (esp. a picture or photograph) 给……镶框；陷害；制定
	n.	镜框，框架；构架
campaign /kæmˈpein/	n.	plan for fighting part of a war 战役；运动
	vi.	参加运动
headquarters /ˈhedˌkwɔːtəz/	n.	司令部，指挥部；总部
unlikely /ʌnˈlaikli/	a.	not expected; not likely to be true 未必的，不大可靠的；不大有希望的
▲crease /kriːs/	n.	line made by folding or pressing 皱折
	v.	to make creases in（使）起皱折
longtime /ˈlɔŋtaim/	a.	（已持续）长时间的，为时甚久的
observer /əbˈzɜːvə/	n.	a person who watches what happens but has no active part in it 观测者，观察员
grandson /ˈɡrændsʌn/	n.	孙子
association /əˌsəusiˈeiʃən/	n.	a society of people joined together for a particular purpose 协会，社团；联合，交往
executive /iɡˈzekjutiv/	n.	a person in a high position, esp. in business 主管，高级行政人员
	a.	执行的，行政的
leader /ˈliːdə/	n.	a person who controls a group of people 领导者
▲motto /ˈmɔtəu/	n.	short sentence or phrase used as a guide or rule of behaviour 座右铭
alike /əˈlaik/	a.	almost the same 相同的，相似的
	ad.	以同样的方式，类似于
hardware /ˈhɑːdwɛə/	n.	metal goods, such as nails, tools, etc. 五金器具；（计算机）硬件
merchant /ˈmɜːtʃənt/	n.	a person who buys and sells things, esp. from and to other countries 商人，批发商，贸易商，店主
	a.	商业的，商人的
★royalty /ˈrɔiəlti/	n.	[pl.] a part of the price of a book, paid to the writer on each copy sold 版税；皇室，王族
cassette /kəˈset/	n.	a container, usually holding magnetic tape, which can be fitted into a tape recorder 盒式录音带

Unit 5 Living a Full Life

rosy /'rəuzi/		a.	玫瑰红色的
supple /'sʌpl/		a.	easily bent or bending 柔软的，灵便的
imagination /iˌmædʒi'neiʃən/		n.	the act of imagining or the ability to imagine 想象（力）；空想，幻觉
vigor /'vigə/		n.	mental or physical strength 精力；活力
freshness		n.	气味清新，精神饱满
temperamental /ˌtempərə'mentl/		a.	caused by one's nature 由于气质的
predominance /pri'dɔminəns/		n.	the state or quality of being most powerful, noticeable, or important 优势，显著
timidity /ti'miditi/		n.	the state of being easily frightened 怯懦
appetite /'æpitait/		n.	a desire or wish for (esp. food) 欲望（尤指食欲）
ease /i:z/		n.	a lack of difficulty 悠闲；安逸；不费力
		vt.	缓和，减轻
		vi.	减弱，减轻，放松，灵活地移动
wrinkle /'riŋkəl/		n.	small line on the surface of sth. 皱纹
		v.	to (cause to) form into lines（使）起皱纹
distrust /dis'trʌst/		n.	不信任
		vt.	不信任
bow /bau/		v.	bend your head or body forward to show respect 鞠躬，弯腰
		n.	鞠躬
★ *lure* /luə/		n.	attraction or interest 吸引力，趣味
unfailing /ʌn'feiliŋ/		a.	经久不衰的，无穷尽的，可靠的
childlike /'tʃaildlaik/		a.	孩子似的，天真烂漫的
wireless /'waiəlis/		a.	无线的
infinite /'infinit/		a.	without limits or end 无限的，无穷的
the Infinite			God 上帝
★ *aerial* /'ɛəriəl/		n.	a wire put up to receive radio or television broadcasts 天线
cynicism /'sinisizəm/		n.	the state of mind or feelings of a person who sees little or no good in anything and who has no belief in human progress 愤世嫉俗，玩世不恭
pessimistic /ˌpesi'mistik/		a.	having the habit of thinking that whatever happens will be bad 悲观的

Part B

Extensive Reading

pessimism /ˈpesimizəm/	*n.*	the state of expecting or believing that bad things will happen 悲观（主义）
★ optimism /ˈɔptimizəm/	*n.*	tendency to look upon the bright side of things 乐观，乐观主义

PHRASES

pick up	to take hold of and lift up 捡起
come up	be put forward 被提出(起)
couldn't get over	couldn't believe 对……感到惊奇，感到难以置信

EXERCISES

Reading Comprehension

Task 1

Find answers to the following questions.

1. Who often referred to Ullman's "Youth" essay?
2. How did General Douglas MacArthur keep his copy of Ullman's "Youth" essay?
3. How important is the essay to many Japanese businessmen?
4. How old was Ullman when he started writing?
5. What is "youth" according to Ullman?
6. How are people grown old according to Ullman?
7. What does the sentence "when the aerials are down" imply?
8. How can people have a youthful spirit even at the age of 80?

Vocabulary

Task 2

Give words or phrases that are close in meaning to the underlined part in each of the following sentences.

1. You can be <u>stronger and healthier</u> if you take exercise regularly.
2. Phillip's manner was <u>polite</u>, though not particularly friendly.

Unit 5 Living a Full Life

3. There is <u>a large range</u> of bank accounts available.

4. It wasn't proper for him to show his <u>affections</u>.

5. One of the good things about teaching young children is their <u>eagerness</u>.

6. This capable group leader has a strong <u>desire</u> for power.

7. Students should have a <u>good supply</u> of reading material.

8. James thought he was being followed, but it was <u>not real</u>.

9. The tone of the meeting was very <u>sad</u>.

10. Our <u>involvement in</u> the project began at the university.

11. I write <u>articles for</u> a local newspaper.

12. It's <u>hardly possible</u> that I'll have any free time next week.

13. Her <u>attitude</u> is "If a job's worth doing, it's worth doing well".

14. Sandy answered the questions <u>without difficulty</u>.

15. In October 1942, General George Patton launched his famous military <u>operation</u> in north Africa.

16. Suzan is a senior <u>manager</u> in a computer company.

II. The Lost Gold Piece

After the first World War, a small group of veterans returned to their village in France. Most of them managed to get along fairly well, but one—Francois Lebeau[1], who had been gassed and never recovered his strength — was unable to work regularly. In time he became poverty-stricken. Yet he was too proud to accept charity from the people in the village.

5 Once each year the veterans held a reunion dinner. On one of these occasions they met in the home of Jules Grandin[2], who had made a good deal of money and had grown fat and self-important. Grandin produced a curiosity — a large gold coin
10 about whose age, rarity and value he talked at some length. Each man examined it with interest as it passed around the long table. All, however, had drunk wine freely and the room was filled with noisy talk, so that the gold piece was soon forgotten. Later, when Grandin remembered it and asked for it, the coin was missing.

---

1. **Francois Lebeau:** masculine name 弗朗索瓦·勒博，男子名
2. **Jules Grandin:** masculine name 于勒·格朗丹，男子名

Instantly there arose a hubbub of questions and denials. Finally the village attorney suggested everyone be searched, to which all agreed — except Lebeau. His companions looked at him with surprise.

"You refuse, then?" asked Grandin.

Lebeau flushed. "Yes," he said, "I cannot allow it."

"Do you realize," asked the owner of the gold piece, "what your refusal implies?"

"I did not steal the gold piece, and I will not submit to a search," Lebeau answered.

One by one, the rest of the group turned out their pockets. When the coin failed to appear, attention was focused once more on poor Lebeau.

"Surely you will not persist in your refusal?" the attorney demanded. Lebeau made no reply. Grandin stepped out of the room in anger. No one addressed another word to Lebeau and, under the pitying stares of his friends, he walked out with the hangdog air of a prisoner and returned to his home.

From that day, Lebeau was a man with a bad reputation. People turned their eyes away when they met him. He grew poorer, and when his wife died not long afterward no one knew or cared whether it was from want or shame.

A few years later, when the incident had become almost legendary, Grandin made some alterations in his house. A workman found the gold coin, buried in dirt between planks of the floor in the room where the reunion dinner had been held.

Self-important though he was, Grandin was a just man and now that he had proof that Lebeau was innocent he was quick to admit his mistake. Hurrying to Lebeau's humble home, he told him of the amazing discovery of the coin and apologized for having suspected him.

"But," he concluded, "you knew that the gold piece was not on your person — why did you not allow yourself to be searched?"

Lebeau, shabby, old before his time, looked at Grandin blankly. "Because I was a thief," he said brokenly. "For weeks my family and I had not had enough to eat?and my pockets were full of food that I had taken from the table to carry home to my wife and hungry children." (527 words)

NEW WORDS

| gas /gæs/ | vt. | to poison (sb.) by gas 用毒气杀伤（人） |
| | n. | any air-like substance 气体；煤气；汽油 |

Unit 5 Living a Full Life

stricken /ˈstrikən/		a.	suffering severely from the effects of sth. 遭殃的，患病的
charity /ˈtʃæriti/		n.	money or gifts which are given to poor people 救济金，施舍物；慈善团体；慈悲，慈善
reunion /riːˈjuːnjən/		n.	团圆，重聚
occasion /əˈkeiʒən/		n.	a time when sth. happens 场合；时机，机会
		vt.	引起
curiosity /ˌkjuəriˈɔsiti/		n.	a strange, interesting or rare object 珍品；好奇心
rarity /ˈrɛəriti/		n.	稀有
arise /əˈraiz/ (**arose** /əˈrəuz/)		v.	to appear 出现；起身
hubbub /ˈhʌbʌb/		n.	a mixture of loud noises 吵闹声，喧哗
attorney /əˈtəːni/		n.	[US] lawyer（美）律师
★ *flush* /flʌʃ/		v.	（使脸）发红；（被）冲洗
		n.	脸红
imply /imˈplai/		vt.	to mean sth. without saying it 暗示，意味
submit /səbˈmit/		v.	to cause (oneself) to agree to obey because of the power of another 屈服，听从；呈送，提交
hangdog /ˈhæŋdɔg/		a.	ashamed, guilty 惭愧的，自觉有罪的
reputation /ˌrepju(ː)ˈteiʃən/		n.	opinion held by others, the degree to which one is well thought of 名气，名声，名望
incident /ˈinsidənt/		n.	an event, esp. one that is either unpleasant or unusual 事件，事变
legendary /ˈledʒəndəri/		a.	传说中的
alteration /ˌɔːltəˈreiʃən/		n.	act of making or becoming different 改变；改动
dirt /dəːt/		n.	stuff that is not clean, for example mud or dust 污垢，泥土
▲ *plank* /plæŋk/		a.	a long usu. heavy piece of board 厚木板
innocent /ˈinəsənt/		a.	not having done wrong 清白的，无罪的；幼稚的；无害的，没有恶意的
humble /ˈhʌmbl/		a.	poor 简陋的；谦逊的，谦恭的；地位(身份)低下的，卑贱的
suspect /səsˈpekt/		v.	to think that sb. has done sth. wrong but not be certain 怀疑；猜想
		n.	嫌疑犯
		a.	不可信的，可疑的

Part B
Extensive Reading

conclude /kən'kluːd/		v.	to end 结束；推断出
★shabby /'ʃæbi/		a.	(of a person) wearing old, worn clothes 衣衫褴褛的；破旧的
blankly /blæŋkli/		ad.	without expression 茫然地，毫无表情地

PHRASES

in time	eventually, in the end; early or soon enough; following the correct time 终于；及时；按时
at length	after a long time, at last; in great detail, thoroughly 最后，终于；详细地
turn out	to happen to be in the end; to empty (one's pocket, drawer) 证明为，结果；腾空，倒出
make no reply	to give no answer 未做答复
now that	as a result of the fact that, since 既然，由于
on one's person	carried about with oneself, as in one's pocket 随身携带

EXERCISES

Reading Comprehension

Task 1

Raise questions that match the following answers.

1. _____
He had been gassed in the war and never recovered his strength.

2. _____
They held a reunion dinner once each year.

3. _____
A large gold coin of the host was missing.

Unit 5 Living a Full Life

4. _____

Because he refused to be searched.

5. _____

The workman found it between planks of the floor in the room where the reunion dinner had been held.

6. _____

Because he had stolen some food.

7. _____

His tone expressed that he was extremely sad.

vocabulary

Task 2

Give words that are close in meaning to the underlined part in each of the following sentences.

1. My brother acted as <u>lawyer</u> for me.
2. I shall tell her what I think if the <u>opportunity</u> arises.
3. It has done so much to build up the <u>honour</u> of the firm.
4. He didn't say so — but he <u>suggested</u> that I was lying.
5. We'll have to get a <u>worker</u> in to fix the window.
6. After a bitter struggle the rebels were forced to <u>surrender</u>.
7. Wipe the <u>mud</u> off your shoes before you come in.
8. Tony always judges other people with <u>mercy</u>.
9. Angela stared <u>expressionlessly</u> out of the window.
10. He firmly believes that she is <u>not guilty</u> of the crime.
11. Various tragic <u>events</u> had made people suspicious.
12. I don't <u>doubt</u> your ability to do the work.
13. Tracy <u>ended</u> her remarks by thanking her supporters.

Part C ► Reading Skill

Transition Words (1)

In order to keep his ideas moving ahead, a writer often uses transition words. These are words or phrases that join one idea to another. By doing so they add coherence to writing. Recognizing transition words enables you to see how the writer develops his thinking, organizes the parts of his writing, and passes the message to the reader. Therefore, familiarizing yourself with transition words will help you follow the writer's ideas and predict what is coming next.

Read the paragraph below carefully, paying special attention to the transition words, which are underlined.

English and Spanish use the same alphabet, but there are differences between their writing systems. <u>To begin with</u>, each letter in Spanish generally represents one sound, while a letter in English may represent many sounds. <u>For example</u>, the letter *i* in Spanish is always pronounced /iː/ (as in the Spanish word *isla*). The same letter in English, <u>however</u>, represents many sounds, as in the words *island*, *Indian*, and *machine*. <u>In addition</u>, Spanish uses some symbols which English does not use. <u>For instance</u>, Spanish includes stress marks on some vowels (televisión). English words do not have stress marks (television). Spanish uses an upside-down question mark before questions (¿Vienes?), but English does not (Are you coming?).

As you can see in the paragraph above, transition words may appear at the beginning, in the middle, and also at the end of a sentence. Wherever they are they stand like signposts telling the reader which way to go and showing the function or purpose of the sentences.

Transition words may be divided into different groups. The most commonly used are shown in the table below:

Unit 5 Living a Full Life

Addition and Sequence	besides, also, moreover, furthermore, likewise, in addition, first, second, then, next, later, finally, while, when
Comparison and Contrast	Like, in the same way, similarly, too, both, also, equally important, likewise, so unlike, while, whereas, instead, in contrast, on the contrary, on the other hand
Cause and Effect	because, for this reason, for, as, since, why so, therefore, consequently, accordingly, hence, as a result
Summary	to sum up, to conclude, in short, in brief, in summary, in conclusion, on the whole, at last, finally, hence, thus
Concession	however, yet, still, but, after all, nevertheless, in spite of, despite, although, instead

The first group of transition words listed in the table can be used to add supporting details to an argument.

EXERCISES

Task 1

Below is a paragraph discussing personal qualities. However, some transition words are missing. You are to select the proper ones from the above table to complete the paragraph to make it meaningful.

　　Looking forward to the year 2000, one wonders what personal qualities will be needed for success. Possibly the four most essential qualities are flexibility, honesty, creativity, and perseverance. __1__, our rapidly changing society requires flexibility — the ability to adapt oneself to new ideas and practices. __2__, honesty, the capacity both to tell and face the truth courageously, will be important in all aspects of personal and public relations. __3__, creativity will be required to meet the constantly changing world around us. __4__, perseverance, the ability to hold on at all costs will be required in a society where competition for space, food, and shelter will increase with a growing population.

Task 2

Below is a paragraph which tells the 4 steps a student should do while taking notes. But the sentences are jumbled. Number them in the correct order so that

they sound logical.

a. First, he has to understand what's written or what's said.
b. Finally, the student's notes must show the relations between the various points he has noted.
c. The second thing the student has to do is to decide what's important in the passage or in the lecture.
d. When a student takes notes in reading or in a lecture, he has to do four things.
e. The third task for the student is to write down the important points with clarity.

   1._____ 2._____ 3._____ 4._____ 5._____

Practicing classification of transition words.

Task 3

The same sentence below appears five times. Each time it is followed by a different transition word. Match sentences 1~5 to sentences a~e respectively. Then note down in the bracket which class the transition word in each sentence belongs to. You may refer to the above table.

a. A calm, quiet atmosphere is necessary to effective study. However, _____ ( )
b. A calm, quiet atmosphere is necessary to effective study. This is because, _____ ( )
c. A calm, quiet atmosphere is necessary to effective study. For example, _____ ( )
d. A calm, quiet atmosphere is necessary to effective study. In fact, _____ ( )
e. A calm, quiet atmosphere is necessary to effective study. Therefore, _____ ( )

1. _____ noise distracts and reduces concentration.
2. _____ without such an atmosphere it is actually impossible to study at all.
3. _____ not all students are able to find this kind of environment.
4. _____ it is worth making an effort to create or find such an atmosphere.
5. _____ a section of a library well away from the lending counter may be suitable.

Unit 6

On Personal Qualities

Aims and Objectives

In this unit you will learn:
1. Genre/Style: Exposition/Narration
2. Word Power: Phrasal Verbs
3. Grammar Focus: Past Continuous Tense
4. Writing Skill: Cause and Effect
5. Translation Skill: Translation of English Pronouns
6. Reading Skill: Transition Words (2)

Brief Introductions to the Texts

The passages in this unit deal with personal qualities.

In the first passage "Man at His Best," the author recalls his argument with a man over a parking space and how this fleeting encounter showed him a man at his best.

The other two passages are both concerned with intelligence. In "Emotions Help with Success," the author draws the readers' attention to emotional intelligence and the positive role it plays in people's success. "What Is Intelligence, Anyway?" is a piece in which the author illustrates through his own experience the fact that there are different kinds of intelligence besides what just comes from academic learning.

Unit 6 On Personal Qualities

 Intensive Reading

Pre-Reading

Task 1

Tell each other about a person you admire. Describe the qualities you most admire in this person and explain why you consider these qualities important. Give specific reasons and examples to support your opinion. The following words are for your reference:

hardworking	gentle	honest	humorous
intelligent	patient	knowledgeable	generous
imaginative	kind	creative	tolerant

Task 2

Pair work: You apologize to your partner for certain things.

You:

1) spill tea on his/her book

2) step on his/her foot on a crowded bus

3) forget his/her birthday

4) haven't finished your homework on time

5) drop his/her tape-recorder and it stops working

Useful expressions:

I'm sorry.   Forget it!
I apologize.   No problem.
I'm sorry that / about ...   Oh, that's all right, don't worry.
Please let me apologize.   That's OK.

Please accept my apology.   It's not really your fault.
Will you forgive me?   That's too bad.

Reading and Thinking

Man at His Best

I cry easily. I once burst into tears when the curtain came down on the Kirov Ballet's[1] "Swan Lake[2]". I still choke up every time I see a film of Roger Bannister[3] breaking the "impossible" four-minute mark for the mile. I figure I am moved by witnessing men and women at their best. But they need not be great men and women, doing great things.

> What function do sentences 2 and 3 serve?

Take the night, some years ago, when my wife and I were going to dinner at a friend's house in New York City. It was sleeting. As we hurried toward the house, with its welcoming light, I noticed a car pulling out from the curb. Just ahead, another car was waiting to back into the parking space — a rare commodity in crowded Manhattan[4]. But before he could do so, another car came up from behind and sneaked into the spot. That's dirty pool[5], I thought.

> What does "a rare commodity" refer to?

While my wife went ahead into our friend's house, I stepped into the street to give the guilty driver a piece of my mind. A man in work clothes rolled down the window.

"Hey," I said, "this parking space belongs to that guy." I gestured toward the man ahead, who was looking

---

1. **Kirov Ballet:** It is one of the two major ballet companies of Russia. In 1991 it was officially renamed the St. Petersburg Maryinsky Ballet; however, on its frequent tours abroad it is still called the Kirov Ballet. 基洛夫芭蕾舞团，现在的圣彼得堡芭蕾舞团
2. ***Swan Lake***：《天鹅湖》，四幕芭蕾舞剧，由柴可夫斯基（Tchaikovsky）作曲，是古典芭蕾的代表作。
3. **Roger Bannister:** 罗杰·班尼斯特，1954年在英国牛津以3分59.4秒的成绩跑完一英里，成为第一个打破该赛事4分钟纪录的人。
4. **Manhattan** /mæn'hætən/: 曼哈顿（美国纽约市一区）
5. **dirty pool:** [*slang*] the use of unfair or dishonest tactics 不诚实的行为，不公正的行为

Unit 6 On Personal Qualities

20 back angrily. I thought I was being a good Samaritan[1], I guess—and I remember that at the moment I was feeling pretty manly in my new trench coat.

"Mind your own business!" the driver told me.

"No," I said. "You don't understand. That fellow was waiting to
25 back into this space."

Things quickly heated up until finally he leaped out of the car. My God, he was colossal! He grabbed me and bent me back over the hood of his car as if I were a rag doll. That sleet stung my face. I glanced at the other driver, looking for help, but he gunned[2] his engine
30 and hightailed it[3] out of there.

The huge man shook his rock of a fist at me, brushing my lip and cutting the inside of my mouth against my teeth. I tasted blood. I was terrified. He snarled and threatened, and then told me to beat it[4].

Almost in a panic, I scrambled to my friend's front door. As a
35 former Marine, as a man, I felt utterly humiliated. Seeing that I was shaken, my wife and friends asked me what had happened. All I could bring myself to say was that I had had an argument about a parking space. They had the sensitivity to let it go at that.

> What did the author use to be?

I sat stunned. Perhaps half an hour later, the doorbell rang. My
40 blood ran cold. For some reason I was sure that the bruiser had returned for me. My hostess got up to answer it, but I stopped her. I felt morally bound to answer it myself.

> Who is "the bruiser"?

I walked down the hallway with dread. Yet I knew I had to face up to my fear. I opened the door. There he stood, towering. Behind
45 him, the sleet came down harder than ever.

"I came back to apologize," he said in a low voice. "When I got home, I said to myself, 'What right did I have to do that?' I'm ashamed of myself. All I can tell you is that the Brooklyn Navy Yard[5] is closing.

---

1. **good Samaritan** /sə'mærɪtən/: 慈善的撒马利亚人，对苦难者给予同情帮助的好心人，乐善好施者（源自基督教《圣经》）
2. **gun:** [*slang*] to advance the throttle of an engine so as to increase the speed 加大油门
3. **hightail it:** [*infml.*] to go or leave in a great hurry 迅速逃走
4. **beat it:** [*slang*] go away at once 走，滚
5. **Brooklyn Navy Yard:** 布鲁克林海军工厂

I've worked there for years. And today I got laid off. I'm not myself.
50 I hope you'll accept my apology."

> What happened to the big man today?

I often remember that big man. I think of the effort and courage it took for him to come back to apologize. He was man at his best.

And I remember that after I closed the door, my eyes blurred, as I stood in the hallway for a few moments alone. (618 words)

NEW WORDS

choke /tʃəuk/		v.	使窒息，呛；塞满，塞住
witness /'witnis/		vt.	to see at first hand 目击，注意到；为……作证，证明
		n.	目击者，见证人；证据，证言
sleet /sliːt/		n.	rain and snow or hail falling together 冰雨，雨夹雪
		vi.	下雨雪，下冰雹
curb /kəːb/		n.	the stone or concrete edge of a pavement at the side of a road（街道或人行道的）路缘，路边；控制，约束
		vt.	控制，约束
★commodity /kə'mɔditi/		n.	article of trade 商品，货物
★sneak /sniːk/		vi.	to go quietly and secretly, so as not to be seen 偷偷地走，溜
		vt.	偷偷地做（或拿、吃）
spot /spɔt/		n.	a particular place 地点，处所；斑点，污点；少量
		vt.	认出，发现；玷污
hey /hei/		int.	嗨！（用于引起注意或表示疑问、惊奇、赞许或喜悦）
★trench /trentʃ/		n.	沟渠，战壕
trench coat			胶布雨衣
leap /liːp/		vi.	to make a sudden powerful jump 跳，跃，跳动；急速行动，冲
		vt.	跃过
		n.	跳，跳跃；激增，骤变
▲colossal /kə'lɔsl/		a.	very large 巨大的
grab /græb/		vt.	to grasp suddenly, snatch 抓取，攫取；赶紧做；抓住（机会）
		vi.	抓住，夺得

Unit 6 On Personal Qualities

	n.	抓，夺
▲hood /hud/	n.	车盖，引擎罩；风帽；排风罩
doll /dɔl/	n.	small model of a human being, used as a toy 洋娃娃，玩偶
sting /stiŋ/	vt.	to cause sharp pain to 刺痛，使痛苦；刺，蛰，叮；激怒
	vi.	刺，蛰，叮；感到剧痛
	n.	（昆虫的）蛰刺；刺痛，剧痛
engine /ˈendʒin/	n.	发动机，引擎；机车，火车头
★terrified /ˈterifaid/	a.	very afraid, badly frightened 恐惧的，受惊吓的
	n.	商业广告
▲snarl /snɑːl/	vi.	to speak or say in an angry bad-tempered way 咆哮，叫着表达；狂吠，嗥叫
	vt.	咆哮着说
	n.	咆哮，怒吼
threaten /ˈθretn/	vt.	to express a threat against sb. 威胁，恐吓；预示（危险）快要来临，是……的征兆
	vi.	构成威胁，可能发生
panic /ˈpænik/	n.	(a state of) sudden uncontrollable quickly-spreading terror or anxiety 恐慌，惊慌，慌乱
	v.	（使）恐慌，（使）惊慌失措
★scramble /ˈskræmbl/	vi.	to move or climb quickly 爬，攀登；争夺，抢夺
	vt.	扰乱，搞乱
	n.	爬，攀登；争夺，抢夺
marine /məˈriːn/	n.	[often M-] a member of the Marine Corps 海军陆战队士兵
	a.	海洋的，海生的；海军的；海运的，海事的
utterly /ˈʌtəli/	ad.	completely 完全地，绝对地，彻底地
▲humiliate /hjuːˈmilieit/	vt.	to cause to feel ashamed or to lose the respect of others 使蒙羞，羞辱，使丢脸
argument /ˈɑːgjumənt/	n.	quarrel 争论，争吵，辩论；理由，论据；说理，论证
sensitivity /ˌsensiˈtiviti/	n.	the condition or quality of being sensitive 敏感，灵敏（度），灵敏性
★stun /stʌn/	vt.	to shock or surprise very greatly 使震惊，使目瞪口呆；把……打昏，使昏迷

Part A
Intensive Reading

doorbell /'dɔ:bel/		n.	门铃
★ bruiser /'bru:zə/		n.	a big rough strong man 彪形大汉，粗壮的人
bound /baund/		a.	having a duty, legally or morally, to do sth. 受约束的，有义务的；一定的，必然的；准备到……去的，开往（或驶往）……的
		vi.	跳跃，跳跃着前进；弹回
		vt.	成为……的界线，给……划界
		n.	跳跃；界限，限制
hallway /'hɔ:lwei/		n.	走廊
blur /blə:/		v.	to make or become vague or less distinct （使）变模糊
		n.	模糊，模糊的东西

PHRASES

at one's best	处于最佳状态；（演员）达到个人最高水平；（花等）在盛开期
burst into	to start sth. suddenly, to enter a state suddenly 突然开始，突然进入（某状态）
choke up	（因激动等）说不出话来
pull out	to move away from （车、船等）驶出，开上路
come up	to move near 走近，接近
give sb. a piece of one's mind	对某人直言不讳，责备某人
heat up	to become more lively 变激烈，加剧
let it go at that	to say or do no more about sth. 谈论到此为止，就此罢休
face up to	to show courage in accepting, bearing, or dealing with sth. difficult or painful 勇敢地面对、承担
lay off	to dismiss sb. from work, esp. for a short time 解雇（通常用于被动语态）
be oneself	to function physically and mentally as one normally does （人）处于正常状态

Unit 6 On Personal Qualities

EXERCISES

Reading Comprehension

Task 3

Answer the following questions.

1. What is the main idea of the passage? Locate the sentence(s) in which the author states his main idea.
2. What was the weather like when the incident happened?
3. Was it easy to find a parking space in Manhattan?
4. All of the following words can describe the author except _____.
   a. emotional   b. courageous
   c. indifferent   d. forgiving
5. What did the other driver do when the author looked at him for help?
6. What did the author expect the bruiser to do when the doorbell rang?
7. The author makes reference to his own experience—his argument with a man over a parking space. How does this use of firsthand experience help him make his point?

Task 4

Paraphrase the following sentences.

1. ... give the guilty driver a piece of my mind.
2. Things quickly heated up ...
3. ... and then told me to beat it.
4. They had the sensitivity to let it go at that.
5. My blood ran cold.
6. I felt morally bound to answer it myself.
7. I'm not myself.

Vocabulary

Task 5

Find the words and phrases in the text which fit the following definitions.

1. _____ : to be unable to speak because of feeling strong emotions
2. _____ : in the best state or form
3. _____ : to become difficult to see through clearly
4. _____ : a fear that spreads quickly through a group of people

Part A
Intensive Reading

5. _____: to take sth. firmly and suddenly, roughly or rudely
6. _____: a particular place or area, location
7. _____: to prevent sth. from getting out of control
8. _____: being to blame for sth.
9. _____: to be present at sth. and see it
10. _____: to accept and deal with sth. unpleasant or difficult

Task 6

Complete the following sentences with the phrases from the text.

1. 还要解雇几百名员工 if the company does not get any new orders soon.
2. Much to my surprise John 突然唱起歌来。
3. You must learn to 勇敢地承担你的责任。
4. We watched from the bridge 当火车驶离车站的时候。
5. I don't entirely agree 但是我不再讨论了。
6. 比赛才激烈起来 until the second half.
7. 我从来都不是处于最佳状态 early in the morning.

Task 7

Using its proper form, choose the correct word for each sentence.

| grab | sting | commodity | argument | threaten |
| utterly | bound | curb | blur | witness |

1. A woman who _____ the accident said that the car was going at more than 80 mph when it crashed.
2. The country's most valuable _____ include tin and diamonds.
3. There will be new _____ on drunk-driving starting next week.
4. The mixture of industrial pollution and dust _____ her eyes.
5. He's very unhappy about her promotion; he seems to feel that his own job is _____.
6. You're _____ to feel nervous about your interview.
7. Do you agree that male and female roles are becoming _____?
8. The meeting was an (a) _____ waste of time.
9. If you don't _____ this opportunity, you might not get another one.
10. Liz and John spent a long time _____ over which film to go and see.

Task 8

Cloze: Fill in the blanks with appropriate words. The first letter of each expected word is given to help you.

    Are some people born clever, and others born stupid? Or is intelligence developed by our

Unit 6 On Personal Qualities

environment and our experiences? Strangely enough, the answer to both these questions is yes. To some extent our intelligence is given us at (1) b___ , and no amount of special education can (2) m___ a genius out of a child born with (3) l___ intelligence. On the other hand, a child who lives in a (4) b___ environment will develop his intelligence less than (5) o___ who lives in rich and varied (6) s___ . Thus the limits of a person's intelligence are fixed at birth but whether or not he reaches those limits will (7) d___ on his environment. This view, now (8) h___ by most experts can be supported in a number of ways.

Relations (9) l___ brothers and sisters, parents and children, usually have similar intelligence, and this clearly (10) s___ that intelligence depends on birth.

Task 9

The word "bound" may have different meanings in different sentences. Match the sentences with the proper Chinese equivalents of the word.

1. He bounded into the room and announced that he was getting married.	受约束的，有义务的
2. They are bound by contract to deliver the goods on time.	开往（或驶往）……的
3. We boarded a plane bound for New York.	必然的
4. These two young musicians are bound for international success.	成为……的界线
5. Germany is bounded on the west by France and on the south by Switzerland.	跳跃着前进

Grammar

Task 10

Choose the best answer to complete each of the following sentences.

1. If there were life on Mars（火星）, such life forms _____ unable to survive on earth.
   a. would   b. will be   c. would be   d. are
2. Liz suggested that we _____ a while before making any firm decisions.
   a. waited   b. wait   c. shall wait   d. would wait
3. He talks as if he _____ the incident.
   a. had witnessed   b. witnesses   c. witness   d. have witnessed
4. The presidential report urged that more attention _____ to languages less commonly studied.
   a. is given   b. was given   c. be given   d. must be given
5. _____ the rain we would have had a nice holiday.
   a. For but   b. But for   c. In spite   d. In case of

172

6. I wish you _____ me yesterday.
   a. tell   b. could tell   c. would tell   d. had told
7. It's about time people _____ notice of what women did during the war.
   a. took   b. take   c. have taken   d. will take

Task 11

Choose the best answer to complete each of the following sentences.

1. By the end of next month, the airport which is under construction now surely _____ in use.
   a. is   b. will be
   c. will have been   d. will have to be
2. By the late 1800s, the development of electric power and advances in chemical processing _____ the fields of electrical and chemical engineering.
   a. were creating   b. created
   c. have created   d. had created
3. The boy won't have his lunch before he _____ his homework.
   a. will finish   b. finishes
   c. had finished   d. finished
4. I asked her to be quiet. I _____ to hear what the teacher was saying.
   a. tried   b. was trying
   c. have tried   d. am trying
5. No sooner _____ mowing（割草）the lawn than it started raining.
   a. had I started   b. I had started
   c. was I started   d. I was starting

因果法 (Cause and Effect)

我们日常对话中，经常会听到别人问为什么，自己也经常问同样的问题，所以我们对于因果推理并不陌生。

实际上，任何一个因果推理都有可能是以下三个模板中的一种或多种。

Unit 6 On Personal Qualities

模板1：一种原因导致一种结果
模板2：一种原因导致多种结果
模板3：多种原因导致一种结果

模板1是一种理想化的因果模板，原因和结果一一对应，在解决一些简单问题的时候还是可能的，但在日常生活中的因果对应往往很复杂，所以我们经常使用的因果模板是模板2或模板3。

模板的确定与推理模式的确定有密切的联系。在因果法的应用中，我们或者把原因放在前面，把结果放在后面，或者反之。模式的选择主要取决于我们要回答的问题是"WHY"还是"HOW"。如果是前者，结果一般放在前面，原因放后面；如果是后者，原因一般放前面，结果放后面。

在模板2和模板3的使用中，我们还必须注意多个原因或多个结果的排列次序，原则上我们应该把最重要的原因或结果放在最后面，起到强调的作用。那么下面这篇文章使用了哪个模板呢？

As a successful person, a celebrity（名人）understands that being in the public eye can be very awful. For one thing, celebrities don't have the privacy an ordinary person has. The most personal details of their lives are printed all over the front pages of newspapers and magazines. In addition, celebrities are under constant pressure. Their physical appearance is always under observation. Famous people are always under pressure to act calm under any circumstance. Most important, celebrities must deal with the stress of being in constant danger. The friendly hugs（拥抱）and kisses of enthusiastic fans can quickly turn into uncontrolled attacks on a celebrity's hair, clothes, and car.

因果法常用的动词和动词短语：
cause, lead to, give rise to, result in, bring about, be due to, be caused by, result from, be the result of , be the effect of

Part A
Intensive Reading

Task 12

The following paragraph which is organized by cause and effect is incomplete. Please find 3 or 4 causes of student failure.

Notice: The causes lie in the students themselves, that is, students cause their own failure.

Causes of Student Failure

  Thirty-six percent of the freshmen entering a large New York university are dismissed during or at the end of the first year. Studies indicate that this alarming rate of failure is due to a variety of causes, some of which are beyond the control of the student. Among these are inadequate academic and personal counseling services, inferior quality of instruction in very large freshman classes, and the computerized anonymity (匿名) of most administrative procedures. But many of the causes of early student failure can be traced to non-adaptive behavior on the part of the student himself.

_____
_____
_____
_____

Task 13

Please rearrange the following sentences into a meaningful and complete paragraph:

___ (a) At campus dorms, there are no parking spaces for students cars.
___ (b) For these reasons, Susan likes to live off-campus.
___ (c) Finally, she can keep her car at a house.
___ (d) For example, she paid $ 120 a month to live in a dorm, but it costs her only $ 90 to live in a private home.
___ (e) Second, she has more privacy in a home.
___ (f) Susan likes living in a private house better than in a dormitory for a number of reasons.
___ (g) Third, it is easier to study in a private home.
___ (h) First, it costs less.
___ (i) In a dorm, she shared a room with another girl, but in a home, she has a room all to herself.
___ (j) A dorm is often too noisy, but a home rarely is.

Task 14

Which quality do you think is the most important to personal success? Please explain your reasons in a paragraph of about 100 words, and support your opinion with detailed examples.

Unit 6 On Personal Qualities

Translation

英语代词的翻译 (Translation of English Pronouns)

英语使用代词的频率总体说来要比汉语高，而且还有一个比较特别的"it"，所以，有必要专门介绍一下英语代词的翻译技巧。

首先我们来看一看英语的第一人称代词（I/me, we/us）的翻译。"I/me"虽说相当于汉语的"我"，但翻译时绝对不能看到"I/me"就清一色全译成"我"，而应根据特定的上下文和汉语的行文习惯采用不同的译法："我、本人、敝人、鄙夫、鄙人、人家、小的、咱、笔者、在下、寡人、朕"，甚至可以译成"老娘、老夫、老朽、老子"等等。同样，"we/us"除了译作"我们"外，还可以根据情况译成"咱们、我方、咱们大伙儿、你我"等。如：

- *We* met in secret; / I grieve in silence.

  当年**你我**偷偷幽会；/ 如今我暗自伤悲。

其他人称代词及物主代词、反身代词等可以依次类推。此外，并非代词就一定要译作代词，有时还可以还原为所代的名词：

- With September comes a sense of autumn. *It* creeps in on a misty dawn and vanishes in the hot afternoon.

  九月，秋意隐隐。**隐隐的秋意**乘着蒙蒙朝雾而来，躲着炎炎烈日而去。

汉语使用代词的频率较低，还有一个原因，就是汉语喜欢用一些别的字眼来代替前文中提到的名词，如：

- He wasn't sure what had awakened *him*.

  是什么把**自己**给弄醒了，他不是很有把握。

- *I* can't stand ties — *they* choke *you*.

  我这个人打不惯领带——勒死人。

以上谈的是需要译出来的情形，除此，很多情况下，英语代词还可以省去不译，而且有时还硬是不能译出来，如：

- He put his hands into his pockets and shrugged his shoulders.

如果原句中的每个代词都一个不落全部译出来，即：

他把他的手放进他的口袋，然后耸了耸他的肩。

看到这样的句子，中国人还以为是"他把张三的手放进了张三/李四或者他自己的口袋，然后耸了耸张三/李四/王五或者他自己的肩"呢。在中国人看来，如果"他"是把自己的手放进了自己的口袋，耸的也是他自个儿的肩的话，就无需一一说明。所以，该句只能译成：

他把手插进口袋/兜儿里，（然后）耸了耸肩。

又如：

- He took off *his* shoes and stretched *himself* out on the bed.

他脱了鞋，伸开四肢舒舒服服地躺在了床上。

另外，英语中的物主代词在译成汉语时，有时可以省去"的"，如：

- After *I* retired last year, *my* wife and I began walking for exercise to help the back problem I have had for years. I have noticed over the past few months that *I* get a burning pain in *my* legs after walking about 10 minutes. *It* goes away if *I* rest but then comes back again. Is this something *I* should be worried about?

去年退了休之后，我便和（**我**）妻子开始散步，想通过这种锻炼，帮助解决我背疼了好些年这个老毛病。过去的几个月里，我发现散了10来分钟的步之后，双腿就火辣辣地疼。停下来就不疼了，可一走就又疼起来了。这种情况用不用担心？

像"my wife and I"这种情况，最多只需译成"我和我妻子/老婆"，因为"我和妻子"在中文里只能有一种解释，绝对不会因为没有"我的"两个字而引起误解。

英语中"it"是一个很复杂的词，翻译时更得视具体情况而定：

- Yes, it's old, but it can still be used.

不错，（旧）是旧了点，但还能用。

- About your sister, she had a baby this morning. I haven't found out whether it's a girl or a boy.

说到你姐姐，她今儿早上生了。我还不清楚是个闺女还是个小子。

Unit 6 On Personal Qualities

Task 15

Translate the following sentences into Chinese. Pay special attention to the pronouns.

1) I cry easily. I once burst into tears when the curtain came down on Kirov Ballet's "Swan Lake". I still choke up every time I see a film of Roger Bannister breaking the "impossible" four-minute mark for the mile.

2) Take the night, some years ago, when my wife and I were going to dinner at a friend's house in New York City. It was sleeting. As we hurried toward the house, with its welcoming light, I noticed a car pulling out from the curb.

3) "Hey," I said, "this parking space belongs to that guy." I gestured toward the man ahead, who was looking back angrily. I thought I was being a good Samaritan, I guess—and I remember that at the moment I was feeling pretty manly in my new trench coat.

Quotation

When the original merely hints and is obscure, the translator has no right to give the text an arbitrary clarity.

— *Wilhelm von Humboldt* (1769 — 1858)

原文若是拐弯抹角、含糊其词，译者便无权自作聪明，按照自己的武断臆测将原文译得清晰明了。

——威廉·冯·洪堡特(1769 — 1858)

▶ **Extensive Reading**

I. Emotions Help with Success

ver thought you were really clever but just didn't have the exam results to back it up? Anyone who has ever felt academically thick can let out a sigh of relief, because

IQ[1] does not and cannot predict success in life, says a new book by Steven Stein and Howard Book called *The EQ[2] Edge-Emotional Intelligence (EI[3]) and Your Success*.

Hallelujah[4], praise the Lord! It would seem that the brain has been far too over-rated an organ for too long. As Antoine de Saint-Exupery[5] says in *The Little Prince*[6]: "It is with the heart that one sees rightly; what is essential is invisible to the eye."

So what is emotional intelligence? Occupational psychologist and management consultant Chris Watkins describes it as "the capacity to recognize your own feelings and those of other people, to be able to motivate yourself, and to manage emotions in yourself and in your relationships." Gulp...And who coined this terrifying form of intelligence — any money it was an American? Yep.

Dr. Daniel Goleman, a States-side academic defined it back in 1996 in his best-selling book, *Emotional Intelligence: Why It Can Matter More Than IQ*. Psychologist and author Anne Dickson also talks of it at length in *Trusting the Tides: Self-Empowerment Through Emotions*.

"Emotional intelligence is about using emotions to learn and understand. To use them the way we use thought. Feelings are too often dismissed as messy, irrational and childish and most of the time we try and suppress them because they embarrass us and because we fear that they are uncontrollable. Often we end up swallowing them down or else they just erupt. For too long and unfortunately, intelligence has too often been associated with the cognitive and rational which are distinctively unemotional," says Dickson.

How and why have we been ignoring our emotions? Educational establishments do not appear to teach us what to do with our feelings. Apart from the odd spurt of expression in the nativity play[7] or a heated debate on the relationship between Jane Eyre[8] and Mr. Rochester[9], emotions, on the whole, are largely unaddressed by the national curriculums. Instead of paying heed and learning from the constant dialogue of emotions inside us, we are led to believe the

---

1. **IQ:** intelligence quotient 的缩写，智商
2. **EQ:** emotional quotient 的缩写，情商
3. **EI:** emotional intelligence 的缩写，情感智力
4. **hallelujah** /ˌhæl'luːjə/：哈利路亚（犹太教和基督教的欢呼用语，意为"赞美神"）
5. **Antoine de Saint-Exupery:** French aviator and writer, real life hero who looked at adventure and danger with poet's eyes — sometimes from the viewpoint of a child. His most famous work is *The Little Prince* (1943), which he also illustrated. It has become one of the classics of children's literature of the 20th century.
6. **The Little Prince:**《小王子》
7. **nativity play:** a play telling the story of the birth of Christ, esp. one performed by children at school 耶稣诞生记（戏剧）
8. **Jane Eyre:**《简·爱》（夏洛蒂·勃朗特著）中的女主人公
9. **Mr. Rochester:**《简·爱》中的男主人公

Unit 6 On Personal Qualities

intelligence is swotting for high school graduation exams, and then going through several years of fast food-eating poverty to get that lauded degree.

But it is the world of work which has finally realized the way to motivate, lead and manage people. And it is not by the traditional method of employing some dusty dysfunctional Ivy League[1] graduate with a list of exam results the length of his/her old school tie, but rather someone who has strong people skills. "With regard to IQ's relevance in the workplace, studies have shown that it can serve to predict between 1 and 20 per cent (the average is 6 per cent) of success in a given job. EQ, on the other hand, has been found to be directly responsible for between 27 and 45 per cent of job success depending on which field was under study," says Stein and Book.

And if you need further evidence, a survey of 733 multimillionaires in the US revealed that when asked to rate the factors that were most responsible for their success, the top five answers were: being honest with all people; being well disciplined; getting along with people; having a supportive spouse; working harder than most people. It's the simple things really. You probably want to know where you can get some emotional intelligence? No, you can't buy it and, no, it can't be e-mailed or sent in a text message to your mobile phone. EI is about going inwards, taking a good hard look at the black hole inside us which we tend to avoid at all costs.

Dickson offers some words of advice. "Drugs and alcohol are too often used as a way of suppressing emotions, there's an awful lot of people struggling with socially negative feelings while pretending they are not. It's about understanding that all feelings are OK, there's no such thing as good or bad feelings. By understanding what you are feeling you will begin to understand how to deal with them." (702 words)

NEW WORDS

academically /ˌækəˈdemikli/	ad.	学术上，学问上	
relief /rɪˈliːf/	n.	feeling of comfort at the ending of anxiety, pain, or dullness 轻松、宽慰；（痛苦等）缓解、减轻；救济、救援；接替、替换	
predict /prɪˈdɪkt/	vt.	to tell about in advance 预言，预测，预告	
lord /lɔːd/	n.	[the L-] God 上帝；领主，君主；贵族	
overrate /ˌəʊvəˈreit/	vt.	to put too high a value on 估计（估价）过高	
prince /prɪns/	a.	a son or other near male relation of a king or queen 王	

1. Ivy League:（美国东北部哈佛、哥伦比亚等八所名牌大学组成的）常春藤联合会

Part B

Extensive Reading

			子，亲王
essential /i'senʃəl/		a.	basic or fundamental; vitally important 本质的，实质的；必不可少的，绝对必要的
		n.	[常 pl.] 要素，要点；必需品
occupational /ˌɔkju'peiʃənəl/		a.	of, about, or caused by one's job 职业的；占领的
consultant /kən'sʌltənt/		n.	specialist who gives professional advice 顾问；会诊医生
▲ gulp /gʌlp/		vi.	to make a sudden swallowing movement as if surprised or nervous 哽住
		vt.	狼吞虎咽地吃，吞咽；大口地吸；抑制，忍住
		n.	吞咽；一大口（尤指液体）
★ terrify /'terifai/		vt.	to fill with fear 使害怕，使惊吓
yep /jep/		ad.	[slang] yes 是
define /di'fain/		vt.	to give the meaning of a word or idea 给……下定义，解释；限定，规定
tide /taid/		n.	a feeling or tendency that moves or changes like the tide 潮流，趋势；潮，潮汐
empower /im'pauə/		vt.	to enable; to authorize 使能够；授权与
messy /'mesi/		a.	dirty, confused, or untidy 肮脏的，凌乱的
★ suppress /sə'pres/		vt.	to prevent from being shown 抑制（感情等）；镇压；查禁；阻止……的生长（或发展）
uncontrollable /ˌʌnkən'trəuləbl/		a.	无法控制的
swallow /'swɔləu/		vt.	to hold back, not to show or express 压制，抑制；吞，咽；轻信，轻易接受
		vi.	吞，咽
		n.	燕子；吞，咽
★ erupt /i'rʌpt/		vi.	to burst forth suddenly and violently 爆发，突然发生；（火山等）喷发
rational /'ræʃənl/		a.	based on or according to reason; sensible, reasonable 理性的，理智的；合理的
irrational /i'ræʃənəl/		a.	not (done by) using reason, against reasonable behavior 不合理的，荒谬的
distinctively /dis'tiŋktivli/		ad.	区别地，独特地

Unit 6 On Personal Qualities

unemotional /ˌʌniˈməuʃnl/	a.	不诉诸感情的，不易动感情的，缺乏感情的
ignore /igˈnɔː/	vt.	to take no notice of, to refuse to pay attention to 不顾，不理，忽视
establishment /isˈtæbliʃmənt/	n.	commercial or other institution 机构，企业；建立，确立
apart /əˈpɑːt/	ad.	（空间、时间）成距离，相间隔；分离，分开
	a.	分离的，分隔的
spurt /spəːt/	n.	a sudden, brief burst of energy, etc. 短促突然的爆发
nativity /nəˈtiviti/	n.	birth, the birth of Christ 出生，[the N-] 耶稣诞生
unaddressed /ˌʌnəˈdrest/	a.	not brought up for discussion or solution 未被提出商议或解决的
curriculum /kəˈrikjuləm/	n.	all the courses of study offered by a school or college 课程，（学校等的）全部课程
swot /swɔt/	v.	[Br.E.] to study hard 用功读书，死用功
poverty /ˈpɔvəti/	n.	the state of being poor 贫穷，贫困
laud /lɔːd/	vt.	to praise 赞美，称赞
dysfunctional /disˈfʌŋkʃənəl/	a.	unable to function normally, properly 机能不良的
▲ ivy /ˈaivi/	n.	常春藤
relevance /ˈrelivəns/	n.	关联，中肯，适当
workplace /ˈwəːkpleis/	n.	工作场所
multimillionaire /ˌmʌltiˌmiljəˈneə/	n.	拥有数百万家产的富翁，大富豪
supportive /səˈpɔːtiv/	a.	giving encouragement, help, etc. 支持的，支援的
spouse /spauz/	n.	a husband or wife 配偶
mobile /ˈməubail/	a.	able to move or be moved 运动的，活动的；流动的，机动的；多变的，易变的
	n.	移动电话
phone /fəun/	n.	电话，电话机；听筒，耳机
	v.	打电话（给）
inwards /ˈinwədz/	ad.	towards the inside 向内地，向内部地
alcohol /ˈælkəhɔl/	n.	酒精，酒
negative /ˈnegətiv/	a.	without any active, useful, or helpful qualities 反面的，消极的；否定的；负的，阴性的
	n.	（照相的）底片；负数

Part B

Extensive Reading

PHRASES

back up	to support 支持
let out	to express (a sound) 发出（某声音）
at length	using many words, in great detail 详细地
swallow down	to control (a feeling) 压制，抑制（感情等）
associate with	to find a connection between 把……与……联系在一起，联想
apart from	except; besides 除……之外
on the whole	generally, considering everything 大体上，基本上
pay heed to	to pay attention to 注意，留心
with regard to	关于
get along with	to form or have a friendly relationship with 与……相处（融洽）
at all costs	无论如何，不惜任何代价
deal with	to take action about 处理，对付

EXERCISES

Reading Comprehension

Task 1

Write short answers to the following questions according to the text.

1. The word "thick" (Par. 1) can be best interpreted as _____.
2. Chris Watkins defines emotional intelligence as _____.
3. "Any money it was an American" (Par. 3) can be paraphrased as _____.
4. Often we _____ our emotions or they just erupt.
5. _____ are to blame for people ignoring their emotions.
6. "Several years of fast food-eating poverty" (Par. 6) implies _____.
7. According Stein and Book, _____ rather than _____ seems to play a more vital role in job success.
8. The "black hole" (Par. 8) refers to _____.
9. People usually turn to _____ and _____ as ways of suppressing their emotions.

Unit 6 On Personal Qualities

vocabulary

Task 2

Choose the correct phrase for each sentence.

| back up | at length | associate with | deal with |
| apart from | on the whole | get along with | at all costs |

1. I always _____ the smell of those flowers _____ my childhood.
2. He works until nine o'clock every evening, and that's quite _____ the work he does over the weekend.
3. We need further facts to _____ our statements.
4. _____ I prefer to listen to classical music.
5. Bank staff are to be given more training to help them _____ armed robbers.
6. We must prevent them from finding it _____.
7. Our new manager is very easy to _____.
8. This issue has already been examined _____ great _____ in these columns.

II. What Is Intelligence, Anyway?

What is intelligence, anyway? When I was in the army, I received a kind of aptitude test that all soldiers took and, against a normal of 100, scored 160. No one at the base had ever seen a figure like that, and for two hours they made a big fuss over me. (It didn't mean anything. The next day I was still a private with KP[1] as my highest duty.)

5   All my life I have been registering scores like that, so that I have the satisfied feeling that I'm highly intelligent, and I expect other people to think so, too. Actually, though, don't such scores simply mean that I am very good at answering the type of academic questions that are considered worthy of answers by the people who make up the intelligence tests — people with intellectual ability similar to mine?

10   For instance, I had an auto repair man once, who, on these intelligence tests, could not possibly have scored more than 80, by my estimate. I always took it for granted that I was far more intelligent than he was. Yet, when

---

1. **KP:** kitchen police （军队中）炊事值勤（员）

anything went wrong with my car I hurried to him with it, watched him anxiously as he explored its vitals, and listened to his pronouncements as though they were authoritative statements — and he always fixed my car.

Well, then, suppose my auto repair man devised questions for an intelligence test. Or suppose a carpenter did, or a farmer, or, indeed, almost anyone but a scholar. By every one of those tests, I'd prove myself stupid. And I'd be stupid, too. In a world where I could not use my academic training and my verbal talents but had to do something sophisticated or hard, working with my hands, I would do poorly. My intelligence, then, is not absolute but is a function of the society I live in and of the fact that a small subsection of that society has managed to impose itself on the rest as a judge of such matters.

Consider my auto repair man, again. He had a habit of telling me jokes whenever he saw me. One time he raised his head from under the automobile hood to say: "Doc[1], a deaf-and-dumb guy went into a hardware store to ask for some nails. He put two fingers together on the counter and made hammering motions with the other hand. The clerk brought him a hammer. He shook his head and pointed to the two fingers he was hammering. The clerk brought him nails. He picked out the sizes he wanted, and left. Well, doc, the next guy who came in was a blind man. He wanted scissors. How do you suppose he asked for them?"

I lifted my right hand and made scissoring motions with my first two fingers. At once my auto repair man laughed harshly and said, "Why, you dumb guy, he used his voice and asked for them." Then he said, contentedly, "I've been trying that on all my customers today." "Did you catch many?" I asked. "Quite a few," he said, "but I knew for sure I'd catch you." "Why is that?" I asked. "Because you're so educated, doc, I knew you couldn't be very smart."

And I have an uneasy feeling he had something there. (547 words)

NEW WORDS

register /ˈredʒistə/	vt.	to put into an official list or record 登记，注册；（仪表等）指示，自动记下；表示，表达；注意到，记住；把（邮件）挂号
	vi.	登记，注册
	n.	登记，注册；登记表，注册簿

---

1. **doc:** [*infml.*] doctor

Unit 6 On Personal Qualities

instance /'instəns/	n.	particular example 例子，实例，事例
estimate /'estimeit/	n.	a calculation or judgment of the nature, value, size, amount, etc., of sth. 估计，估量；评价，看法
	vt.	估计，估量
vital /'vaitl/	n.	[pl.] the essential parts of anything, indispensable for its existence, continuance, etc. 要害，命脉，主要部件
	a.	生死攸关的，极其重要的；有生命的，充满生机的
pronouncement /prə'naunsmənt/	n.	formal announcement 声明
★ **authoritative** /ɔː'θɒritətiv/	a.	recognized as being reliable, possessing authority 权威性的，可信的；专断的，命令式的
devise /di'vaiz/	vt.	to plan or invent, esp. cleverly 发明，策划，想出
carpenter /'kɑːpintə/	n.	workman who makes the wooden parts of buildings 木匠
scholar /'skɒlə/	n.	person with much knowledge 学者
★ **verbal** /'vɜːbəl/	a.	connected with words and their use 用言词的，用文字的；口头的；动词的
sophisticated /sə'fistikeitid/	a.	highly complex, refined or developed 精密的，复杂的，尖端的；老于世故的，老练的
absolute /'æbsəluːt/	a.	complete, not relative 绝对的，完全的，不受任何限制的
subsection /'sʌbsekʃən/	n.	分部，分段，小部分
impose /im'pəuz/	vt.	to force (oneself, one's presence or will, etc.) on another or others without right or invitation 把……强加于；征（税等）
automobile /ɔːtəmə'biːl/	n.	motor car 汽车
auto /'ɔːtəu/	n.	[infml.] an automobile
deaf /def/	a.	unable to hear at all, unable to hear well 聋的，听力不佳的；不愿意听的
dumb /dʌm/	a.	lacking the power to speak 哑的；（因惊恐等）说不出话的，沉默的
hardware /'hɑːdwɛə/	n.	metal tools or implements 五金器具，硬件
hammer /'hæmə/	n.	锤，榔头
	vt.	锤击，敲打
scissor /'sizə/	vt.	剪，剪取
scissors /'sizəz/	n.	剪子

Part B
Extensive Reading

harsh /hɑːʃ/	a.	rough and disagreeable 粗糙的，刺耳的，刺目的；严厉的，严酷的
harshly /hɑːʃli/	ad.	粗糙地，刺耳地，刺目地；严厉地，严酷地
▲**contentedly** /kən'tentidli/	ad.	满足地，满意地

PHRASES

make up	to invent 捏造，临时编造
have a habit of	有……的习惯
pick out	to choose 选择

EXERCISES

Reading Comprehension

Task 1

Write short answers to the following questions according to the text.

1. The word "function" (Par. 4) can be best interpreted as _____.
2. The expression "such matters" (Par. 4) refers to _____.
3. The clerk brought nails to the deaf-and-dumb person when _____.
4. The auto repair man laughed harshly because _____.
5. From the article, we can know that at the beginning the writer regarded his auto repair man as _____.
6. The writer considered himself _____.
7. The last sentence, "I have an uneasy feeling he had something there", implies that the writer _____.
8. This article describes _____.

Vocabulary

Task 2

A. Choose the best answer to complete each of the following sentences.

1. The age of this prehistoric skeleton（骨骼）is _____ at 30,000 years.

Unit 6 On Personal Qualities

    a. instructed   b. valued

    c. estimated   d. counted

2. Within two weeks of arrival all foreigners had to _____ with the local police.

    a. register   b. label

    c. list   d. check

3. He's very good at _____ language games that you can play with students in class.

    a. figuring   b. answering

    c. devising   d. supposing

4. The pair of _____ Betty bought was sharp enough to cut iron.

    a. knives   b. hammers

    c. nails   d. scissors

5. She was a harsh mother and _____ severe discipline on her children.

    a. taught   b. imposed

    c. appeared   d. educated

B. Spell out the following words according to the definitions given in the brackets.

1. d _ _ _   (a person who can't speak)

2. d _ _ _   (a person who can't hear)

3. sc _ _ l _ _   (a person with much knowledge)

4. c _ _ p _ _ _ _ _   (a workman who makes the wooden parts of buildings)

5. h _ _ dw _ _ _   (metal goods for home use)

6. au _ _ _ _ _ _ _ _   (car)

7. e _ _ _ _ _ _ _   (to value)

8. d _ _ _ _ _   (to think out, to plan)

9. h _ _ _ _   (sharp)

10. s _ _ _ _ _ t _ _ _ _ _ _   (complex and refined)

Part C
Reading Skill

Transition Words (2)

The second group of transition words shown in the table (Unit 5, Part C) signal to what extent people or things are similar or different. When the writer stresses comparison or similarities, he uses *like, both, in the same way...*; when he stresses contrast or differences he uses *unlike, on the contrary*, etc.

EXERCISES

Below are two paragraphs, one of them stresses comparison, the other focuses on contrast.

Task 1

Choose proper transition words from the table (Unit 5, Part C) to complete the paragraph below.

Jane and Karen have many things in common. First, __1__ girls have the same background. Jane was born and raised in New England, and __2__ was Karen. Next, __3__ girls are interested in the same kinds of courses at college. Jane likes higher mathematics, economics management, and French. __4__ , Karen is interested in differential and integration (微分和积分). Furthermore, Jane has a deep love for music; __5__ , Karen is a pop (通俗音乐) fan and plays the guitar skillfully. In short, the two girls are almost twins.

Task 2

Using the given transition words, complete the numbered blanks in the paragraph below.

a. Above all
b. on the contrary
c. Unlike the unsafe driver
d. In (sharp) contrast

There are two extremes of drivers behind the wheels today. The first type is the unsafe driver, the one who disregards traffic rules and makes life difficult for pedestrians (行人) and other drivers.

Unit 6 On Personal Qualities

___1___ is the safe driver, who obeys traffic rules and practices courtesy (礼让) on the road. The unsafe driver is also impatient and honks his horn (喇叭) repeatedly or signals his lights unnecessarily. He slows down or speeds up just to annoy other drivers. ___2___, the safe driver is always considerate of pedestrians and other drivers. He is a careful driver. The first type of driver, ___3___, is irresponsible, taking risks and causing accidents. ___4___, it is often the latter type of driver who, through quick actions, is able to prevent a dangerous situation from turning into a bad accident.

The third group of transition words signal cause and effect as is shown in the table in Unit 5, Part C.

Task 3

Choose proper transition words that signal cause and effect to complete the following paragraph.

When the television was invented in 1923, parents had no idea of the harmful effects this wonderful invention would one day have on children. ___1___ children spend tremendous amounts of time watching TV, they become passive observers. Child psychologists say that children learn best by doing, not by watching. ___2___, television has a negative effect on children's learning abilities and their creativity. ___3___ children spend more time in front of the TV and less time behind a good book, their reading abilities have also suffered. Another harmful effect of television is caused by the excessive (过多的) violence in many popular programs. Studies show that aggressive behavior in children is a direct result of this violence. Young people imitate the behavior they see on TV. ___4___, youngsters have been known to "fly" out of windows like Superman and kill their enemies like Kojak. ___5___, television has evolved (演变) from the miracle (奇迹) it once was into the monster (怪物) it is today.

Task 4

Choose from among words and phrases given to complete the following passage.

1. a. First   b. Of course   c. Thus
2. a. Of course   b. In addition/Besides c. In contrast
3. a. Moreover   b. To sum up   c. As a result
4. a. Otherwise   b. Thus   c. In condition
5. a. Accordingly   b. Consequently   c. In short/To sum up

Advertising is an American way of life. ___1___, Americans like advertising (广告). ___2___, people depend on advertisements in their daily life because they are consumers. The advertisers are manufacturers. ___3___, some advertisers are salesmen. Their merchandise (商品) needs advertising. ___4___, every product is advertised. Most merchants buy ads for their products. ___5___, good advertising means success; bad advertising can mean failure.

Unit 7

Stories of a Pet, a Young Writer

Aims and Objectives

In this unit you will learn:
1. Genre/Style: Narration / Description
2. Word Power: The Word "Wake" and Its Synonyms
3. Grammar Focus: Introductory "It" in Cleft Sentences
4. Writing Skill: The Beginning of an Essay
5. Translation Skill: Translation of English Prepositions
6. Reading Skill: Transition Words (3)

Brief Introductions to the Texts

The articles in this unit are examples of descriptive narrations. Each author gives detail to describe the stories they are revealing. As the passages are read, images are created in the mind of the reader. The effective narrations create a "movie of the mind" which the reader sees as the stories unfold. Each of the passage takes an unexpected turn at the end.

Unit 7 Stories of a Pet, a Young Writer

Part A — Intensive Reading

Reading

Pre-Reading

Task 1

Answer the following questions briefly.

1. What are the advantages and disadvantages of keeping a pet?
2. Do you agree with the Chinese saying that "Keeping a pet will lead to one's having no more ambition"?

Reading and Thinking

The Capybara[1]

By **Gerald Durrell**, from *Three Singles to Adventure*

With the arrival of the capybara, things came to a head. A man led the huge rodent in on a string late one evening. It was half grown, very tame, and it sat there with a noble expression on its
5 face while we bargained with its owner. We bargained for a long time, for the owner had noticed the acquisitive gleam in our eyes when we first saw the beast, but at last the capybara was ours. He was housed in a large, coffin-shaped box with a wire net front that seemed strong enough to with-
10 stand any attacks he might make upon it. We showered him with choice fruits and grasses, which he accepted with royal condescension, and congratulated ourselves on

> What is this passage going to be about?
>
> How do you understand the linking word "for"?
>
> What does "it" refer to?

---

1. **capybara:** It is a tailless, largely aquatic (水的) South American rodent often exceeding four feet in length. It is allied (同源) to the guinea pig (豚鼠), and mainly vegetarian. It damages sugarcane plantations. 南美洲产的一种大而无尾的啮齿类动物，以食草为主，常常给甘蔗园造成损坏。

having acquired such a lovely animal. We gazed at him spellbound while he ate, tenderly pressed a few more mangoes through the bars, and went upstairs to sleep. We lay in the dark for a while, talking about our wonderful new specimen, and then eventually dropped off. At about midnight it began.

I was awakened by a most curious noise coming from the garden beneath our window; it sounded like someone playing on a Jew's harp[1] accompanied rather strangely by someone else beating on a tin can. I was lying there listening to it, and wondering what it could be, when I suddenly remembered the capybara. With a cry of "the capybara's escaping!" I leapt out of bed and fled downstairs to the garden, barefoot and in my pajamas, closely followed by my sleepy companion. When we reached the garden all was quiet; the capybara was sitting on its haunches, looking down its nose in a superior manner. We had a long argument as to whether or not it was the capybara that had been making the noise; I said it was and Smith said it was not. He insisted that the creature looked too calm and innocent, and I maintained that that was exactly why I thought it was the criminal. The capybara just sat in its moonlit cage and stared through us. There was no repetition of the sound, so we went back to bed, arguing in fierce whispers. No sooner had we settled down than the noise started again, and, if possible, it sounded louder than ever. I got out of bed and peered out of the window. The capybara cage was vibrating gently in the moonlight.

"It is that blasted animal," I said triumphantly.

"What's he doing?" enquired Smith.

"God knows, but we'd better go and stop him or he'll have the whole place awake."

We crept downstairs and from the shelter of a convenient cluster of bushes we surveyed the cage. The capybara was sitting by the wire looking very noble. He would lean forward and place his enormous curved teeth round a string of wire, pull hard and then release it so that the whole cage front vibrated like a harp. He listened until the

---

1. **Jew's harp:** 犹太齿琴

Unit 7 Stories of a Pet, a Young Writer

noise had died away, and then he raised his large bottom and beat the tin tray with his hind feet, making a noise like stage thunder. I suppose he was applauding.

50 "Do you think he's trying to escape?" asked Smith.

"No, he's just doing it because he likes it."

The capybara played another little tune.

"Let's stop him, or he'll wake everyone."

"What can we do?"

55 "Remove the tin tray," said Smith practically.

"He'll still get that harpsichord effect with the wire."

"Let's cover the front of the cage up," said Smith.

So we removed the tray and covered the front of the cage with sacks, in case it was the moonlight that was making the animal feel musical. He waited until we were in bed before he started twanging again. (631 words)

> What is the implication of this sentence?

NEW WORDS

capybara /ˌkæpɪˈbɑːrə/		n.	水豚
rodent /ˈrəʊdənt/		n.	啮齿动物
string /strɪŋ/		n.	thin pieces of tightly-stretched wire or nylon; thin rope; series of things 弦；细绳；一串，一行
		vt.	string (strung /strʌŋ/, strung) to tie with a string 缚，捆
tame /teɪm/		a.	(of animals) used to living with human beings, not wild; dull 驯服的，温顺的；平淡，乏味的
		vt.	to bring people or things under control 驯服，制服
acquisitive /əˈkwɪzɪtɪv/		a.	tending to acquire, often greedily 渴望得到的
★ *gleam* /gliːm/		n.	a shining light 闪光
coffin /ˈkɔfɪn/		n.	the box in which a dead person is buried 棺材，灵柩
withstand /wɪðˈstænd/		vt.	(-stood, -stood) to resist or oppose, esp. successfully 经受，承受，抵住
condescension /ˌkɔndɪˈsenʃən/		n.	the act of condescending or an instance of acting in a manner that makes one appear of a higher social rank

Part A
Intensive Reading

			高傲的态度
congratulate /kənˈgrætjuleit/		vt.	to express one's joy to a person, as on a happy occasion 祝贺，向……道喜
spellbound /ˈspelbaund/		a.	having your attention completely held by sth., so that you cannot think about anything else 入迷的，出神的
bar /bɑː/		n.	a place where one can buy and drink alcoholic drinks; a counter on which alcoholic drinks are served; a long, straight piece of hard material; barrier 酒吧间；售酒的柜台；棒，条；栅，拦；障碍
		vt.	to block 阻止，拦阻
specimen /ˈspesimən/		n.	a single typical thing or example 标本，样本
awaken /əˈweikən/		vt.	to cause to wake up 唤醒，觉醒
▲harp /hɑːp/		n.	stringed musical instrument played with the finger 竖琴
leap /liːp/		vt.	(BrE., leapt or leaped) to jump over 跃过
		vi.	to spring through the air, often landing in a place, to act, pass, rise, etc. rapidly as if with a jump 跳、跃，跳动
		n.	a sudden jump, spring, or movement 跳，跳跃；激增，骤变
by/in leaps and bounds			very quickly 极其迅速地
flee /fliː/		v.	(fled, fled) to run away 逃走，逃避
bare /bɛə/		a.	without clothing or covering, empty; not more than, only 赤裸的，光秃秃的；仅仅的，勉强的
		v.	to uncover, to reveal 露出，暴露
barefoot /ˈbɛəfut/		a./adv.	without shoes or other covering on the feet 赤脚的
pyjamas /piˈdʒɑːməz/		n.	[pl.] loose-fitting jacket and trousers for sleeping in 睡衣裤
haunch /hɔːntʃ/		n.	the back leg of an animal 腰腿部分
creature /ˈkriːtʃə/		n.	living animal; living person 动物；人
moonlight /ˈmuːnlait/		n.	the light reflected from the surface of the moon 月光
blast /blɑːst/		vt.	to break sth. up by explosions; to injure (用炸药)炸毁，炸掉；毁灭
		n.	the sound of an explosion; strong, sudden rush of wind 爆炸；一阵（疾风等），一股（强烈的气流）

Unit 7 Stories of a Pet, a Young Writer

blasted /ˈblæstid/		a.	damn 该死的
enquire, inquire /inˈkwaiə/		v.	(of) to ask; (about) to ask for information 打听，询问
inquire after			问起（某人情况），问候
inquire into			调查，探究
creep /kriːp/		vi.	(crept, crept) to move or advance slowly and quietly 蔓延，爬行
curve /kəːv/		n.	a line of which no part is straight and which contains no angles 曲线，弧线，弯曲
		vt.	to make sth. curve 使弯曲
release /riˈliːs/		vt.	to allow to go; to allow (a film) to be exhibited; to set free 释放，解放；发布，发行，放开，松开
vibrate /vaiˈbreit/		v.	to (cause to) move rapidly and continuously back and forth （使）振动，（使）摇摆
hind /haind/		a.	at the back 后面的
applaud /əˈplɔːd/		v.	to praise by striking one's hands together 鼓掌
tune /tjuːn/		n.	arrangement of musical sounds; agreement 曲子，曲调；和谐，协调
		vt.	to set (a musical instrument) at the proper musical level; to adjust for proper functioning 为（乐器）调音；调整
tune in (to)			to set a radio to receive broadcasts from a particular radio station 收听
harpsichord /ˈhɑːpsikɔːd/		n.	大键琴
sack /sæk/		n.	a large bag made of strong material 麻袋，包
		vt.	to take away the job of 解雇
twang /twæŋ/		n.	sound of a tight string 弦声
		v.	to (cause to) make this kind of sound （使）发弦声

PHRASES

come to a head	to reach a crisis 达到紧急关头
shower sb. with sth.	to send or give sth. to sb. in a shower 大量地给某人某物
drop off	fall asleep 睡着
sit on its haunches	蹲着

Part A

Intensive Reading

look down one's nose	to consider sb./sth. unworthy, to disapprove of sb./sth. 轻视，瞧不起
as to	about, with regard to 至于，关于
no sooner...than	when / at once 一………，刚……就
die away	become weak 渐渐消失
in case	for fear that 假使，以防万一

EXERCISES

Reading Comprehension

Task 2

Answer the following questions.

1. What is your first impression of the capybara?
2. What can be inferred from the second sentence in Par. 1?
3. Why did the writer use "he" instead of "it" to refer to the capybara most of the time?
4. How can you describe the cage for the capybara?
5. What did the new owners treat the animal to?
6. What evidence is there in the passage to infer that the new owners were particularly pleased with their purchase?
7. Which sentence indicates that the new owners were concerned that the animal might try to escape?
8. What made the writer think that it was the capybara that had been making the noise?
9. When would the capybara start to make the noise again?
10. How did the capybara make the sound of a Jew's harp?
11. What evidence is there in the passage to infer that the writer assumed the capybara liked the noise he was making?
12. Name the six different words that the writer used to refer to the capybara.

Task 3

Below are 11 statements, four of which are true according to the text. Read the statements carefully and circle the correct ones.

1. The capybara is a member of the rodent family, which includes rats, mice, rabbits and beavers.
2. Smith and the writer hesitated about buying the animal.

Unit 7 Stories of a Pet, a Young Writer

3. A strong wire net front was put up to resist any attacks the capybara might make upon it.
4. Smith and the writer wanted to use their new specimen, the capybara, for a test.
5. The noise was made by one playing on a harp and the other beating on a tin can.
6. The writer and Smith quarreled for a long time about how to calm the capybara down.
7. Smith and the writer wanted the capybara to keep them company because they were living in complete isolation.
8. The thundering sound was made by the capybara's striking the tin tray with his teeth.
9. The capybara achieved the effect of a Jew's harp with the wire net front of the cage.
10. It can be inferred from the passage that it was not exactly the moonlight that was causing the capybara to make the noise.
11. The passage is about how delightful a capybara is.

Task 4

The writer describes the capybara as having many human qualities. Use information from the passage to decide whether the following statements in the table are facts or examples of personification. Put a check in the appropriate box.

	Fact	Example of Personification
1. The rodent was half grown.		
2. It was very tame.		
3. It sat there with a noble expression on its face.		
4. He accepted the fruits with royal condescension.		
5. The capybara was sitting on its haunches.		
6. He looked down his nose in a superior manner.		
7. The creature looked calm and innocent.		
8. The capybara stared through us.		
9. The capybara was sitting by the wire.		
10. The capybara looked very noble.		
11. He had enormous curved teeth.		
12. He had a large bottom.		
13. He beat the tin tray with his hind feet.		
14. The capybara played another little tune.		
15. He was applauding.		

Part A
Intensive Reading

Vocabulary

Task 5

Complete the following sentences by putting the Chinese into English.

1. applaud, applause
    a. The audience _____ (喝彩鼓掌) anything that pleases it in a play or concert.
    b. The singer received _____ (热烈的掌声).
    c. His first novel was _____ (值得称赞).
2. release
    a. He was _____ (从监狱里放出来) yesterday.
    b. No details of the murder _____ (公布) to the press.
    c. After the match the coach had a _____ (如释重负之感).
    d. Death has _____ (使他从痛苦中解脱出来).
3. creep
    a. We _____ (蹑手蹑脚地上了楼梯) so as not to wake the baby.
    b. Mist is _____ over the lake (悄悄升起了).
4. enquire, inquire
    a. They _____ (查询飞往北京的航班).
    b. She _____ (打听) her results in the examinations.
    c. When I met him in the USA, he _____ (问候) you.
5. creature
    a. Don't _____ (所有的生物) have certain rights?
    b. What a lovely _____ (女人) she is!
    c. The novel is _____ (想象力的产物).
6. tune
    a. The piano is _____ (走调了).
    b. Many politicians are totally _____ (与普通人的需要完全不一致).
    c. He _____ (收听) to this music station every day at lunch.
7. bare, barely
    a. This room looks _____ (空落落的) — you need some pictures on the walls.
    b. It was 37 degrees and the air conditioning _____ (好容易才) cooled the room.
8. congratulate, congratulation
    a. We all lined up to _____ (向……贺喜) the newly-weds.
    b. "_____," (恭喜你) the doctor said, "You have a son."

Unit 7 Stories of a Pet, a Young Writer

Task 6

A. Choose from Column B words or phrases that are opposite in meaning to those in Column A. Note there are some extra items in Column B.

Column A
1. wild
2. tiny
3. wake up
4. stay
5. reveal
6. submit
7. defeat
8. straighten

Column B
a. curve
b. flee
c. triumph
d. vibrate
e. cover up
f. tame
g. convenient
h. drop off
i. peer
j. withstand
k. enormous

B. Give words or phrases that are close in meaning to the underlined part in each of the following sentences.

1. The wild <u>animal</u> was caught in a trap.
2. Poverty is not always a <u>barrier</u> to happiness.
3. The doctor took a <u>sample</u> of the patient's blood.
4. His shoulders <u>shook</u> with anger.
5. He was <u>fired from his</u> job for laziness.
6. Potatoes were put into <u>bags</u>.
7. The soldiers <u>resisted</u> the attack from the air.
8. What are you <u>gazing</u> at?
9. The new play achieved a great <u>victory</u>.
10. Long ago there were <u>huge</u> beasts in the world.
11. The little boy raised many <u>domestic</u> animals.
12. The winner was <u>offered</u> congratulations <u>from many people</u>.
13. Take warm clothes <u>for fear that</u> it gets cold.
14. This talented student asked a <u>series</u> of questions.

Task 7

Translate the following sentences into English.

1. 大约是在午夜，我被一种奇怪的噪音给吵醒了。这音来自我们的后院。它听起来像是有人在敲钟。
2. 关于这首歌的曲子是不是 Tom 写的，我们争论了好久；后来证明我是对的。
3. 在附近一片灌木丛的掩蔽下，我悄悄地靠近了他们，看到他们正试图用土将什么东西埋在树下。

Task 8

Fill in the blanks with appropriate words.

　　Apes (类人猿) are most highly developed animals. The gorilla (大猩猩) is the largest of the apes. The ___1___ is as tall as six feet when standing upright. Many people think that gorillas are very ___2___. These beasts are often described ___3___ standing upright like a man, beating their fists and roaring. They are in fact peaceful ___4___ and never use their great strength unless ___5___. Even then, they retreat if they can. When there is danger, they use bushes for ___6___. They feed during the day on plants and fruit.

　　The chimpanzee is like a gorilla, ___7___ it is only five feet high. It lives in the same way as a gorilla. Chimpanzees are more lively than gorillas, and it is easier to ___8___ them and teach them tricks.

Grammar

Task 9

Make sentences according to the model, emphasizing the underlined part.

Example: 1. It was the capybara that had been making the noise.
　　　　　2. It was the moonlight that was making the animal feel musical.

1. John and Henry first met in London.
2. Tom went to Shanghai on Tuesday.
3. Mary's father was surprised at the price.
4. At the station, we were met by a man carrying a copy of the *Times*.
5. Our motherland suffered from aggression in the 20th century.
6. He didn't commit this mistake through ignorance.
7. We should guard against this kind of thing.
8. She didn't know anything about it until I told her.
9. We are not working hard for ourselves alone.
10. How did you miss such a fine lecture?

Stories of a Pet, a Young Writer

文章的开头 (The Beginning of an Essay)

俗话说:"好的开头是成功的一半"。在英文写作中,文章的开头段往往表达整篇文章的主题或中心论点,对文章的其他段落起驾驭作用。因此,一个明确、清晰的开头段有助于读者一开始就把握写作者的意图,对写作内容一目了然。

文章的开头段由一个或几个句子组成。若开头段只有一个句子,这个句子本身往往就是文章的中心论点。一般来讲,文章的开头段有以下几种常见的方式:

1) 直接提出中心论点

如:I think it is fair to pay tuition fees for higher education in China.

2) 由某一普遍现象或概念开始,逐渐缩小范围,引出中心论点

如:Knowledge may be acquired through many ways. One way of getting knowledge is from traveling. Another way is by conversation, especially one with a great man. A person may also become knowledgeable through other ways such as listening to the radio or watching television. The best way to acquire knowledge, however, is through reading.

3) 由某一具体事实或数据引出主题

如:During the past five years, the number of Americans killed annually in car accidents has climbed to more than 55,000. These needless deaths on streets and highways can be attributed to three general causes: mechanical failures, environmental conditions and errors of human judgment.

4) 由名言或谚语引出中心论点

如:Nearly every civilization has its equivalent to the proverb "No pains, no gains". It means that nothing that is really worth doing can be gained without painstaking efforts and that no knowledge or skill can be acquired without sweat or effort.

5) 设问开头,引发读者兴趣,导入中心论点

如:Most of the ill health we suffer could be prevented if people made effort to change their life styles. Instead, many people continue to smoke, to drink excessively and to eat unbalanced diets. How can governments help people protect their health and avoid premature(过早的) death?

注意：在写作文章开头段时应避免提出多个主题或论点。

Task 10

A. Please write at least two different beginning paragraphs of an essay describing an anecdote of a pet you have raised.

B. Please finish the following outline of "Looking After Old People Should Be the Responsibility of the Family", and then write a complete paragraph based on the outline.

1. Reasons FOR old people living with their families
   a. They can help look after children.
   b. ...
   c. ...
   d. ...

2. Reasons AGAINST old people living with their families
   a. They may need special care.
   b. ...
   c. ...
   d. ...

C. Read the following four paragraphs, and decide which one is the most suitable beginning paragraph? Why aren't the others suitable?

1. My next door neighbor is 73 years old and she lives on her own. Her son lives quite nearby. He comes round twice a week to check on her.

2. Throughout this century it has become more and more common for old people in some cultures, such as England and America, to live on their own or in old people's homes rather than with their families. People from other cultures often find this practice uncivilized, but are they right?

3. Of course old people should be looked after by their families — after all, they looked after their children when they were young.

4. In some ways it is a good idea for old people to live with their families, and in some ways it is not. Some people might be very happy to have their older relatives living with them. Some old people might not want to live with their family.

Unit 7 Stories of a Pet, a Young Writer

Task 11
Below are four beginning paragraphs of students' samples on the following writing task:

Present a written argument to an educated reader on the following topic:
Lecturing as a method of teaching results in passive learning. This teaching method tends to be less effective than those that fully engage the learner.
To what extent do you agree or disagree with this opinion?

Can you tell their attitudes from the beginning paragraphs? If you are asked to write on this topic, which paragraph would you prefer? Why?

1. I think lecturing and discussion classes that fully engage the learner are both very important and effective means of studying, especially in China. Active learning requires the application of knowledge that has been learned, while lecturing is more effective in teaching new knowledge.
2. Because of the limitation of time and the lack of professors in most universities of China, lecturing is still the most important teaching method. Though it can't be replaced completely, it really needs to be improved.
3. Some people argue that lecturing as a method of teaching results in passive learning and this teaching method tends to be less effective than those that fully engage the learner. I agree with them.
4. I've heard many classmates of mine complain about the boring lectures they had. It seems that everyone wants the classes which are active and effective rather than ones where the teacher just lectures. But is it necessarily the case?

英语介词的翻译 (Translation of English Prepositions)

介词是中国人学英语的一大难点，同时也是英汉互译的一大难点。很多人用英语作文或者将汉语译成英语时，写出来的英语不像英语，一个很重要的原因就在于没有掌握好英语的介词。英语介词的翻译概括起来，可以分为以下几种情况：

1) 依然译作介词：

- He told me not to sit *on* the ground.

  他叫我别坐**在地上**/地下。

- She had herself locked *in* the room.

  她把自己锁**在**了屋**里**。

2) 转换为动词：

- She is married *with* children.

  她已**成**了家，**有**了孩子。

- We had a chat *over* a cup of tea.

  我们边**喝**茶边聊天。

- The car has been damaged *with* the branch of a tree.

  车让人**用**树枝划坏了。

- The car has been damaged *by* the branch of a tree.

  车**让**树枝给划坏了。

- "You are disappointed," Ausable said *over* his shoulder.

  "你失望了吧，"奥瑟布尔**扭**过头来说道。

- The pressure changes *with* the temperature.

  压力**随**温度变化而变化。

- No one is yet *in occupation of* the house.

  那所房子现在还没**住人**。

- Mother is *on the phone* with father.

  母亲与父亲**在通电话**。

- The wheat then was *in the milk*.

  那时小麦**正在灌浆**。

3) 省去不译：

- The boy is slow *of* understanding.

  这孩子反应迟钝。

- She tried to make a fool *of* me.

  她想愚弄我。

- Happiness cannot be bought *with* money.

Unit 7 Stories of a Pet, a Young Writer

金钱买不来幸福。/快乐不是用钱能买到的。

- She has an eye *for* beauty.

  她有审美眼光。

- Which do you prefer, word-*for*-word translation or sense-*for*-sense translation?

  你是喜欢逐字翻译还是喜欢意译?

- We are enemies of all wars, but above all *of* dynastic wars.

  我们反对一切战争,尤其是王朝战争。

- He emerged *from* the game *of* chess an exhausted man.

  下完棋,他已精疲力竭。

Task 12

Translate the following sentences into Chinese. Pay special attention to the prepositions.

1) *With* the arrival *of* the capybara, things came to a head.
2) A man led the huge rodent in *on* a string late one evening. It was half grown, very tame, and it sat there *with* a noble expression *on* its face while we bargained *with* its owner.
3) We bargained *for* a long time, *for* the owner had noticed the acquisitive gleam *in* our eyes when we first saw the beast, but at last the capybara was ours.
4) I was awakened *by* a most curious noise coming *from* the garden *beneath* our window; it sounded *like* someone playing *on* a Jew's harp accompanied rather strangely *by* someone else beating *on* a tin can.
5) It is not good *for* all our wishes to be filled; *through* sickness we recognize the value of health; *through* evil, the value of good; *through* hunger, the value of food; *through* exertion, the value of rest.

Quotation

The art of translation lies less in knowing the other language than in knowing your own.

— *Ned Rorem*

翻译这门艺术精不精通外语尚在其次,更要紧的是要精通自己的母语。

——内德·罗勒姆

Part B ▶Extensive Reading

I. The Luncheon[1]

(Adapted)

By William Somerset Maugham[2]

I caught sight of her at the play and in answer to her signaling I went over during the interval and sat down beside her. It was long since I had last seen her and if someone had not mentioned her name I hardly think I would have recognized her. She addressed me brightly.

"Well, it's many years since we first met. How time does fly! We're none of us getting any
5 younger. Do you remember the first time I saw you? You asked me to luncheon."

It was twenty years ago and I was living in Paris. I had a tiny apartment in the Latin Quarter[3] overlooking a graveyard and I was earning barely enough money to keep body and soul together. She had read a book of mine and had written to me about it. I answered, thanking her, and soon I received from her another letter saying that she was passing through Paris and would like to
10 have a chat with me; but her time was limited and the only free moment she had was on the following Thursday; she was spending the morning at the Luxembourg[4] and would I give her a little luncheon at Foyot's afterwards? Foyot's is a restaurant at which the French senators eat and it was so far beyond my means that I had never even thought of going there. But I was flattered and I was too young to have learned to say no to a woman. (Few men, I may add, learn this until
15 they are too old to make it of any importance to a woman what they say.) I had eighty francs (gold francs) to last me the rest of the month and a modest luncheon should not cost more than fifteen. If I cut out coffee for the next two weeks I could manage well enough.

I answered by letter that I would meet my friend at Foyot's on Thursday at half-past twelve. She was not so young as I expected and in appearance imposing rather than attractive. She was in
20 fact a woman of forty (a charming age, but not one that excites a sudden and burning passion at first sight), and she gave me the impression of having more teeth, white and large and even, than

---

1. **luncheon** /ˈlʌntʃən/ n. [fml.] for lunch (正式用语)午餐
2. **Maugham, William Somerset** (1874—1965) English novelist and dramatist 威廉·萨默塞特·毛姆,英国小说家和剧作家
3. **quarter**: a part of a town, often typical of certain people (城市中的)区
4. **Luxembourg** /ˈlʌksəmbɜːg/ : a country of northwest Europe 卢森堡,西欧一公国(文中此处指巴黎市一地名。)

Unit 7 Stories of a Pet, a Young Writer

were necessary for any practical purpose. She was talkative, but since she seemed inclined to talk about me I was prepared to be an eager listener.

I was frightened when the bill of fare was brought, for the prices were a great deal higher than I had anticipated. But she reassured me.

"I never eat anything for luncheon," she said.

"Oh, don't say that!" I answered generously.

"I never eat more than one thing. I think people eat far too much nowadays. A little fish, perhaps. I wonder if they have any salmon."

Well, it was early in the year for salmon and it was not on the bill of fare, but I asked the waiter if there was any. Yes, a beautiful salmon had just come in, it was the first they had had. I ordered it for my guest. The waiter asked her if she would have something while it was being cooked.

"No, she answered, I never eat more than one thing. Unless you had a little caviare. I never mind caviare."

My heart sank a little. I knew I could not afford caviare, but I could not very well tell her that. I told the waiter by all means to bring caviare. For myself I chose the cheapest dish on the menu and that was a mutton chop.

"I think you're unwise to eat meat," she said. "I don't know how you can expect to work after eating heavy[1] things like chops. I don't believe in overloading my stomach."

Then came the question of drink.

"I never drink anything for luncheon," she said.

"Neither do I," I answered promptly.

"Except white wine," she proceeded as though I had not spoken. "These French white wines are so light[2]. They're wonderful for the digestion."

"What would you like?" I asked, hospitable still, but not exactly effusive.

She gave me a bright flash of her white teeth.

"My doctor won't let me drink anything but champagne."

I fancy I turned a little pale. I ordered half a bottle. I mentioned casually that my doctor had absolutely forbidden me to drink champagne.

"What are you going to drink, then?"

"Water."

She ate the caviare and she ate the salmon. She talked gaily of art and literature and music.

---

1. **heavy**: rich, difficult to digest 油腻且难消化的
2. **light**: (of beer, wines) not very strong; (of food) easily digested 清淡的；易消化的

But I wondered what the bill would come to. When my mutton chop arrived she took me quite seriously to task.

"I see that you're in the habit of eating a heavy luncheon. I'm sure it's a mistake. Why don't you follow my example and just eat one thing? I'm sure you'd feel ever so much better for it."

"I am only going to eat one thing," I said, as the waiter came again with the bill of fare.

She waved him aside with an airy[1] gesture.

"No, no. I never eat anything for luncheon. Just a bite, I never eat more than that, and I eat that more as an excuse for conversation than anything else. I couldn't possibly eat anything more — unless they had some of those giant asparagus. I should be sorry to leave Paris without having some of them."

My heart sank. I had seen them in the shops and I knew that they were horribly expensive. My mouth had often watered[2] at the sight of them.

"Madame[3] wants to know if you have any of those giant asparagus," I asked the waiter.

I tried with all my might to will[4] him to say no. A happy smile spread over his broad face, and he assured me that they had some so large, so splendid, so tender, that it was a marvel.

"I'm not in the least hungry," my guest sighed, "but if you insist I don't mind having some asparagus."

I ordered them.

"Aren't you going to have any?"

"No, I never eat asparagus."

"I know there are people who don't like them. The fact is, you ruin your palate by all the meat you eat."

We waited for the asparagus to be cooked. Panic seized me. It was not a question now how much money I should have left over for the rest of the month, but whether I had enough to pay the bill. It would be shameful to find myself ten francs short and be obliged to borrow from my guest. I could not bring myself to do that. I knew exactly how much I had and if the bill came to more I made up my mind that I would put my hand in my pocket and with a dramatic cry start up and say it had been picked[5]. Of course it would be awkward if she had not money enough either to pay the bill. Then the only thing would be to leave my watch and say I would come back and

---

1. **airy:** not sincere [口] 做作的
2. **water:** *v.* to form or let out water or sth. like water 出水，流口水
3. **Madame:** a title for married women 夫人
4. **will:** *v.* to make use of one's mental powers in an attempt to do sth. or get sth. 意欲，想要
5. **pick:** *v.* to steal 偷

Unit 7 Stories of a Pet, a Young Writer

pay later.

The asparagus appeared. They were enormous, juicy and appetising. I watched the woman thrust them down her throat in large mouthfuls and in my polite way I discussed about the condition of the drama in the Balkans[1]. At last she finished.

"Coffee?" I said.

"Yes, just an ice-cream and coffee," she answered.

I was past caring now, so I ordered coffee for myself and an ice-cream and coffee for her.

"You know, there's one thing I thoroughly believe in", she said, as she ate the ice-cream. "One should always get up from a meal feeling one could eat a little more."

"Are you still hungry?" I asked faintly.

"Oh, no, I'm not hungry; you see, I don't eat luncheon. I have a cup of coffee in the morning and then dinner, but I never eat more than one thing for luncheon. I was speaking for you."

"Oh, I see!"

Then a terrible thing happened. While we were waiting for the coffee, the head waiter, with a smile on his face, came up to us with a large basket full of huge peaches in his hand. But surely peaches were not in season then? Lord knew what they cost. I knew too — a little later, for my guest, going on with her conversation, absentmindedly took one.

"You see, you've filled your stomach with a lot of meat and you can't eat any more. But I've just had a snack and I shall enjoy a peach."

The bill came and when I paid it I found that I had only enough for a quite inadequate tip. Her eyes rested for an instant on the three francs I left for the waiter and I knew that she thought me mean. But when I walked out of the restaurant I had the whole month before me and not a penny in my pocket.

"Follow my example," she said as we shook hands, "and never eat more than one thing for luncheon."

"I'll do better than that," I answered back. "I'll eat nothing for dinner tonight."

"Humorist!" she cried gaily, jumping into a taxi. "You're quite a humorist!"

But I have had my revenge at last. I do not believe that I am a vindictive man, but when the immortal gods take a hand in the matter it is pardonable to observe the result with pleasure. Today she weighs 294 pounds. (1587 words)

---

1. **the Balkans** /ˈbɔːlkəns/ countries on the peninsula of Southeast Europe 巴尔干半岛各国; the name of a theatre 这里是剧院名。

Part B

Extensive Reading

NEW WORDS

luncheon /ˈlʌntʃən/		n.	a usually formal lunch 午宴，正式的午餐
overlook /ˌəuvəˈluk/		vt.	to ignore, to fail to notice or consider; disregard; to look down on from above 忽略，忽视，未注意到；宽舒，宽容；俯瞰，俯视
grave /greiv/		n.	the place in the ground where a dead person is buried 坟墓
		a.	requiring careful consideration; serious 严重的；严肃的，庄严的
graveyard /ˈgreivjɑːd/		n.	piece of land used for burying the dead 墓地
barely /ˈbɛəli/		ad.	only just, hardly 仅仅，只不过，几乎不
senator /ˈsenətə/		n.	a member of the smaller and more important of two law-making groups in some countries 参议员
★ flatter /ˈflætə/		vt.	to praise too much; to give pleasure to 向……献媚，奉承；使满意，使高兴
appearance /əˈpiərəns/		n.	act of appearing; that which can be seen, look 出现，露面；外观，外貌
impose /imˈpəuz/		vt.	(on) to force the acceptance of; to force into unwelcome closeness with; to establish (an additional payment) officially 把……强加于；征税等，处以（罚款，监禁等）
imposing /imˈpəuziŋ/		a.	powerful in appearance, strong or large in size 使人难忘的，壮丽的
charming /ˈtʃɑːmiŋ/		a.	very pleasing 迷人的，娇媚的
impression /imˈpreʃn/		n.	effect produced on the mind or feelings; mark made by pressing 印象，感想；印记，压痕
talkative /ˈtɔːkətiv/		a.	likely to talk a lot 多话的，爱说话的，多嘴的
inclined /inˈklaind/		a.	encouraged; feeling a wish (to); likely, tending (to) 倾向……的，赞同
fare /fɛə/		n.	the money charged for a journey (by bus, ship, etc.); food provided at a meal；（车、船等）费，票价；饮食，伙食；bill of fare: list of dishes, menu 菜单
anticipate /ænˈtisipeit/		n.	to realize in advance that an event may happen, to look

Unit 7 Stories of a Pet, a Young Writer

		forward to 预料，期望
assure /ə'ʃuə/	vt.	to inform positively, to feel certain, to cause (sb.) to be sure; to make certain; to insure esp. against death 断然地说；确告，保证，担保
★reassure /ˌriːə'ʃuə/	vt.	to comfort and make free from fear 使安心
▲salmon /'sæmən/	n.	沙文鱼，鲑鱼
caviare /'kævɑː/	n.	鱼子酱
▲mutton /'mʌtn/	n.	flesh of sheep as food 羊肉
chop /tʃɔp/	vt.	to cut sth. into pieces by hitting it with an axe or a knife 砍，劈，斩
	n.	a small piece of meat usu. containing a bone 排骨
overload /'əuvə'ləud/	vt.	to load too heavily 使超载，超过负荷
	n.	the fact or amount of overloading 超载，负荷过多
proceed /prə'siːd/	vi.	to begin and continue; to continue (after stopping); to advance, move forward, move along a course 进行，继续下去，（沿特定路线）行进，前进
digest /dai'dʒest/	vt.	to (cause to) be changed into a form that the body can use 消化
digestion /dai'dʒestʃən/	n.	消化
hospitable /'hɔspitəbl/	a.	showing the wish to give attention to the needs of others 殷勤的
effusive /i'fjuːsiv/	a.	pouring out feelings without control 洋溢的
flash /flæʃ/	n.	a sudden quick bright light 闪光，闪烁；（比喻用法）闪现
	vi.	to send a sudden bright light; to come suddenly; to appear or exist for a moment 闪光，闪烁，飞驰，掠过，闪现，闪耀
★champagne /ʃæm'pein/	n.	a French wine 香槟酒
fancy /'fænsi/	vt.	to like; to imagine; to believe without evidence or certainty 想要，喜欢；想象，设想；猜想，认为
	n.	liking, inclination; imagination; taste 爱好，迷恋；想象力
	a.	excessive, of particular excellence; not plain 昂贵的，高档的；别致的，花俏的
casual /'kæʒjuəl/	a.	happening by chance; informal; employed for a short

			period of time 偶然的，碰巧的；随便的，非正式的；临时的
casually /ˈkæʒjuəli/	ad.		informally, temporarily 偶然地，随便地，临时地
forbid /fəˈbid/	vt.		(forbade, forbidden) to command (sb. or sth.) not to do sth. 不许，禁止
airy /ˈɛəri/	a.		of, relating to air, open to the air 空气的，空中的，通风的
asparagus /əsˈpærəgəs/	n.		芦笋
tender /ˈtendə/	a.		easily chewed or not hard; delicate, too easily crushed; painful, sore; gentle and loving 嫩的；疼痛的，一触即痛的；温柔的
	vt.		a formal offer in payment; to present for acceptance （正式）提出
	vi.		(for) to bid for 投标
	n.		a bid 投标
▲marvel /ˈmɑːvəl/	n.		wonderful thing 令人惊奇的事物
palate /ˈpælit/	n.		sense of taste 味觉
shameful /ˈʃeimful/	a.		causing shame, disgraceful, indecent 不体面的
franc /fræŋk/	n.		the standard coin of France, Switzerland, etc. 法郎
juicy /ˈdʒuːs/	a.		full of juice; richly interesting 多汁的；有趣的
appetising /ˈæpitaiziŋ/	a.		美味可口的，促进食欲的
thrust /θrʌst/	vt.		to push forcefully and suddenly; to pierce or stab as if with a pointed weapon to issue or extend 插，挤
	vi.		(at) to push, or force one's way; to pierce or stab with or as if with a pointed weapon 刺，戳
	n.		a forceful push; a driving force or pressure 戳，刺；要点，要旨；推力
mouthful /ˈmauθˌful/	n.		the amount of food or other material that can be placed or held in the mouth at one time 一口，满口
faintly /ˈfeintli/	ad.		weak and about to lose consciousness; lacking courage or spirit 微弱地，朦胧地，模糊地
absent /ˈæbsənt/	a.		not present; showing lack of attention to what is happening 缺席，不在；心不在焉的
absent-minded /ˈæbsəntˈmaindid/	a.		so concerned with one's thought as not to notice what is happening, what one is doing, etc. 心不在焉的,茫

Unit 7 Stories of a Pet, a Young Writer

		然的
absent-mindedly /ˈæbsəntˈmaindidli/	ad.	心不在焉地，茫然地
★ *snack* /snæk/	n.	light, usu. hurriedly eaten meal 快餐，小吃，点心
inadequate /inˈædikwət/	a.	not enough to fulfill a need or meet a requirement; insufficient 不充分的，不适当的
humorist /ˈhjuːmərist/	n.	a person with a good sense of humor 有幽默感的人；幽默作家，滑稽演员
★ *revenge* /riˈvendʒ/	n.	punishment given to sb. in return for harm done to oneself 报复，报仇
vindictive /vinˈdiktiv/	a.	having the desire to harm sb. from whom harm has been received 报复的
★ *immortal* /iˈmɔːtəl/	a.	living forever 不朽的
pardonable /ˈpɑːdənəb(ə)l/	a.	that can be forgiven 可原谅的，难怪的

PHRASES

catch sight of	to see for a moment 看到，发现
at first sight	at the first time of seeing 初次看见时
believe in	to consider (sth.) to be of worth 主张
come to	to amount to 共计为
take sb. to task	criticize sb. for a fault 责备某人，申斥某人
in the habit of	有……的习惯
ever so	[*infml*] (esp. *BrE*.) very 非常
more ... than	to a greater extent; to a greater degree 倒，倒不如说
in the least	at all 一点，丝毫
leave over	to remain 留下，剩下
make up one's mind	to reach a decision 打定主意，决定
start up	to jump 突然站起，惊起
in season	at the time of usual fitness for eating 正当时令
take a hand in	to be partly the cause of or have an effect on (sth.) 插手，影响

Part B
Extensive Reading

EXERCISES

Reading Comprehension

Task 1

A. Find answers to the following questions in the text.

1. Where and when did the writer suddenly see the woman he had met long ago?
2. How did he possibly manage to earn a living twenty years ago?
3. What did the woman improperly ask him to do?
4. What were his impressions of her appearance?
5. What did the woman eat and drink at the lunch?
6. What did he eat and drink at the lunch?
7. Why did he become a little depressed when the woman ordered caviare?
8. What did the woman say concerning overloading her stomach?
9. What would he feel shame over?
10. Why were peaches extremely expensive at that time?
11. What do you think of the young writer and the woman reader in the story?

B. Paraphrase the following sentences or put them into Chinese.

1. I was earning barely enough money to keep body and soul together.
2. That restaurant was so far beyond my means.
3. Few men learn this until they are too old to make it of any importance to a woman what they say.
4. I had eighty francs to last me the rest of the month.
5. I told the waiter by all means to bring caviare.
6. I tried with all my might to will him to say no.
7. I could not bring myself to do that.
8. I was past caring now.
9. Her eyes rested for an instant on the three francs I left for the waiter.

Vocabulary

Task 2

A. Give words or phrases from the text that are close in meaning to the following.

1. outcome: _____
2. final resting place: _____
3. see suddenly: _____
9. at first glance: _____
10. cut: _____
11. amazing: _____

Unit 7 Stories of a Pet, a Young Writer

4. smooth: _____
5. inconvenient: _____
6. charge: _____
7. reasonable: _____
8. detailed: _____

12. insure: _____
13. terror: _____
14. gleam: _____
15. unexpected: _____
16. emotion: _____

B. Complete the following sentences by choosing a word from the box below, using the proper form.

| absent | tender | forbid | fancy | flash |
| proceed | anticipate | assure | impose | overlook |

1. We are trying to _____ what questions we'll be asked in the examination.
2. Before going to bed she _____ herself that the door was locked.
3. From our house on the hillside, we can _____ the whole port.
4. Love was totally _____ from his childhood.
5. Preparations for the conference are _____ smoothly.
6. In some countries women are _____ from going out without a veil.
7. I don't _____ going all that way in such bad weather.
8. The government _____ a ban on the sale of ivory.

Task 3

Choose the correct word to fit into each sentence, using the proper form.

1. to appear, appearance, reappear, reappearance
   a. The stranger _____ to be rather friendly.
   b. You can change the whole _____ of a room.
   c. There _____ to be some mistake.
   d. The singer's _____ in the news was not unexpected.
2. generous, generously, generosity
   a. It was most _____ of you to lend me the money.
   b. Please give the books _____ to children in need.
   c. Sally's friends take advantage of her _____.
   d. My uncle is very _____ with his money.
3. to digest, digest, digestion, digestive
   a. Some people find that they cannot _____ meat easily.
   b. A monthly _____ is published, giving details of the company's activities.

c. Ever since her illness, her _____ has been poor.

d. The _____ system is the organs of a body which _____ food.

4. to tender, tender
   a. My injured leg is still _____.
   b. She _____ her husband day and night for six days.
   c. The company accepted the lowest _____.
   d. The beef is really _____.

5. passion, passionate, passionately
   a. Philosophy was his lifelong _____.
   b. My brother is _____ about football.
   c. His _____ overcame his reason.
   d. The woman leader gave a _____ speech.
   e. The well-known dancer spoke _____ about her love of music.

6. to impress, impression, impressive
   a. There are some very _____ buildings in the town.
   b. He's got a very _____ collection of modern paintings.
   c. My mother was very much _____ by your behaviour.
   d. I don't tend to trust first _____.
   e. My father _____ on me the importance of work.

II. After Twenty Years

By O. Henry

The policeman on the beat moved up the street with an air of importance[1] as usual. The time was hardly 10 o'clock at night, but the cold wind with a bit of rain in it had almost made the street empty. With a club in his hand, the officer tried doors as he walked, turning now and then to look at the quiet street. He could see the lights of a cigar store or of an all-night counter sometimes, but
5 most of the shops had long since been closed.

Walking towards the middle of the street, the policeman suddenly slowed his walk. In the doorway of a store stood a man with an unlighted cigar in his mouth. As the policeman walked up to him the man spoke up quickly.

"It's all right, officer," he said. "I'm just waiting for a friend. It's an appointment made
10 twenty years ago. Sounds a little funny to you, doesn't it? Well, I'll explain if you'd like to make

---

1. **with an air of importance:** with a look of being important

Unit 7 Stories of a Pet, a Young Writer

certain it's all straight[1]. About that long ago[2] there used to be a restaurant where this store stands — 'Big Joe' Brandy's restaurant."

"Until five years ago," said the policeman. "It was torn down then."

The man in the doorway struck a match and lit his cigar. The light showed a pale, square face with keen eyes, and a little white scar near his right eyebrow. He wore an expression silk tie with a diamond pin.

"Twenty years ago tonight," said the man, "I ate here at 'Big Joe' Brandy's with Jimmy Wells, my best friend and the finest person in the world. He and I were raised here in New York, just like two brothers, together. I was eighteen and Jimmy was twenty. The next morning I was to start for the West to make my fortune. You couldn't have made Jimmy leave New York; he thought it was the only place on earth. Well, we agreed that night that we would meet here again exactly twenty years from that date and time, no matter what our conditions might be or from what distance we might have to come. We thought that in twenty years each of us ought to have our fate worked out and our fortunes made, whatever they were going to be."

"It sounds pretty interesting," said the policeman. "Rather a long time between meets, though, it seems to me. Haven't you heard from your friend since you left?"

"Well, yes, for a time we wrote," said the other. "But after a year or two we stopped. You see, the West is a pretty big proposition, and I kept moving around from place to place. But I know Jimmy will meet me here if he's alive, for he always was the truest old friend in the world. He'll never forget. I came a thousand miles to stand in this door tonight, and it's worth it, if he turns up."

The waiting man pulled out a handsome watch, the lids of it set with small diamonds.

"Three minutes to ten," he said. "It was exactly ten o'clock when we parted here at the restaurant door."

"Did pretty well out West, did you?" asked the policeman.

"Sure. I hope Jimmy had done half as well."

The policeman twirled his club and took a step or two.

"I'll be on my way. Hope your friend comes around all right. Going to stop waiting at 10 sharp?"[3]

---

1. **it's all straight**: It's all honest and truthful.
2. **that long ago**: Here "that" is an adverb, meaning "so, to such a degree". It is used to emphasize "long ago".
3. **at 10 sharp**: exactly at ten 十点整

"I should say not!" said the other. "I'll give him half an hour at least. If Jimmy is alive on earth he'll be here by that time. So long, officer."

"Good-night, sir," said the policeman, passing on along his beat, trying doors as he went.

There was now a rain falling, and the wind was blowing harder. A few people hurried along with coat collars turned high and pocketed hands[1]. And in the door of that store the man who had come a thousand miles to keep an appointment with the friend of his youth, smoked his cigar and waited.

About twenty minutes he waited, and then a tall man in a long overcoat, with collar turned up to his ears, hurried across from the opposite side of the street. He went directly to the waiting man.

"Is that you, Bob?" he asked.

"Is that you, Jimmy Wells?" cried the man in the door.

"Bless my heart![2]" exclaimed the new arrival, holding both of the other's hands. "It's Bob, sure as fate. I was certain I'd find you here if you were still in existence. Well, well, well!— twenty years is a long time. The old restaurant's gone, Bob; I wish it had lasted, so we could have had another dinner there. How has the West treated you, old man?"

"Fine, it has given me everything I asked it for. You've changed lots, Jimmy. I never thought you were so tall by two or three inches."

"Oh, I grew a bit after I was twenty."

"Doing well in New York, Jimmy?"

"Moderately. I have a position in one of the city departments. Come on, Bob, we'll go around to a place I know of, and have a good long talk about old times."

The two men started up the street, arm in arm. The man from the West, proud of his success, was beginning to talk about the history of his career. The other listened with interest.

At the corner stood a drug store, bright with electric lights. When they came into this glare each of them turned at the same time to look at the other's face.

The man from the West stopped suddenly and released his arm.

"You're not Jimmy Wells," he said angrily. "Twenty years is a long time, but not long enough to change a man's nose from a Roman[3] to a pug[4]."

"It sometimes changes a good man into a bad one," said the tall man. "You've been under

---

1. **pocketed hands:** with hands in their pockets
2. **Bless my heart!:** an expression of surprise, similar to "God bless my heart".
3. **a Roman:** a Roman nose 鹰钩鼻子
4. **a pug:** 狮子鼻

Unit 7 Stories of a Pet, a Young Writer

arrest for ten minutes, Bob. Chicago thinks you may have dropped over our way and wires[1] us she wants to talk with you. Going quickly, are you? That's sensible. Now, before we go to the station here's a note I was asked to hand you. You may read it here at the window. It's from Officer Wells."

The man from the West unfolded the little piece of paper handed him. His hand was steady when he began to read, but it trembled a little by the time he had finished. The note was rather short.

Bob: I was at the appointed place on time. When you struck the match to light your cigar I saw it was the face of the man wanted in Chicago. Somehow I couldn't do it myself, so I went around and got a plain clothes man to do the job. (1130 words)

NEW WORDS

beat /biːt/	n.	appointed route of a policemen; route over which sb. goes regularly 警察的规定巡逻路线；某人常走的路
doorway /ˈdɔːwei/	n.	an opening for an entrance door into a building or room 门口
unlighted /ˌʌnˈlaitid/	a.	未被照亮的；未被点燃的
keen /kiːn/	a.	(of the mind, the senses) active, sharp; (of feelings, interest) strong; quick at understanding, deeply felt, etc. 热心的，渴望的；激烈的，强烈的；敏锐的，敏捷的
★ scar /skɑː/	n.	a mark left on the skin after a surface injury or wound has healed; mental injury or damage 伤疤，伤痕；(精神上的)创伤
	v.	to leave lasting signs of damage on (给……) 留下伤痕 (或创伤)
tome /təum/	n.	one of the books in a work of several volumes; a book, especially a large or scholarly one 册，卷，本；著作
▲ proposition /ˌprɔpəˈziʃən/	n.	unproved statement in which an opinion or judgment is expressed; (infml) a person or matter to be dealt with 建议，提议；家伙，事情

---

1. **wire someone:** to send someone a telegram 给……发电报

Part B
Extensive Reading

twirl /twə:l/		v.	to (cause to) turn round and run quickly; (cause to) spin; to (cause to) curl （使）快速转动；旋转；（使）卷曲
		n.	a sudden quick spin or circular movement 转动
▲ **bless** /bles/		vt.	to ask God's favour for sth. 求神赐福于，祝福
exclaim /iks'kleim/		v.	to cry out suddenly and loudly 呼喊，惊呼，大声说
moderate /'mɔdərit/		a.	keeping or kept within reasonable limits; not extreme 温和的，稳健的；适中的，适度的
moderately		ad.	not very 适度地
★ *glare* /glɛə/		v.	to shine with a strong light and in a way unpleasant to the eyes 发射强光，发出刺眼的光线；(at) to look in an angry way 怒目而视
		n.	a hard, unpleasant effect given by a strong light; an angry look or stare; a state which continually draws the attention of the public 强光；怒视，瞪眼；炫耀，张扬
pug /pʌg/		n.	狮子鼻
arrest /ə'rest/		vt./n.	to seize in the name of the law and usu. put in prison 逮捕，拘留
sensible /'sensibəl/		a.	reasonable; practical; able to judge things well 合情合理的；切实的；明智的，有判断力的
★ *unfold* /ʌn'fəuld/		v.	to open from a folded position; to (cause to) become clear, more fully known, etc. 展开，打开；显露，展现
steady /'stedi/		a.	firm, not changing, stable 稳定的，不变的；稳重的
		v.	make or become steady （使）平稳，（使）稳定
appoint /ə'pɔint/		vt.	to choose for a post, to set up by choosing members; to choose or fix (a time, date, etc.) 任命，委派，约定，指定（时间、地点）

PHRASES

get along	to make progress; to manage 进展；过活，生活
be aware of	having knowledge or consciousness of 知道，觉察到，明白
in addition to	as well 除……外(还)，加于……之上
and so forth	and so on 等等

Unit **Stories of a Pet, a Young Writer**

EXERCISES

Reading Comprehension

Task 1

Fill in the blanks with the information from the passage.

1. The policeman walked up the street on a windy night because he was on his way _____.
2. The man standing in the doorway of a store explained to the policeman that he had come _____.
3. According to the appointment made before, they would meet at _____ at _____ o'clock, exactly twenty years from the original date and time, no matter what their condition might be.
4. Jimmy Wells didn't address his friend immediately when the man lit his cigar, because he recognized his friend but _____.
5. The man believed that his friend Jimmy was _____ he had ever made.
6. _____ acted as if he were Jimmy Wells who came to meet his friend.
7. The man suspected that the plain-clothes man was not Jimmy only when he noticed that the man's _____ was different from Jimmy's.
8. When Bob was reading the piece of paper handed to him, his hand trembled because he realized that his best friend did not want to shelter _____.

Vocabulary

Task 2

Match each of the words in Column A with an appropriate expression in Column B to make the collocations meaningful.

Column A	Column B
1. exclaim	a. choice
2. arrest	b. size
3. moderate	c. the prisoner
4. release	d. George in the name of the law
5. sensible	e. the new ambassador
6. appoint	f. with fear

Task 3

Give words or phrases that are close in meaning to the underlined part in each of the following sentences.

1. I wonder how their ideas <u>turn out</u> in practice.
2. She always had had a <u>strong</u> desire for a really comfortable home.
3. He promised to come, but he hasn't <u>arrived</u> yet.
4. Arthur worked hard in order to ensure a <u>stable</u> income.
5. We have got to be <u>practical</u> and buy only what we can afford.
6. A <u>reasonable</u> price is one that is neither cheap nor dear.

Part C — Reading Skill

Transition Words (3)

Transition words that signal conclusion or summary often come at the end of a paragraph. They show that the main point(s) of something which has / have been stated before is / are about to be summarized or concluded.

EXERCISE

Task 1

Choose from among the transition words listed below to complete the following paragraph.

(1) First	For example	Thus
(2) Furthermore	For instance	However
(3) Whereas	On the whole	At last

In my opinion, most Americans are weight conscious. (1)_____, they are very concerned with the size and shape of their bodies. I believe that even though people look and feel healthy,

Unit 7 Stories of a Pet, a Young Writer

fashion insists that they be even thinner and more well-proportioned than they already are. (2)_____, if they are not, then there are endless remedies such as fad(时尚) diets, diet pills, and health spas (矿泉, 温泉) to help them lose the extra weight. (3)_____, it is not at all surprising that Americans spend millions of dollars each year on their remedies to achieve their goal.

Transition words such as *however, although, nevertheless,* ... signal the change of direction of thought. They are classified as words of concession.

Task 2

Below is a story about a person full of contrasts. The sentences in the middle part of the story are jumbled. Number them in the correct order to complete the story.

The most fascinating person I know is Mr. Horace Browning, a neighbor of mine. Mr. Browning has many unusual characteristics which you would not guess from his physical appearance...

(1)
(2)
(3)
(4)
(5)
(6)
(7)

I am sure that you would find him a fascinating person too.

a. Nevertheless, he is the best athlete in our area.

b. Mr. Browning has a reputation as the most generous person in our community, although he is not a wealthy man.

c. He is probably the shortest and thinnest man that I know.

d. Instead, Mr. Browning spends most of his leisure time organizing athletic activities for the poorest and most unfortunate children of our community.

e. However, he entertains these children for hours with stories about the interesting things he does and the people he knows.

f. Thus, he cannot show his generosity by giving large amounts of money to the poor.

g. He may not be a wonderful storyteller.

Task 3

Complete the numbered blanks in the paragraph below, using the transition words in the list. Note two of them are interchangeable in this paragraph.

a. Moreover
b. On the other hand
c. Consequently
d. As a result
e. However
f. One reason for this is that
g. For instance

It has often been claimed that examinations are an unfair means of testing a student's knowledge and ability. (1)_____, they measure only a small part of what a student knows. (2)_____, they give a very limited idea of a student's ability. (3)_____, a good student may perform poorly in an examination for unavoidable health reasons; (4)_____, a toothache can completely destroy a student's concentration. (5)_____, it has been argued that examinations are fair because they are the same for everyone, and that they are the most convenient means of testing large numbers of students. (6)_____, these arguments have not persuaded those who are against examinations. (7)_____, it seems that examinations may gradually disappear.

Dealing with transition words, you may find some of them overlapping. This is because some of the transition words can give more than one kind of signal. For example, contrast and concession have some transition words in common, and so do sequence, addition, and summary. Often the general idea of the paragraph will help you decide which signal is intended in the context. In your everyday reading you should learn to react to transition words quickly and automatically so as to become a mature reader.

Unit 8

Enthusiasm for Work

Aims and Objectives

In this unit you will learn:
1. Genre/Style: Exposition/Narration
2. Word Power: Measure Word
3. Grammar Focus: Noun Clauses
4. Writing Skill: The Ending of an Essay
5. Translation Skill: Repetition
6. Reading Skill: Inferring the Author's Views and Attitudes

Brief Introductions to the Texts

The author of the first passage encourages everyone to engage in a worthwhile cause. The second passage is a letter written by basketball star Michael Jordan to his fans. The third is about keeping up the initial enthusiasm for one's daily work.

Unit 8 Enthusiasm for Work

Part A — Intensive Reading

Reading

Task 1

Which of the following are virtues that one should have and which are not? Discuss them with your partners.

1. Expect no return for one's kindness.
2. Help people who are in trouble.
3. Give up on people who have committed a crime.
4. Quit loving your friends when they have done something silly.
5. Make yourself available to people who need your help.
6. Remain faithful to any cause to which you are called.
7. If possible, embrace every cause with all your heart.

Task 2

How do you think the characters in the story might answer the following questions?

1. Q: What can you do for the prisoners?
   A: _____.
2. Q: Why did you spend time with social outcasts when you could have been watching TV?
   A: _____.
3. Q: Why do you dye your hair purple?
   A: _____.
4. Q: Why do you risk you own health for the sake of others?
   A: _____.
5. Q: Are you still so excited about learning?
   A: _____.
6. Q: Why do you want to organize a new peace group?
   A: _____.
7. Q: Why do you need my leadership?
   A: _____.

How to Be True to You

Give wisely and carry a big stick
By **Scott Russell Sanders**

I knew a man, a very tall and spare and gentle man, for several years before I found out that he visited prisoners in our county jail, week in and week out for decades. He would write letters for them,
5 carry messages, fetch clothing or books, but mainly he just offered himself. He didn't preach to them, didn't pick and choose between the likable and the nasty, didn't look for any return on his kindness. All that mattered was that they were in trouble.

10 Why did he spend time with out-casts when he could have been golfing or watching TV? "I go in case everyone else has given up on them," he told me once. "I never give up."

Never giving up is a trait we honor in athletes, in soldiers, in survivors of disaster, in patients recovering from severe injuries. If
15 you struggle bravely against overwhelming odds, you're liable to end up on the evening news. But in less flashy, less news-worthy forms, fidelity to a mission or a person or an occupation shows up in countless lives all around us.

> What does the sentence imply?

It shows up in parents who will not quit loving their daughter
20 even after she dyes her hair purple and tattoos her belly and runs off with a rock band. It shows up in couples who choose to mend their marriages instead of filing for divorce. It shows up in volunteers at the hospital or library or women's shelter or soup kitchen[1]. It shows up in unsung people everywhere who do their jobs well, not because
25 the supervisor is watching or because they are paid gobs of money,

---

1. **soup kitchen:** a place where soup and other food is supplied free to people, esp. after a disaster such as an earthquake or a flood 施粥所

Unit 8 Enthusiasm for Work

but because they know their work matters.

When my son Jesse was in sixth grade, his teacher was diagnosed with breast cancer. She told the children about the disease, about the surgery and therapy, and about her hopes for recovery. Jesse came home deeply impressed that she had trusted them with her news. She could have stayed home for the rest of the year. When her mastectomy healed, she began going in to school one afternoon a week, then two, then a full day, then two days and three.

When a parent worried that she might be risking her health for the sake of the children, the teacher scoffed, "Oh, heavens, no! They're my best medicine." Besides, these children would only be in sixth grade once, she said, and she meant to help them all she could while she had the chance.

> What does the word "they" refer to?

The therapy must have worked, because ten years later she's going strong. When I see her around town, she always asks about Jesse. Is he still so funny, so bright, so excited about learning? Yes, he is, I tell her, and she beams.

A cause needn't be grand, it needn't impress a crowd to be worthy of our commitment. I have a friend who built houses Monday through Friday for people who could pay him and then built other houses for free on Saturday with Habitat for Humanity. A neighbor makes herself available to international students and their families, unriddling for them the puzzles of living in this new place. Other neighbors coach soccer teams, visit the sick, give rides to the housebound, tutor dropouts, teach adults to read.

> What do these examples show?

I could multiply these examples a hundredfold without ever leaving my county. Most likely you could do the same. Any community worth living in must have a web of people faithful to good work and to one another, or that community would fall apart.

To say that fidelity is common is not to say it's easy, painless or free. It costs energy and time, maybe a lifetime.

And every firm *yes* we say requires many a firm *no*. One Sunday I was talking with the man who visited prisoners in jail, when a young woman approached to ask if he would join the board of a new peace group she was organizing. In a rush of words she told him why the cause was crucial, why the time was ripe, why she absolutely needed his leadership. Knowing this man's sympathies, I figured he would agree to serve. But after listening to her plea, he gazed at her soberly for a moment, then said, "That certainly is a vital concern, worthy of all your passion. But it is not my concern."

> Did the man agree to serve?

The challenge for all of us is to find those few causes that are peculiarly our own — those to which we are clearly called and then to embrace them with all our heart. By remaining faithful to a calling, we can create the conditions for finding a purpose and a pattern in our days.

If you imagine trying to solve all the world's problems at once, though, you're likely to quit before you finish rolling up your sleeves. But if you stake out your own workable territory, if you settle on a manageable number of causes, then you might accomplish a great deal, all the while trusting that others elsewhere are working faithfully in their own places. (855 words)

NEW WORDS

county /ˈkaunti/	n.	an area in Britain, Ireland or the USA which has its own local government 县，郡	
jail /dʒeil/	n.	a prison 监狱	
	vt.	to put sb. in prison 监禁	
★ **preach** /priːtʃ/	v.	to say that sth. is good and to persuade others to accept it 鼓吹	
likable /ˈlaikəbl/	a.	可爱的	
nasty /ˈnɑːsti/	a.	bad 令人厌恶的；困难的；恶劣的	
golf /gɔlf/	vi.	打高尔夫球	
athlete /ˈæθliːt/	n.	a person who is good at sports like running, jumping or throwing 运动员，运动选手	
survivor /səˈvaivə/	n.	生还者，残存物	
disaster /diˈzɑːstə/	n.	sth. very bad that happens and that may hurt a lot of people 灾难，天灾，灾祸	
severe /siˈviə/	a.	very bad 严重的；严厉的；严峻的	

Unit 8 Enthusiasm for Work

injury /'indʒəri/	n.	damage to the body of a person or an animal 受伤处；伤害
★overwhelming /ˌəuvə'welmiŋ/	a.	very great or strong 巨大的；势不可挡的
liable /'laiəbl/	a.	(to) likely to 可能的；(for) 有义务的
flashy /'flæʃi/	a.	浮华的
▲fidelity /fi'deliti/	n.	the quality of being faithful 忠实，精确
mission /'miʃən/	n.	a journey to do a special job 使命，任务，使团，代表团
countless /'kautlis/	a.	无数的，数不尽的
dye /dai/	vt.	to change the colour of sth. 染
	n.	染料，染色
purple /'pə:pl/	a.	a color between red and blue 紫色的
	n.	紫色
tattoo /tə'tu:, tæ'tu:/	v.	刺花样
	n.	纹身
file /fail/	v.	提出；排成纵队
	n.	文件，档案；文件夹
divorce /di'vɔ:s/	n.	the end of a marriage by law 离婚；脱离
	vt.	使离婚；与……脱离
volunteer /ˌvɔlən'tiə(r)/	n.	a person who offers or agrees to do sth. without being forced or paid to do it 志愿者，志愿兵
	v.	自愿
unsung /'ʌn'sʌŋ/	a.	未赞颂的
gob /gɔb/	n.	[pl.] a large quantity 大量
diagnose /'daiəgnəuz/	v.	to find out what is wrong or what illness a person has 诊断
breast /brest/	n.	胸部，乳房
cancer /'kænsə/	n.	a very dangerous illness that makes some cells grow too fast 癌，毒瘤
therapy /'θerəpi/	n.	a way of helping people who are ill in their body or mind, usually without drugs 治疗
recovery /ri'kʌvəri/	n.	a return to good health after an illness or to a normal state after a difficult period of time 恢复，痊愈；追回
impress /im'pres/	vt.	to make sb. have good feelings or thoughts about you or about sth. that is yours 留下印象；印，盖印
mastectomy /mæs'tektəmi/	n.	乳房切除术

Part A
Intensive Reading

heal	/hi:l/	v.	to become well again 治愈，医治
sake	/seik/	n.	缘故，理由
▲scoff	/skɔf/	v.	嘲笑，嘲弄
beam	/bi:m/	v.	to smile happily 面露喜色；播送
		n.	梁；（光线的）束，笑容
grand	/grænd/	a.	very important 重大的；宏伟的；傲慢的
▲habitat	/'hæbitæt/	n.	（动植物的）栖息地
humanity	/hju(:)'mæniti/	n.	the quality of being kind and understanding 博爱，仁慈；人性；人类
unriddle	/'ʌn'ridl/	vt.	解，阐明
soccer	/'sɔkə/	n.	英式足球
housebound	/'hausbaund/	a.	不能离家的
dropout		n.	退学学生,辍学学生
multiply	/'mʌltipli/	v.	to become bigger or greater, to increase 增加，繁殖；乘
hundredfold	/'hʌndrədfəuld/	a.	百倍的
		ad.	百倍地
painless	/'peinlis/	a.	无痛的，不痛的
crucial	/'kru:ʃiəl,'kru:ʃəl/	a.	very important 至关紧要的
★plea	/pli:/	n.	a strong request 恳求，请求；辩护；借口
★soberly	/'səubəli/	ad.	seriously, thoughtfully 严肃地，冷静地
embrace	/im'breis/	vt.	to take up willingly or eagerly 乐意地或渴望地从事于；拥抱；包含；包围
		vi.	拥抱
		n.	拥抱
faithful	/'feiθful/	a.	always ready to help your friends and to do what you have promised to do 忠实的；尽职的；可靠的
		n.	信徒
sleeve	/sli:v/	n.	the part of a coat, dress or shirt, for example, that covers your arm 袖子
stake	/steik/	n.	桩，标桩；利害关系；赌本
		vt.	以……打赌
workable	/'wə:kəbl/	a.	可经营的，可使用的
manageable	/'mænidʒəbl/	a.	易管理的，便于管理的
accomplish	/ə'kɔmpliʃ/	vt.	to succeed in doing sth. requiring effort and/or skill 完成，达到，实现

233

Unit 8 Enthusiasm for Work

elsewhere /'els'hwɛə/   ad.   in or to another place 在别处

PHRASES

week in and week out	every week without exception 每个星期都
in case	because of the possibility of sth. happening 以防万一
give up on sb.	no longer believe that sb. is going to be successful, lose hope in sb. 不再相信某人会成功；对某人失望
show up	appear 出现
run off with	run away with sb. 与人私奔
for the sake of	in order to get or keep sth. 为了……的缘故，看在……的分上
for free	for nothing, without a price or cost 不要钱的
roll up one's sleeve	prepare to work or fight 卷起袖子（准备工作或战斗）
stake out	to put boundaries around 用桩标出地界
settle on sth.	choose sth., decide to take sth. 选择某事物，决定做某事
all the while	始终，一直

EXERCISES

Reading Comprehension

Task 3

The following statements are the main ideas of some paragraphs of the text. Match each statement with its related paragraph number.

A. There are many ways in which you can do something good to help others.

B. People everywhere do their jobs well because they know their work is important.

C. You might achieve a lot if you limit the number of causes to which you are faithfully devoted.

D. Countless examples of never giving up can be shown in our lives.

E. Fidelity to a cause is not easy.

F. The author knew a man who helped prisoners.

G. A school teacher suffering from caner knew the importance of her work and did her best to help her students.

H. It is necessary to refuse to spend energy and time on something that is not your concern.

Part A
Intensive Reading

Task 4

The following sentences explain the meanings or implications of some sentences in the text. Pick out the original sentences in the text.

1. We show our respect to those who have suffered a lot but never give up.
2. It's possible you will make news if you fight against great difficulties to win.
3. We can devote ourselves to a cause which may not be so great and which may catch little public attention.
4. The most difficult thing for us is to find those few causes that we are particularly concerned about.
5. If you attempt to settle all the problems in the world immediately, you will probably give up even before you start.

Vocabulary

Task 5

Matching words with similar meanings.

A	B
1. jail	a. achieve
2. athlete	b. colour
3. disaster	c. prison
4. severe	d. accident
5. liable	e. important
6. dye	f. loyalty
7. fidelity	g. particularly
8. accomplish	h. serious
9. crucial	i. likely
10. peculiarly	j. movement
11. mission	k. sportsperson
12. humanity	l. kindness

Task 6

Fill in the blanks with the words given below. Make changes where necessary.

Unit 8 Enthusiasm for Work

injury	purple	divorce	county	nasty	sake	odds
volunteer	heal	elsewhere	kindness	recovery	impress	cast

1. The state of Texas in the US is divided into 254 _____.
2. Paul _____ a stone into the river.
3. You are just arguing for the _____ of arguing.
4. She was sick yesterday, so the _____ are she won't be in today.
5. Nina frequently _____ for extra work because she really likes her job.
6. As people age, they tend to _____ more slowly.
7. If she doesn't like it here, she can go _____.
8. Be grateful. It was done out of _____.
9. The economy is showing signs of _____.
10. It was _____ of him to do such a thing.
11. Richard was removed from the game with a knee _____.
12. The early morning sun cast deep _____ shadows.
13. Angela got a _____ when the children were small.
14. It _____ me that Kevin understood immediately what I meant.

Task 7

Explain the meanings of the italicized words in the following sentences in Chinese.

1. *Beaming* with pleasure she stepped forward to receive her prize.
2. The programme was *beamed* live by satellite to many different countries.
3. Our house isn't very *grand*, but it has a big garden.
4. They are too *grand* for us.
5. He was wearing a white hat with a black *band* round it.
6. Rick played the drums with the *band*.
7. What do you get if you *multiply* 13 and 11?
8. Our profits have *multiplied* over the last two years.
9. *Stakes* in the ground marked the outline of the new building.
10. We play cards for money, but never for very high *stakes*.

Task 8

The word "file" may have different meanings in different sentences. Match the sentences with the proper Chinese equivalents of the word.

1. Students are given a file to keep their course notes in.	档案
2. I can't remember exactly what I said in the letter. I'll need to look at the file.	申请
3. You'll have to go in single file — the path is very narrow.	文件夹
4. He filed for a civil-service job.	排成纵队

Further Practice

Task 9

Translate the following sentences into English, using the words or phrases given in the parenthesis.

1. 值得我们去献身的一项事业不一定会给他人留下深刻的印象，但它却是我们自己特有的事业。(commitment, peculiar)
2. 以诚待人不是能够轻而易举、无痛无忧地做到的，它或许需要我们一辈子的努力。(fidelity, cost)
3. 只要你尽心尽力地从事一项事业，你就一定能取得成绩。(settle on, accomplish)

Task 10

The following is part of a speech given by a volunteer. Complete it by using words or phrases from the box below. There are more words and phrases than you will need.

contribute to	recovery	shelter	accomplish	sympathy	satisfaction
involved with	cancer	volunteer	disaster	kindness	

Since I was a child I have volunteered at nursing homes and schools. Being ___1___ our community has always just been a fact of life — one that has always been a great source of ___2___. I feel I can ___3___ more and help a more diverse group of individuals. Involvement as a volunteer for the ___4___ Society, the Public Library, or a local homeless ___5___ are just a few of the many opportunities for me to give back to my community and hopefully create benefits for those who are in need. Aside from ___6___ work, I believe to be a respectable citizen it is important to ___7___ society through one's chosen profession. Our society is still filled with problems such as AIDS, natural ___8___, and murders that we hear about through the media on a daily basis. It is our responsibility to try to find solutions to these problems.

Unit 8 Enthusiasm for Work

Grammar

Task 11

Decide what the relationship should be between the two parts of the sentences below, and add an appropriate connector to the sentence to establish that relationship.

1. We depend upon the sun's rays for the light and warmth which keep us alive, _____ there are some kinds of rays from the sun which would burn us to death if we were not protected from them.
2. There are still many who argue that microwaves can do almost anything that lasers can do, _____ do it better and cheaper.
3. A gerund differs from a participle in that one is a noun, _____ the other is an adjective.
4. I am sorry to report that in the competition in the Department of Physics you were unsuccessful, _____, we were unable to admit you.
5. Steve wants to play for the team, _____ he has had trouble meeting the academic requirements.
6. The visitors complained loudly about the heat, _____ they continued to play golf every day.
7. Paul has always been nervous in large gatherings, _____ it is no surprise that he avoids crowds of his adoring fans.
8. Lucy is not the only Olympic athlete in her family, _____ are her brother, sister, and her Uncle Chet.
9. Whether you win this race _____ lose it doesn't matter as long as you do your best.
10. That is not what I meant to say, _____ should you interpret my statement as an admission of guilt.

文章的结尾 (The Ending of an Essay)

文章的结尾与文章的开头一样，往往是读者最注意的地方，其作用是对文章的中心论点进一步强调或对文章就中心论点的论证进行归纳总结，给全文一个圆满的结束。常用的结尾方式如下：

1) 重申开头段中的中心论点，如：

In short, with people's standard of living getting higher and higher, changes in their diet will be more obvious and greater.

2) 提出问题的解决方法，如：

Making cities greener requires more than widespread awareness; it calls for an immediate commitment to planting more trees and growing more flowers.

3) 总结展开段中的论证，表明作者观点，如：

I benefited by working in this factory. For one thing, I learned to exchange my labor for money; for another, I made some new friends.

注意：在文章的结尾段中应避免提出新的论点，以防"画蛇添足"。

Task 12

Please write at least two different ending paragraphs for each of the following titles:

1) Practice Makes Perfect
2) Are Lucky Numbers Really Lucky?
3) Making Cities Greener
4) Playing Computer Games Should Be Forbidden in Universities

Task 13

Please review the paragraph you wrote in the last unit on "Looking after Old People Should Be the Responsibility of the Family" and decide which one of the following four paragraphs is the most suitable ending paragraph. Why?

A. In my country we do not have the terrible situation of old people living in hospitals because they have nowhere else to go. Furthermore, because we look after old people in the family, there are very few old people's homes.

B. They have great knowledge and experience which they can pass on. If they have a pension they can help financially, and of course they can help with the babysitting, housework and so on.

C. As you can see this is a difficult matter. It is both a moral and a practical problem. My feeling is that each family should consider all the arguments carefully and decide what best suits them.

D. I will never live with my family when I grow old. My cousin's parents lived with him and they both survived into their nineties. My cousin never had any independence at all.

Unit 8 Enthusiasm for Work

Task 14

Below is an example of a student's attempt at the following exercise. Please try to make improvements and add an ending paragraph.

> Present a written argument to an educated reader on the following topic:
> Lecturing as a method of teaching results in passive learning. This teaching method tends to be less effective than those that fully engage the learner.
> To what extent do you agree or disagree with this opinion?

Some people argue that lecturing means passive learning and is less effective than those that fully engage the learner. I think in some subjects, such as languages and natural science, it is the case. But in other subjects, lecturing is still quite effective and optimal, for example, math, history and philosophy.

There are subjects which needs practice and experiment. Just imagine, can a pupil who stay in the classroom and listen to the teacher all day, really master spoken English? Can a biology student who has never gone into a lab be an expert? I don't think so. Apparently, lecturing is necessary in these fields, but to study better, other methods are significate. And English corner, English movies, language lab, library and experiment are all good "lecturers". It took me several weeks to memorise the structure of the roots and stems of vegetation; but I think, after I see them in a microscope, it takes me several minutes.

On the other hand, in some subjects, lecturing is of great importance. Take philosophy for example. The knowledge has to be passed from one generation to one generation, through lecturing. Without lecturing, no one can learn this subject well.

Translation

重复法 (Repetition)

翻译中采用重复法，分为两种情况：一是因为原文采用了重复这一修饰手法，翻译中为了体现原文的特点，同样采用重复的手段；二是根据目的语的行文习惯适当进行一些必要的重复。

Part A
Intensive Reading

1) 修辞重复：

- Who *chatters* to you, will *chatter* of you.

  来说**是非**者，必是**是非**人。

- *Believe* not all you can hear, tell not all you *believe*.

  所闻不要全**信**，所**信**不要全讲。

- *What lies* behind us and what lies before us are tiny compared to *what lies* within us.

  身外之物，前面的也好，后面的也罢，与身内之物一比较，都微不足道。

- Learn to *laugh at* your troubles and you'll never run out of things to *laugh at*.

  烦恼面前学会**开开心心**，**开心**之事便会无穷无尽。

- Gentlemen may cry, *Peace*, *Peace* — but there is no peace.

  老爷们尽管可以高呼"**和平**，**和平**"！但是依然没有**和平**。

- *Farewell to* the mountains high covered with snow!

  Farewell to the straths and green valleys below!

  Farewell to the forests and wild hanging woods!

  Farewell to the torrents and loud-pouring floods!

  别了，白雪皑皑的高山！

  别了，山下的平谷碧川！

  别了森林，还有那张牙舞爪的树林！

  别了湍流，还有那咆哮滔滔的洪水！

- I have *written* in bed and *written* out of it, *written* day and night.

  我卧床**写**，起床也**写**；白天**写**，晚上也**写**。

2) 出于目的语行文习惯、译文语气或语义需要而采用选词或其他重复：

- Some cause happiness *wherever* they go; others *wherever* they leave.

  有些人到**哪儿**，**哪儿**就有欢乐；有些人是离开**哪儿**，**哪儿**才有欢乐。

- Walking up and down the *empty* room, he *stopped* here and there to *touch* or look.

  房间里空**空荡荡**，他走来**走**去，这儿**停停**，那儿**停停**，东**摸摸**，西瞧瞧。

- It's a bit fishy that she should have given a villa *like that*.

  真是有点儿叫人不敢相信，那么好的一幢别墅，她居然**白白**地送了人。

- Each art has its own medium: the painter *his pigments*, the musician *his sounds*, and the

Unit 8 Enthusiasm for Work

writer, *words*.

每种艺术都有自己的**表现手段**。画家的**表现手段**是颜料．音乐家的**表现手段**是声音，作家的**表现手段**是词语。

- *A* bird in the hand is worth *two* in the bush.

一鸟在手胜于两鸟在林。

Task 15

Translate the following sentences into Chinese, using the method of repetition.

1) I knew a man, a very tall and spare and gentle man, for several years before I found out that he visited prisoners in our county jail, *week in and week* out for decades.

2) Never giving up is a trait we honor *in* athletes, *in* soldiers, *in* survivors of disaster, *in* patients recovering from severe injuries.

3) But in less flashy, less news-worthy forms, fidelity to a mission or a person or an occupation shows up in countless lives all around us.

4) *It shows up in* parents who will not quit loving their daughter even after she dyes her hair purple and tattoos her belly and runs off with a rock band. *It shows up in* couples who choose to mend their marriages instead of filing for divorce. *It shows up in* volunteers at the hospital or library or women's shelter or soup kitchen. *It shows up in* unsung people everywhere who do their jobs well, not because the supervisor is watching or because they are paid gobs of money but because they know their work matters.

5) She told the children about the disease, about the surgery and therapy, and about her hopes for recovery.

6) On mastectomy healed, she began going in to school one afternoon a week, then two, then a full day, then two days and three.

7) Any community worth living in must have a web of people faithful to good work and to one another, or that community would fall apart.

8) To say that fidelity is common is not to say it's easy, painless or free. It costs energy and time, maybe a lifetime.

9) And every firm *yes* we say requires many a firm *no*.

10) In a rush of words she told him why the cause was crucial, why the time was ripe, why she absolutely needed his leadership.

Part B
Extensive Reading

Quotation

A badly written book is only a blunder. A bad translation of a good book is a crime.

— *Gilbert Arthur Highet* (1906 — 1978)

一本书写差了不过是大错一个；一本好书译差了则是罪过一桩。

——吉尔伯特·海特(1906 — 1978)

Part B ▶Extensive Reading

I. Michael Jordan's Farewell Letter to Basketball

By **Michael Jordan**

ear Basketball,

It's been almost 28 years since the first day we met. 28 years since I saw you in the back of our garage. 28 years since my parents introduced us.

If someone would have told me then, what would become of us, I'm not sure
5 I would have believed them. I barely remembered your name.

Then I started seeing you around the neighborhood and watching you on television. I used to see you with guys down at the playground. But when my older brother started paying more attention to you, I started to wonder. Maybe you were different.

We hung out a few times. The more I got to know you, the more I liked you. And as life
10 would have it, when I finally got really interested in you, when I was finally ready to get serious, you left me off the varsity. You told me I wasn't good enough.

I was crushed. I was hurt. I think I even cried.

Then I wanted you more than ever. So I practiced. I hustled. I worked on my game. Passing. Dribbling. Shooting. Thinking. I ran. I did sit-ups. I did push-ups. I did pull-ups[1]. I lifted weights.

---

1. **Sit-up, push-up, pull-up:** 仰卧起坐，俯卧撑，引体向上

Unit 8 Enthusiasm for Work

15 I studied you. I began to fall in love and you noticed. At least that's what Coach Smith said.

At the time, I wasn't sure exactly what was going on. But now I know. Coach Smith was teaching me how to love you, how to listen to you, how to understand you, how to respect you and how to appreciate you. Then it happened. That night, at the Louisiana Superdome in the final seconds of the championship game against Georgetown, you found me in the corner and we
20 danced. Since then, you've become much more than just a ball to me. You've become more than just a court. More than just a hoop. More than just a pair of sneakers. More than just a game.

In some respects, you've become my life. My passion. My motivation. My inspiration.

You're my biggest fan and my harshest critic. You're my dearest friend and my strongest ally. You're my most challenging teacher and my most endearing student. You're my ultimate
25 teammate and my toughest competitor. You're my passport around the world and my visa into the hearts of millions.

So much has changed since the first day we met, and to a large degree, I have you to thank. So if you haven't heard me say it before, let me say it now for the world to hear. Thank you. Thank you, Basketball. Thank you for everything. Thank you for all the players who came before
30 me. Thank you for all the players who went into battle with me. Thank you for the championships and the rings[1]. Thank you for the All-Star Games[2] and the Playoffs. Thank you for the last shots, the buzzer-beaters, the hard fouls, the victories and the defeats. Thank you for making me earn my keep. Thank you for #23. Thank you for North Carolina and Chicago. Thank you for the air and the nickname. Thank you for the moves[3] and the hang time[4]. Thank you for the Slam-
35 Dunk Contest[5]. Thank you for the will and the determination, the heart and the soul, the pride and the courage. Thank you for the competitive spirits and the competition to challenge it. Thank you for the failures and the setbacks, the blessings and the applause. Thank you for the triangle. Thank you for baseball and the Barons. Thank you for forgiving me. Thank you for the assistant coaches, the trainers, and the physical therapists. Thank you for the announcers, the refs, the
40 writers, the reporters, the broadcasters and the radio stations. Thank you for the Pistons and the Lakers, the Cavs and the Knicks, the Sixers and the Celtics[6]. Thank you for Phoenix, Portland,

---

1. **ring:** 冠军戒指
2. **All Star Games:** 明星赛
3. **move :** 移动
4. **hang time:** 滞空时间
5. **Slam-Dunk Contest:** 扣篮大赛
6. **the Pistons and the Lakers, the Cavs and the Knicks, the Sixers and the Celtics:** 活塞队、湖人队、骑士队、尼克斯队、七六人队、凯尔特人队

Seattle and Utah. Thank you for the Wizards[1]. Thank you for the believers and the doubters. Thank you for Coach Smith, Coach Loughery, Coach Albeck, Coach Collins and Coach Jackson[2]. Thank you for the education and the experience. Thank you for teaching me the game behind, beneath, within, above and around the game. Thank you for every fan who has ever called my name, put their hands together for me and my teammates, slapped me five or patted me on the back. Thank you for everything you've given my family. Thank you for the moon and the stars, and last but not least, thank you for Bugs and Mars.

I know I'm not the only one who loves you. I know you have loved many before me and will love many after me. But, I also know what we had was unique. It was special. So as our relationship changes yet again, as all relationships do, one thing is for sure.

I love you, Basketball. I love everything about you and I always will. My playing days in the NBA are definitely over, but our relationship will never end.

Much Love and Respect,
Michael Jordan (848 words)

NEW WORDS

barely /ˈbɛəli/	ad.	almost not, only just 仅仅，刚刚，几乎不能
varsity /ˈvɑːsiti/	n.	大学运动代表队，大学
crush /krʌʃ/	vt.	to defeat completely 压垮；压碎
▲ **hustle** /ˈhʌsl/	vi.	催促，催赶
	n.	忙碌，奔忙
dribble /ˈdribl/	vt.	带球，运球
championship /ˈtʃæmpjənʃip/	n.	锦标赛
hoop /huːp/	n.	篮筐
sneaker /ˈsniːkə(r)/	n.	运动鞋
inspiration /ˌinspəˈreiʃn/	n.	灵感
harsh /hɑːʃ/	a.	not kind, cruel 严酷的；刺耳的，刺目的
critic /ˈkritik/	n.	a person who writes about a book, film or play and says

1. **Phoenix, Portland, Seattle and Utah; the Wizards:** 菲尼克斯太阳队、波特兰开拓者队、西雅图超音速队及犹他爵士队；奇才队
2. **Coach Smith, Coach Loughery, Coach Albeck, Coach Collins and Coach Jackson:** 乔丹的五位教练

Unit 8 Enthusiasm for Work

			if he/she likes it or not 批评家，评论家
challenge	/'tʃælindʒ/	n.	a new or difficult thing that makes you try hard 挑战
		vt.	向……挑战
endearing	/in'diəriŋ/	a.	令人钟爱的
ultimate	/'ʌltimit/	a.	the best 最好的；最后的，最终的
		n.	极点，顶点
competitor	/kəm'petitə/	n.	竞争者
passport	/'pɑ:spɔ:t/	n.	a small book with your name and photograph 护照
visa	/'vi:zə/	n.	a special piece of paper or mark in your passport to show that you can go into a country 签证
playoff	/'pleiɔ:f/	n.	季后赛
buzzer-beaters		n.	比赛结束前的最后投篮
★ foul	/faul/	n.	犯规
★ nickname	/'nikneim/	n.	诨号，绰号，昵称
slam-dunk		n.	扣篮
contest	/'kɔntest/	n.	a game or competition that people try to win 竞赛
	/kən'test/	v.	争夺；辩驳
determination	/di,tə:mi'neiʃən/	n.	being certain that you want to do sth. 决心，果断
competitive	/kəm'petitiv/	a.	involving people competing against each other 竞争的
competition	/,kɔmpi'tiʃən/	n.	trying to win or be best 竞争，竞赛
★ setback	/'setbæk/	n.	挫折，退步
blessing	/'blesiŋ/	n.	祝福
applause	/ə'plɔ:z/	n.	when a lot of people clap their hands together to show that they like sth. 鼓掌欢迎，欢呼
triangle	/'traiæŋgl/	n.	a shape with three straight sides 三角组合；[数] 三角形
baseball	/'beisbɔ:l/	n.	棒球，棒球运动
trainer	/'treinə/	n.	训练者，驯服者
physical	/'fizikəl/	a.	of or for your body 身体的；物质的，自然的；物理的
		vt.	体格检查
therapist	/'θerəpist/	n.	队医
announcer	/ə'naunsə/	n.	广播员，报幕员
ref	/ref/	n.	referee 裁判员
writer	/'raitə/	n.	a person who writes books, stories, etc. 作者，作家

Part B

Extensive Reading

broadcast /'brɔːdkɑːst/	n.	to send out sound or pictures by radio or television 广播，播音；广播节目	
	v.	广播	
broadcaster /'brɔːdkɑːstə/	n.	广播员；播放设备，撒播物；广播公司	
▲wizard /'wizəd/	n.	奇才，男巫	
believer /bi'liːvə/	n.	信徒	
doubter /dautə/	n.	怀疑者	
slap /slæp/	vt.	hit sb. with the flat inside part of your hand 拍，掌击，拍击	
	n.	拍，掌击，拍击	
pat /pæt/	v./n.	touch sb. or sth. lightly with your hand flat 轻拍，轻打	
	a.	非常恰当地，适时的	
bug /bʌg/	n.	小虫，臭虫	
	v.	装置窃听器，打扰	
▲mar /mɑː/	v.	弄坏，毁坏，损害	
	n.	损伤，毁损，障碍	
Bugs and Mars	n.	缺点与不足	
definitely /'definitli/	ad.	certainly 明确地，干脆地	

PHRASES

become of	to happen to sb./ sth. 降临, 遭遇
hang out	to spend a lot of time in a place or with sb. 闲荡，厮混
as life would have it	好像命中注定一样
leave off	no longer wear or put on 不再使用
fall in love	爱上
in some respects	在某些方面
work on sth.	engage in physical or mental activity 从事于, 致力于
to a large degree	在很大程度上
earn one's keep	to work hard enough to cover the costs of one's food accommodation, etc. 挣钱维持生活
slap sb. five	双手平伸互相击掌
pat sb. on the back	congratulate sb. 对某人表示祝贺、鼓励或赞扬
for sure	确实

Unit 8 Enthusiasm for Work

EXERCISES

Reading Comprehension

Task 1

Choose the best answer to each question with the information from the passage.

1. This letter is actually addressed to ___.
   A. basketball
   B. basketball players
   C. people who are interested in basketball
   D. Jordan's coaches and his teammates

2. The pronoun "you" in the letter refers to ___.
   A. the game of basketball
   B. the basketball fans
   C. all the teams that Jordan had played for
   D. the NBA (National Basketball Association)

3. Jordan's first attempt to play for his university ___.
   A. made him famous overnight
   B. had attracted the attention of millions of people
   C. was a complete failure
   D. had caught the attention of coach Smith

4. To Jordan, basketball had become more than just a game after ___.
   A. a hard-won victory
   B. his tour about the world
   C. a talk with coach Smith
   D. a period of hard training

5. All of the following pairs of words stand for people from different standpoints EXCEPT ___.
   A. fan and critic
   B. friend and ally
   C. teacher and student
   D. teammate and competitor

6. The expression "the players who went into battle with me" are his ___.
   A. competitors and critics
   B. teammates and coaches
   C. fans and friends

D. schoolmates and teachers

Task 2

Fill in the blanks with the words given below. Make changes where necessary.

| crush | passion | bug | harsh | broadcast | critic | challenge | ultimate |
| slam | competitive | applause | triangle | pat | | definite | barely | physical |

1. Because of the way this research was done, its findings are open to _____.
2. If we have to lower our prices to remain _____, we will.
3. The _____ liked his new film.
4. We _____ can't afford such a high price.
5. He was _____ by the news of his wife's death.
6. The performance got terrific _____ from the audience.
7. Mike grew up in the _____ environment of a small town.
8. Bob _____ the door shut.
9. He _____ me on the shoulder.
10. Her earrings were in the shape of _____.
11. You've _____ eaten anything — are you feeling all right?
12. Parents must consider their children's _____ and emotional needs.
13. The Olympics are _____ live by satellite.
14. There is a _____ in the software.

II. A Pair of Socks

By William Lyon Phelps

One fine afternoon I was walking along Fifth Avenue, when I remembered that it was necessary to buy a pair of socks. Why I wished to buy only one pair is unimportant. I turned into the first sock shop that caught my eye, and a boy clerk who could not have been more than seventeen years old came forward. "What can I do for you, sir?" "I wish to buy a pair of socks."

5 His eyes glowed. There was a note of passion in his voice. "Did you know that you had come into the finest place in the world to buy socks?" I had not been aware of that, as my entrance had been accidental. "Come with me," said the boy, ecstatically.

Unit 8 Enthusiasm for Work

I followed him to the rear of the shop, and he began to haul down from the shelves box after box, displaying their contents for my delight.

"Hold on, lad, I am going to buy only one pair!" "I know that," said he, "but I want you to see how marvellously beautiful these are. Aren't they wonderful!" There was on his face an expression of solemn and holy rapture, as if he were revealing to me the mysteries of his religion.

I became far more interested in him than in the socks. I looked at him in amazement. "My friend," said I, "if you can keep this up, if this is not merely the enthusiasm that comes from novelty, from having a new job, if you can keep up this zeal and excitement day after day, in ten years you will own every sock in the United States."

My amazement at his pride and joy in salesmanship will be easily understood by all who read this article. In many shops the customer has to wait for some one to wait upon him. And when finally some clerk does design to notice you, you are made to feel as if you were interrupting him. Either he is absorbed in profound thought in which he hates to be disturbed or he is skylarking with a girl clerk and you feel like apologizing for thrusting yourself into such intimacy.

He displays no interest either in you or in the goods he is paid to sell. Yet possibly that very clerk who is now so apathetic began his career with hope and enthusiasm. The daily grind was too much for him; the novelty wore off; his only pleasures were found outside of working hours. He became a mechanical, not an inspired, salesman. After being mechanical, he became incompetent; then he saw younger clerks who had more zest in their work, promoted over him. He became sour and nourished a grievance.

That was the last stage. His usefulness was over. I have observed this melancholy decline in the lives of so many men in so many occupations that I have come to the conclusion that the surest road to failure is to do things mechanically.

It is simple enough for any one to be attracted by the novelty of a new job. The real difficulty is to keep up that initial enthusiasm every day of one's life, to go to work every morning with zest and excitement. I believe that a man should live every day as if that day were his first and his last day on earth.

Every person needs some relaxation, some recreation; but a man's chief happiness should not lie outside his daily work, but in it. The chief difference between the happiness of child-hood and the happiness of maturity is that the child's happiness is dependent on something different from the daily routine—a picnic, an excursion, a break of some kind. But to the right sort of men and women happiness is found in the routine itself, not in departures from it. Instead of hoping for a change, one hopes there will be no change, that one will have sufficient health to continue in one's chosen occupation.

The child has pleasures; the man has happiness. But unfortunately some men remain children all their lives. (687 words)

NEW WORDS

seventeen /'sevən'ti:n/	*num.*	十七	
	n.	十七个	
glow /gləu/	*vi.*	to send out soft light 发光；发热	
aware /ə'wɛə/	*a.*	to know about sth. 知道的，明白的，意识到的	
accidental /ˌæksi'dentl/	*a.*	happening by chance 意外的，偶然的	
ecstatically /eks'tætikli/	*ad.*	心醉神迷地，入神地	
rear /riə/	*n.*	the back part 后面，背后，后方，屁股	
	a.	后面的，背面的，后方的	
	vt.	培养，饲养，栽种	
haul /hɔ:l/	*v.*	to pull or drag sth. with great effort 拖，拉；拖拉，拖运	
	n.	拖，拉，拖拉	
display /di'splei/	*vt.*	to show sth. 显示，表现；陈列，展览	
	n.	陈列，展览，显示	
lad /læd/	*n.*	a boy or young man 男孩，小伙子	
marvelous /'mɑ:vələs/	*a.*	wonderful 绝妙的，了不起的	
solemn /'sɔləm/	*a.*	sincere, done or said in a formal way 庄严的，隆重的；严肃的	
holy /'həuli/	*a.*	very special because it is about God or a god 神圣的，圣洁的	
rapture /'ræptʃə/	*n.*	兴高采烈，欢天喜地	
mystery /'mistəri/	*n.*	sth. strange that you cannot understand or explain 神秘，神秘的事物	
★ **novelty** /'nɔvəlti/	*n.*	the quality of being new and different 新奇感；新奇的事物	
▲ **zeal** /zi:l/	*n.*	great energy or enthusiasm 热心，热情，热诚	
salesmanship /'seilzmənʃip/	*n.*	推销术，销售	
deign /dein/	*vi.*	屈尊	

Unit 8 Enthusiasm for Work

interrupt /ˌintə'rʌpt/	vt.	to stop sb. speaking or doing sth. by saying or doing sth. yourself 打扰，打断；中止
	vi.	打断
lark /lɑːk/	vi.	嬉耍
thrust /θrʌst/	vt.	插入，猛推；冲
intimacy /'intiməsi/	n.	亲密，隐私
apathetic /ˌæpə'θetik/	a.	缺乏兴趣的，缺乏感情的
grind /graind/	n.	difficult or unpleasant activity that is tiring or repetitious 苦差事；枯燥乏味的工作
	v.	磨（碎），碾（碎）；折磨
mechanical /mi'kænikl/	a.	done like a machine as if you are not thinking about what you are doing 机械似的，呆板的；机械的；力学的
salesman /'seilzmən/	n.	a person whose job is selling things to people 售货员，推销员
incompetent /in'kɔmpitənt/	a.	不合格的，不胜任的
zest /zest/	n.	强烈的兴趣，热情，热心
nourish /'nʌriʃ/	vt.	to allow a feeling or belief to grow stronger 怀有（希望，仇恨等）；滋养，使健壮
grievance /'griːvəns/	n.	委屈，冤情，不平
▲*melancholy* /'melənkəli/	a.	feeling or expressing sadness 忧郁的，悲伤的
	n.	忧郁
decline /di'klain/	n.	a process or period of becoming weaker, smaller or less satisfactory 衰败，衰落；下降
	vi.	下倾；衰退；拒绝
	vt.	拒绝
conclusion /kən'kluːʒən/	n.	a belief or opinion that you reach after considering sth. carefully 结论；结尾；缔结
failure /'feiljə/	n.	not being successful 失败；失败者；失灵；<美>不及格
initial /i'niʃəl/	a.	at the beginning, first 最初的，初始的
	n.	词首大写字母
recreation /ˌrekri'eiʃ(ə)n/	n.	enjoying yourself and relaxing when you are not working 消遣，娱乐
maturity /mə'tjuəriti/	n.	成熟

Part B

Extensive Reading

routine /ruːˈtiːn/		n.	your usual way of doing things 例行公事，常规，日常事务
		a.	例行的，常规的
departure /diˈpɑːtʃə/		n.	an action which is different from what is usual or expected 背离；启程，出发，离开
sufficient /səˈfiʃənt/		a.	as much or as many as you need or want, enough 充分的，足够的

PHRASES

turn into	to enter 走进
catch one's eye	to attract sb.'s attention 吸引某人的注意
keep sth. up	to not allow (one's spirits, strength, etc.) to decline, to maintain 不让（精力等）衰退，保持
wait upon/on sb.	to act as a servant for sb. 照料或伺候某人
wear off	to disappear or be removed gradually 逐渐消失或除去

EXERCISES

Reading Comprehension

Task 1

Complete the following outline with the information from the text.

1. The first three paragraphs of the text describe one of the author's experiences of _____.
2. He was deeply impressed by _____ of a boy clerk working in the sock shop.
3. The author gives a visual picture of how most clerks _____ in paragraph 4.
4. One's lack of interest _____ can result in harmful consequences.
5. The author has concluded that doing things mechanically will surely _____.
6. The real difficulty lies in _____ the initial enthusiasm.
7. A man's chief happiness should lie in his _____ or the routine itself.
8. It is suggested in the last paragraph that some men only _____ but no happiness all their lives.

253

Unit 8 Enthusiasm for Work

vocabulary

Task 2

Fill in the blanks with the words given below. Make changes where necessary.

| marvelously | grind | decline | initial | conclusion | routine | accidental | delay |
| solemn | holy | mystery | initial | mechanical | recreation | departure | |

1. What do you do for _____?
2. Despite years of study, sleepwalking remains a _____.
3. Her _____ face told us that the news was bad.
4. The fire began shortly after 1:30 a.m. and appears to have been _____.
5. The company did not have _____ funds to pay for the goods it had received.
6. If you work out a _____ you will get things done more quickly.
7. We came to the _____ that he was right.
8. My _____ reaction was to refuse, but I later changed my mind.
9. As an industrial power, the country is in _____.
10. Our picnic was _____ because of bad weather.
11. Kate came to the hotel for a rest from the daily _____.
12. Thank you for the invitation but I'm afraid I have to _____.

Task 3

Fill in the blanks with the right words. Pay attention to grammatical collocations （语法搭配） or lexical collocations （词义搭配）.

1. aware
   a. I suddenly felt aware _____ somebody watching me.
   b. I am aware _____ you will face difficulties.
   c. People's awareness _____ healthy eating has increased in recent years.

2. conclusion
   a. We _____ to the conclusion that Mike was right.
   b. The jury reached the conclusion _____ the men were guilty.
   c. _____ conclusion, I would like to wish you continued success in the future.

3. grind
   a. He sometimes grinds his _____ during his sleep.
   b. This mill grinds wheat into _____.
   c. Karen came to the hotel for a rest from the _____ grind.

4. mystery
   a. Detectives are still trying to solve the mystery _____ his disappearance.
   b. It is a mystery _____ me why she married him in the first place!
   c. The case is shrouded (隐藏) _____ mystery.
5. failure
   a. Mary was upset by her failure _____ the exam.
   b. I was very disappointed at his failure _____ come to the meeting.
   c. Martin is a failure _____ a businessman.

Part C  Reading Skill

Inferring the Author's Views and Attitudes

Inferring the views and attitudes of an author is a difficult skill. A reader often has to be able to work out what the author's views and attitudes are, particularly since they are not always directly stated. An author's attitude will be determined by his purpose. It could be serious, sympathetic, angry, positive, neutral, suspicious, critical, negative, etc. And the tone of a passage could be emotional, personal, optimistic, calm, amused, serious, happy, humorous, etc.

A question which asks the reader to determine the author's view or attitude could be stated in any of these ways:

1. The author's attitude toward...is _____.
2. The author gives the impression that _____.
3. The author suggests/thinks that _____.
4. The tone of the passage can be best described as _____.
5. Which of the following can best describe the author's attitude toward ...?
6. The author's point of view is _____.

Unit 8 Enthusiasm for Work

EXERCISES

Read the following passages and choose the best answer to each question.

Passage 1

To the Editor:

   I pay a good amount of my income in taxes. I think I have a right to be able to get out of my driveway the day after a snowstorm. Why pay taxes if you can't depend on getting satisfactory service from them?

1. This author's tone would be best described as _____.
   a. angry   b. serious   c. bored   d. happy

Passage 2

   You shop for credit the way you shop for anything else. It's best to shop at more than one place. And it's best to know what to look for. A typical household with a good credit rating can save enough for an annual vacation by shopping for the money it "rents" in order to buy now and play later.

   Here are some pointers to help you shop for money for installment buying through credit cards. This article will not deal with financing a home or other real property.

2. The author _____.
   a. wants to save your money
   b. doesn't approve of credit buying
   c. is personally in debt
   d. wants to loan money

3. The author thinks that _____.
   a. you should not buy on credit
   b. you should shop for credit
   c. all people should have the same credit rating
   d. credit ratings are not accurate

Passage 3

   Throughout human history there have been many social prohibitions concerning watching other people eat or eating in the presence of others. There have been attempts to explain these social prohibitions in terms of inappropriate social relationships either between those who are involved and those who are not simultaneously involved in the satisfaction of a bodily need, or between those who already had their meals and those who appear to be shamelessly stuffing themselves with food. Undoubtedly such elements exist in the social prohibitions, but there is an additional element with a much more fundamental importance. In prehistoric times, when food was so precious and the on-lookers so hungry, not to offer half of the little food one had was unthinkable, since every glance was an eager request for life. Further, during those times, people existed in nuclear or extended family groups, and the sharing of food was quite literally supporting one's family or, by extension, preserving one's self.

4. If the argument in the passage is logical, social prohibitions against eating in the presence of others who are not eating would be LEAST likely in a society that _____.
   a. emphasized the value of privacy
   b. emphasized the need to share personal possessions
   c. discouraged yielding too much to one's desires
   d. had always had a plentiful supply of food

5. According to the passage, the author believes that past attempts to explain some social prohibitions concerning eating are _____.
   a. unimaginative   b. unreasonable
   c. incomplete   d. unclear

Glossary

aback /ə'bæk/	ad.	向后地 3BI
abandon /ə'bændən/	vt.	丢弃，离弃，抛弃；放弃 4A
ability /ə'biliti/	n.	能力，才能 1A,6BII
absent /'æbsənt/	a.	缺席，不在；心不在焉的 7BI
absent-minded /'æbsənt'maindid/	a.	心不在焉的，茫然的 7BI
absent-mindedly	ad.	心不在焉地，茫然地 7BI
absolute /'æbsəlu:t/	a.	绝对的，完全的；不受任何限制的 6BII,8A
academically /ˌækə'demikli/	ad.	学术上，学问上 6BI
acceptance /ək'septəns/	n.	接受，接纳，承认；容忍 1A
accidental /ˌæksi'dentl/	a.	意外的，偶然的 8BII
accomplish /ə'kɔmpliʃ/	vt.	完成，达到，实现 8A
accuse /ə'kju:z/	vt.	控告，谴责，非难 2BII
acknowledge /ək'nɔlidʒ/	vt.	承认，确认；报偿 2BII
acquaintance /ə'kweintəns/	n.	相识，熟人 3BI
acquire /ə'kwaiə/	vt.	学到，取得，获得 1BI,7A
acquisitive /ə'kwizitiv/	a.	渴望得到的 7A
action /'ækʃən/	n.	行为；行动；作用；情节 3BII,4BII
activity /æk'tiviti/	n.	活动，行动；活跃，活力 1A
adequate /'ædikwət/	a.	充足的，足够的；适当的，胜任的 4BI
adjust /ə'dʒʌst/	vt.	校准，调整；调节 2A
	vi.	(*to*) 适应 2A
adjustment /ə'dʒʌstmənt/	n.	调整，调节器 2A
★ *administer* /əd'ministə/	v.	管理，给予；执行 2BII
administrator /əd'ministreitə/	n.	管理人，行政官 2BII
admission /əd'miʃən/	n.	允许进入，入场费；供认 2BII
★ *aerial* /'ɛəriəl/	n.	天线 5BI
affection /ə'fekʃən/	n.	爱，感情 4BII
agency /'eidʒənsi/	n.	作用，手段；代理行；专业行政部门 2A
airy /'ɛəri/	a.	空气的，空中的，通风的 7BI
alcohol /'ælkəhɔl/	n.	酒精，酒 6BI

alike /ə'laik/	a.	相似的，同样的 1BII	
	ad.	相似地；同样程度地 1BII, 5BI	
★allege /ə'ledʒ/	vt.	宣称，断言 3BI	
allowance /ə'lauəns/	n.	津贴，补助 2A	
alone /ə'ləun/	a.	单独的，独一无二的，孤独的，独自的 4A	
aloneness /ə'ləunis/	n.	孤独 4A	
aloof /ə'lu:f/	a.	冷淡的 3BI	
alteration /ɔ:ltə'reiʃən/	n.	改变；改动 5BII	
alternative /ɔ:l'tə:nətiv/	a.	两者择一的，供选择的，供替代的 1A	
	n.	取舍，抉择；选择的自由 1A, 2A	
amaze /ə'meiz/	vt.	使吃惊 2A	
amazement /ə'meizmənt/	n.	惊愕，惊异 2A	
ambassador /æm'bæsədə/	n.	大使 3BI	
announcer /ə'naunsə/	n.	广播员，报幕员 8BI	
anticipate /æn'tisipeit/	n.	预料，期望 7BI	
anxiety /æŋ'zaiəti/	n.	焦虑，挂念；渴望，热望 5A	
apart /ə'pɑ:t/	ad.	相间隔；分离，分开 4A	
	a.	分离的，分隔的 4A	
apart /ə'pɑ:t/	ad.	（空间、时间）成距离，相间隔；分离，分开 6BI	
	a.	分离的，分隔的 6BI	
apathetic /æpə'θetik/	a.	缺乏兴趣的，缺乏感情的 8BII	
apparent /ə'pærənt/	a.	显然的，外观上的 3A	
apparently /ə'pærəntli/	ad.	显然地 3A	
appealingly /ə'pi:liŋli/	ad.	上诉地，哀求地 2A	
appearance /ə'piərəns/	n.	出现，露面；外观，外貌 7BI	
appetising /'æpitaiziŋ/	a.	美味可口的，促进食欲的 7BI	
appetite /'æpitait/	n.	欲望（尤指食欲）5BI	
applaud /ə'plɔ:d/	v.	鼓掌 7A	
applause /ə'plɔ:z/	n.	鼓掌欢迎，欢呼 8BI	
applicant /'æplikənt/	n.	申请人 1BI	
application /æpli'keiʃən/	n.	申请，申请表；应用，实施；敷用，涂抹 1BI	
appoint /ə'pɔint/	vt.	任命，委派；约定，指定（时间、地点）7BII	
appropriate /ə'prəupriit/	a.	适当的 2BII	
architectural /ɑ:ki'tektʃərəl/	a.	建筑上的，建筑学的 3A	
argument /'ɑ:gjumənt/	n.	争论，争吵，辩论；理由，论据；说理，论证 3BI	

arise /əˈraiz/ (arose /əˈrəuz/)	v.	出现；起身 5BII
arrest /əˈrest/	vt./n.	逮捕，拘留 7BII
★arrogant /ˈærəgənt/	a.	傲慢的，自大的 3BI
asparagus /əsˈpærəgəs/		芦笋 7BI
aspect /ˈæspekt/	n.	（问题等的）方面；方向；面貌 3BI
assertion /əˈsəːʃən/	n.	主张，断言，声明 1BI
association /əˌsəusiˈeiʃən/	n.	协会，社团；联合，交往 5BI
assure /əˈʃuə/	vt.	断然地说，确告，保证，担保 7BI
astonish /əsˈtɔniʃ/	vt.	使惊讶 5A
▲astronaut /ˈæstrənɔːt/	n.	宇航员，太空人 3BII
athlete /ˈæθliːt/	n.	运动员，运动选手 8A
athletic /æθˈletik/	a.	运动的 2BI, 8BII
attorney /əˈtəːni/	n.	（美）律师 5BII
★authoritative /ɔːˈθɔritətiv/	a.	权威性的，可信的；专断的，命令式的 6BII
auto /ˈɔːtəu/	n.	[infml] an automobile 6BII
automobile /ˈɔːtəməˌbiːl/	n.	汽车 6BII
★aviation /ˌeiviˈeiʃən/	n.	航空，飞行；飞机制造业 1A
awaken /əˈweikən/	vt.	唤醒，觉醒 7A
aware /əˈwɛə/	a.	知道的，明白的，意识到的 3BII, 8BII
backstab /ˈbækstæb/	v.	以卑鄙的手段陷害 2BII
bar /bɑː/	n.	酒吧间；售酒的柜台；棒，条；栅，栏；障碍 7A
	vt.	阻止，拦阻 7A
bare /bɛə/	a.	赤裸的，光秃秃的；仅仅的，勉强的 7A
	v.	露出，暴露 7A
barefoot /ˈbɛəfut/	a.	赤脚的 7A
barely /ˈbɛəli/	ad.	仅仅，只不过，几乎不 7BI, 8BI
baseball /ˈbeisbɔːl/	n.	棒球，棒球运动 8BI
bat /bæt, bɑːt/	n.	球棒；蝙蝠 3BI
	v.	用球棒击球 3BI
beam /biːm/	v.	面露喜色；播送 8A
	n.	梁；（光线的）束，笑容 8A
beat /biːt/	n.	警察的规定巡逻路线；某人常走的路 7BII
believer /biˈliːvə/	n.	信徒 8BI
berry /ˈberi/	n.	浆果 2A
bicker /ˈbikə/	vi.	斗嘴 3BI

Glossary

261

		n.	口角 3BI
biological /baiə'lɔdʒikəl/		a.	生物学的 2A
blank /blæŋk/		a.	空白的，空着的；茫然的,无表情的 2BI
		n.	空白；空白处；空白表格 2BI
blankly /blæŋkli/		ad.	茫然地,毫无表情地 5BII
blast /blɑːst/		vt.	（用炸药）炸毁，炸掉；毁灭 7A
		n.	炸毁，炸掉；毁 7A
blasted /'blæːstid/		a.	该死的 7A
★ bleak /bliːk/		a.	凄凉的，黯淡的 2BII
▲ bless /bles/		vt.	求神赐福于，祝福 7BII
blessing /'blesiŋ/		n.	祝福 8BI
blouse /blauz/		n.	（妇女的）罩衫，宽大的短外套 2BI
blur /bləː/		v.	（使）变模糊 6A
		n.	模糊，模糊的东西 6A
★ booth /buːθ/		n.	（隔开的）小房间，公用电话亭；货摊，售货亭 1BII
★ botany /'bɔtəni/		n.	植物学 2A
boundary /'baundəri/		n.	边界，界线 1A
bound /baund/		a.	受约束的，有义务的；一定的，必然的；准备到……去的，开往（或驶往）……的 6A
		vi.	跳跃，跳跃着前进，弹回 6A
		vt.	成为……的界线，给……划界 6A
		n.	跳跃；界限，限制 6A
bow /bəu/		n.	蝴蝶结 4BII
bow /bau/		v.	鞠躬，弯腰 5BI
		n.	鞠躬 5BI
★ brace /breis/		vt.	支住，撑牢 3BI
		n.	支柱 3BI
breast /brest/		n.	胸部，乳房 8A
broach /brəutʃ/		vt.	开始讨论，提出 3BI
broadcast /'brɔːdkɑːst/		n.	广播，播音；广播节目 8BI
		v.	广播 8BI
broadcaster /'brɔːdkɑːstə/		n.	广播员 8BI
★ bronze /brɔnz/		n.	青铜色 14BII
★ bruiser /'bruːzə/		n.	彪形大汉，粗壮的人 6A
bug /bʌg/		n.	小虫，臭虫 8BI

		v.	装置窃听器，打扰 8BI
Bugs and Mars		n.	缺点与不足 8BI
burden	/'bəːdən/	n.	担子，负担 4A
buzzer — beaters		n.	比赛结束前的最后投篮 8BI
calculate	/'kælkjuleit/	v.	计算，核算；估计，推测；计划，打算 4BII
calculation	/kælkju'leiʃən/	n.	计算；估计 4BII
camel	/'kæməl/	n.	骆驼 1BII
campaign	/kæm'pein/	n.	运动；战役 3BI
		vi.	参加活动 3BI,5BI
campus	/'kæmpəs/	n.	校园 2BII
cancer	/'kænsə/	n.	癌，毒瘤 8A
candy	/'kændi/	n.	糖果 1BII
capture	/'kæptʃə/	vt.	夺得，占领；俘房，捕获 1BI
		n.	俘获，捕获 1BI
capybara	/ˌkæpi'bɑːrə/	n.	水豚 7A
cargo	/'kɑːgəu/	n.	（船、飞机或车辆所载的）货物 1BII
carpenter	/'kɑːpintə/	n.	木匠 6BII
cassette	/kə'set/	n.	盒式录音带 5BI
casual	/'kæʒuəl/	a.	偶然的，碰巧的；随便的，非正式的；临时的 7BI
casually	/'kæʒuəli/	ad.	偶然地，随便地，临时地 7BI
caviare	/'kæviɑː/	n.	鱼子酱 7BI
cell	/sel/	n.	细胞；单人房间；电池 2A
certificate	/sə'tifikit/	n.	证（明）书 4A
challenge	/'tʃælindʒ/	n.	挑战 2BII,8BI
		vt.	向……挑战 8BI
★champagne	/ʃæm'pein/	n.	香槟酒 7BI
champion	/'tʃæmpjən/	n.	冠军；捍卫者，拥护者 3BII
championship	/'tʃæmpjənʃip/	n.	锦标赛 8BI
character	/'kæriktə/	n.	性格，品质；特性；特征；人物；角色；符号；(汉)字 3A
charity	/'tʃæriti/	n.	救济金，施舍物；慈善团体；慈悲，慈善 5BII
charm	/tʃɑːm/	n.	吸引力；给人快感之能力 4A，7BI
charming	/'tʃɑːmiŋ/	a.	迷人的，娇媚的 7BI
cheat	/tʃiːt/	v.	欺骗，骗取，作弊 2BII
		n.	欺骗，骗子 2BII

cheerily	/'tʃiərili/	ad.	快活地，兴高采烈地 2A
childhood	/'tʃaildhud/	n.	孩童时期 3A
childlike	/'tʃaildlaik/	a.	孩子似的，天真烂漫的 5BI
choke	/tʃəuk/	v.	使窒息，呛；塞满，塞住 6A
chop	/tʃɔp/	vt.	砍，劈，斩 7BI
		n.	排骨 7BI
cite	/sait/	vt.	引用；传唤；表彰 2BII
★clasp	/klɑ:sp/	v.	扣子，钩；握，抱住 3BII,4BII
classification	/ˌklæsifi'keiʃən/	n.	分类，分级 4BI
classify	/'klæsifai/	vt.	把……分类，把……分级 1A
closet	/'klɔzit/	n.	(壁) 橱 4BII
★coalition	/ˌkəuə'liʃən/	n.	同盟；结合 3BI
coffin	/'kɔfin/	n.	棺材，灵柩 7A
▲colossal	/kə'lɔsl/	a.	巨大的 6A
column	/'kɔləm/	n.	专栏（文章）；柱，圆柱；直行 5BI
commercial	/kə'mə:ʃəl/	a.	商业的，商务的 1A
		n.	商业广告 1A
★commodity	/kə'mɔditi/	n.	商品，货物 6A
community	/kə'mju:niti/	n.	团体，界；社区，社会；（动植物的）群落 1A
compete	/kəm'pi:t/	vi.	比赛，竞争 4A
competition	/ˌkɔmpi'tiʃən/	n.	竞争，竞赛 2BII,8BI
competitive	/kəm'petitiv/	a.	竞争的 3BI,8BI
competitor	/kəm'petitə/	n.	竞争者 8BI
complain	/kəm'plein/	v.	抱怨；控告 3A
complaint	/kəm'pleint/	n.	抱怨，怨言；控告，申诉 4BI
compose	/kəm'pəuz/	v.	组成；创作（乐曲、诗歌等）；使平静，使镇静 1A
▲comprehend	/ˌkɔmpri'hend/	vt.	理解 1A
concept	/'kɔnsept/	n.	观念，概念 3A
★conception	/kən'sepʃən/	n.	构想，设想，思想，观念，概念 3A
concern	/kən'sə:n/	vt.	使关心；涉及 2A
		n.	关切的事；关心；关系；企业 2A
concerned	/kən'sə:nd/	a.	关心的 2A
conclude	/kən'klu:d/	v.	结束；推断出 5BII
conclusion	/kən'klu:ʒən/	n.	结论，结尾；缔结 8BII
condescension	/ˌkɔndi'senʃən/	n.	高傲的态度 7A

Glossary

conduct /ˈkɔndʌkt, -dəkt/	v.	进行，管理；引导 2BII	
	n.	行为，举止；管理 2BII	
confidence /ˈkɔnfidəns/	n.	信心；信任 2BI	
conflict /ˈkɔnflikt/	n.	冲突，争论，抵触 4A	
/kənˈflikt/	vt.	相反，抵触，冲突 4A	
confuse /kənˈfjuːz/	vt.	搞乱，使糊涂 2BI, 5A	
confused /kənˈfjuːzd/	a.	困惑的，烦恼的 2BI, 5A	
confusion /kənˈfjuːʒən/	n.	混乱，模糊 3A	
congratulate /kənˈgrætjuleit/	vt.	祝贺，向……道喜 7A	
constitute /ˈkɔnstitjuːt/	vt.	建成，组成；设立 3A	
consultant /kənˈsʌltənt/	n.	顾问；会诊医生 6BI	
consumer /kənˈsjuːmə/	n.	消费者，用户 3BII	
contact /ˈkɔntækt/	vt.	与……取得联系，与……接触 1BI	
	n.	接触，联系；熟人，社会关系；（电路的）触点，接头 1BI, 3A	
▲contentedly /kənˈtentidli/	ad.	满足地，满意地 6BII	
contest /ˈkɔntest; kənˈtest/	n.	竞赛 8BI	
	v.	争夺；辩驳 8BI	
context /ˈkɔntekst/	n.	背景，环境；语境，上下文 3BII	
convenience /kənˈviːnjəns/	n.	方便，合宜；便利设施 1A	
convince /kənˈvins/	vt.	使确信，使信服 2BII, 8BII	
★counterpart /ˈkauntəpɑːt/	n.	与对方地位相当的人，与另一方作用相当的物 1BI	
countless /ˈkautlis/	a.	无数的，数不尽的 8A	
county /ˈkaunti/	n.	县，郡 8A	
cranberry /ˈkrænbəri; ˈkrænberi/	n.	酸果蔓的果实 4A	
▲crease /kriːs/	n.	皱折 5BI	
	v.	（使）起皱折 5BI	
creature /ˈkriːtʃə/	n.	动物；人 7A	
creep /kriːp/	vt.	悄悄地或小心地移动	
	vi.	(crept, crept) 蔓延，爬行 4BII, 7A	
critic /ˈkritik/	n.	批评家，评论家 8BI	
crucial /ˈkruːʃiəl, ˈkruːʃəl/	a.	至关紧要的 8A	
crush /krʌʃ/	vt.	压垮；压碎 8BI	
curb /kəːb/	n.	（街道或人行道的）路缘，路边；控制，约束 6A	
	vt.	控制，约束 6A	

curiosity /ˌkjuəriˈɔsiti/	n.	珍品；好奇心 5BII
curriculum /kəˈrikjuləm/	n.	课程，(学校等的) 全部课程 6BI
curve /kəːv/	n.	曲线，弧线，弯曲 7A
	vt.	使弯曲
cynicism /ˈsinisizəm/	n.	愤世嫉俗，玩世不恭 5BI
daisy /ˈdeizi/	n.	雏菊 5A
deaf /def/	a.	聋的，听力不佳的，不愿意听的 6BII
decisive /diˈsaisiv/	a.	决定性的；坚定的，果断的 4BII
decisiveness /diˈsaisivnis/	n.	决定性；坚定 4BII
decline /diˈklain/	v.	下降，减少，衰落；谢绝 4BII
	n.	下降，减少，衰落 4BII, 8BII
▲ *defer* /diˈfəː/	vt.	推迟，延期 2A
	vi.	听从，服从 2A
deferred	a.	延期的，缓召的 2A
define /diˈfain/	vt.	给……下定义，解释；限定，规定 6BI
definitely /ˈdefinitli/	ad.	明确地，干脆地 8BI
deign /dein/	vi.	屈尊 8BII
delightful /diˈlaitful/	a.	令人愉快的，可喜的 5A
democratic /ˌdeməˈkrætik/	a.	民主的，有民主精神的 3BI
demonstrate /ˈdemənstreit/	vt.	显示，表露；论证，证明；说明，演示 1BI
	vi.	举行示威游行 (或集会) 1BI
denial /diˈnaiəl/	n.	否认，否定；拒绝 4A, 5BII
deny /diˈnai/	vt.	否认；拒绝给予，拒绝……的要求 1A, 4BII
departure /diˈpɑːtʃə/	n.	背离；启程，出发，离开 8BII
dependable /diˈpendəbl/	a.	可靠的 5A
dependent /diˈpendənt/	a.	取决于；(on/upon) 依靠的，依赖的 4BI
deserve /diˈzəːv/	vt.	应受，值得，值得 2BII
despair /disˈpɛə/	n.	绝望 2BI
determination /diˌtəːmiˈneiʃən/	n.	决心，果断 8BI
devise /diˈvaiz/	vt.	发明，策划，想出 6BII
diagnose /ˈdaiəgnəuz/	v.	诊断 8A
digest /daiˈdʒest/	vt.	消化 7BI
digestion /daiˈdʒestʃən/	n.	消化 7BI
dimension /diˈmenʃən/	n.	尺寸，大小；方面 1A
diploma /diˈpləumə/	n.	毕业证书，毕业文凭 2BII

Glossary

diplomacy /di'pləuməsi/	n.	外交 1A
dirt /də:t/	n.	污垢，泥土 5BII
disagree /ˌdisə'gri:/	vi.	不一致，不适宜 3BI
disappoint /ˌdisə'pɔintmənt/	n.	失望 2BI
disarm /dis'ɑ:m, diz-/	vt.	解除武装 3BI
disaster /di'zɑ:stə/	n.	灾难，天灾，灾祸 8A
discomfort /dis'kʌmfət/	n.	不便之处，不适 3A
disguise /dis'gaiz/	vt.	伪装；隐藏 3A
disgust /dis'gʌst/	n.	厌恶 2BI
	v.	使厌恶 2BI
disinformation /disˌinfə'meiʃən/ n.		故意的假情报 3BI
display /di'splei/	vt.	显示，表现；陈列，展览
	n.	陈列，展览，显示 3BI, 8BII
disqualify /dis'kwɔlifai/	vt.	取消……的资格 1BI
distinction /dis'tiŋkʃən/	n.	差别，不同，区分，辨别；优秀 2BI
distinctively /dis'tiŋktivli/	ad.	区别地，独特地 6BI
distinguish /di'stiŋgwiʃ/	v.	区别，辨别，分清 4BII
distinguished /di'stiŋgwiʃt/	a.	卓著的，著名的，高贵的
distribution /ˌdistri'bju:ʃən/	n.	分配，分发；散布 2A
distrust /dis'trʌst/	n.	不信任 5BI
	vt.	不信任 5BI
division /di'viʒən/	n.	分，分开；分配，分担，除（法），部门 3A
divorce /di'vɔ:s/	n.	离婚；脱离 8A
	vt.	使离婚；与……脱离 8A
doll /dɔl/	n.	洋娃娃，玩偶 6A
domestic /də'mestik/	a.	家庭的；国内的；驯服的 3BI
doorbell /'dɔ:bel/	n.	门铃 6A
doorway /'dɔ:wei/	n.	门口 7BII
dot /dɔt/	n.	点，圆点 2A
	vt.	打点于；散布于 2A
doubter /dautə/	n.	怀疑者 8BI
dribble /'dribl/	vt.	带球，运球 8BI
driveway /'draivwei/	n.	车道 1BII
dropout /'drɔpaut/	n.	退学学生，辍学学生 8A
dumb /dʌm/	a.	哑的；（因惊恐等）说不出话的；愚蠢的；沉默的

267

			2A,6BII
dusk	/dʌsk/	n.	薄暮，黄昏 4BII
dye	/dai/	vt.	染 8A
		n.	染料，染色 8A
dysfunctional	/dɪsˈfʌŋkʃənəl/	a.	机能不良的 6BI
ease	/iːz/	n.	悠闲，安逸；不费力
		vt.	缓和，减轻
		vi.	减弱，减轻，放松，灵活地移动 2BII,5BI
economic	/iːkəˈnɔmik/	a.	经济的；经济学的 1A,4A
economical	/iːkəˈnɔmikəl/	a.	节俭的，节约的 4BI
economically	/iːkəˈnɔmikəli/	ad.	节俭地 4BI
economics	/iːkəˈnɔmiks, ˌekə-/	n.	经济学 2A
ecstatically	/eksˈtætikli/	ad.	心醉神迷地，入神地 8BII
effusive	/ɪˈfjuːsiv/	a.	洋溢的 7BI
eggplant	/ˈegplɑːnt/	n.	茄子 1BII
ego	/ˈiːgəu/	n.	自我，自我意识 4A
eighteen	/ˈeiˈtiːn/	a.	十八的，十八个的 3BII,7BII
electrical	/iˈlektrikəl/	a.	电的，电气科学的 2A
electrically	/iˈlektrikəli/	ad.	电力地，有关电地 2A
elementary	/ˌeliˈmentəri/	a.	初级的；基本的 2BII
elsewhere	/ˈelsˈhwɛə/	ad.	在别处 8A
embarrass	/imˈbærəs/	vt.	使不好意思，使尴尬 2A,4BII
embarrassment	/imˈbærəsmənt/	n.	尴尬 4BII
embrace	/imˈbreis/	v.	信奉，拥抱；包含；包围 3BI
		n.	拥抱 3BI,8A
emotional	/iˈməuʃnl/	a.	情感的，情绪的，诉诸情感的 1A
emperor	/ˈempərə/	n.	皇帝 3BII
emphasis	/ˈemfəsis/	n.	强调，重点 2BI,8BII
empower	/imˈpauə/	vt.	使能够；授权与 6BI
encouragingly	/inˈkʌridʒiŋli/	ad.	鼓励地 2A
endearing	/inˈdiəriŋ/	a.	令人钟爱的 8BI
engage	/inˈgeidʒ/	vt.	使从事于，使参加；雇佣 2BII
		vi.	(in) 从事于 2BII
engine	/ˈendʒin/	n.	发动机，引擎；机车，火车头 6A
enlarge	/inˈlɑːdʒ/	vt.	扩大，扩展 4A

Glossary

	vi.	扩大，(on, upon) 详述 4A	
enquire，inquire /in'kwaiə/	*v.*	打听，询问 7A	
inquire after		问起（某人情况），问候 7A	
inquire into		调查，探究 7A	
enrage /in'reidʒ/	*vt.*	激怒 3BI	
entertain /ˌentə'tein/	*v.*	招待，款待；使娱乐 4BI	
entitlement	*n.*	权利 2BII	
equation /i'kweiʃən/	*n.*	方程式,等式 2BI	
error /'erə/	*n.*	错误，差错 1BI	
★ erupt /i'rʌpt/	*vi.*	爆发，突然发生；（火山等）喷发 6BI	
essay /'esei/	*n.*	散文，随笔 1BII,5BII	
essential /i'senʃəl/	*a.*	要素，要点；必需品 1BI,6BI	
establishment /is'tæbliʃmənt/	*n.*	机构，企业；建立，确立 6BI	
estimate /'estimeit/	*n.*	估计，估量；评价，看法 6BII	
	vt.	估计，估量 6BII	
eventually /i'ventjuəli/	*ad.*	终于，最后 1A,3A	
exception /'ikˈsepʃən/	*n.*	例外 1A	
exclaim /iks'kleim/	*v.*	呼喊，惊呼，大声说 7BII	
excursion /ik'skə:ʃən/	*n.*	远足，短途旅行，（集体）游览 5A,8BII	
executive /ig'zekjutiv/	*n.*	主管，高级行政人员 5BI	
	a.	执行的，行政的 5BI	
existence /ig'zistəns/	*n.*	存在，实在，生活，存在物，实在物 5A,7BII	
explore /iks'plɔ:/	*vt.*	仔细察看，探索，探究；探险 1BII,6BII	
extent /iks'tent/	*n.*	程度，范围；广度，宽度 1A	
extremely /iks'tri:mli/	*ad.*	极端地，非常地 3BI	
▲ eyebrow /'aibrau/	*n.*	眉毛 2A,7BII	
fade /feid/	*vi.*	褪色；逐渐消失，变弱 4BII	
failure /'feiljə/	*n.*	失败；失败者；失灵；<美>不及格 2BI,8BII	
faintly /'feintli/	*ad.*	微弱地，朦胧地，模糊地 7BI	
faithful /'feiθful/	*a.*	忠诚的，忠实的；如实的；尽职的；可靠的	
	n.	信徒 4BI,8A	
fancy /'fænsi/	*vt.*	想要，喜欢；想象，设想；猜想，认为 7BI	
	n.	爱好，迷恋；想象力 7BI	
	a.	昂贵的，高档的；别致的，花俏的 7BI	
fare /fɛə/	*n.*	（车、船等）费，票价；饮食，伙；菜单 7BI	

269

fatal /ˈfeitl/	a.	致命的，毁灭性的 4BII
fate /feit/	n.	命运 4BII
★ **feast** /fiːst/	n.	宗教节日；盛宴 4A
	v.	参加宴会；款宴 4A
fee /fiː/	n.	费，酬金 1BI
fertile /ˈfəːˈtail/	a.	肥沃的，丰产的，丰富的 4A
fictional /ˈfikʃənəl/	a.	虚构的，想象的 1A
▲ *fidelity* /fiˈdeliti/	n.	忠实，精确 8A
fierce /fiəs/	a.	凶猛的，残忍的；可怕的；强烈的，猛烈的
fiercely /ˈfiəsli/	ad.	猛烈地，厉害地 4A
file /fail/	v.	提出；排成纵队 8A
	n.	文件，档案；文件夹 8A
finding /ˈfaindiŋ/	n.	[常 *pl.*] 调查（或研究的）结果；（陪审团的）裁决 1BI
fireside /ˈfaiəsaid/	a.	炉边的，亲切的，无拘无束的 4BII
	n.	炉边，家庭 4BII
flash /flæʃ/	n.	闪光，闪烁；（比喻用法）闪现 7BI
	vi.	闪光，闪烁；飞驰，掠过；闪现，闪耀 7BI
flashy /ˈflæʃi/	a.	浮华的 8A
flatten /ˈflætən/	vt.	变平；变单调 4A
★ **flatter** /ˈflætə/	vt.	向……献媚，奉承；使满意，使高兴 7BI
flee /fliː/	v.	逃走，逃避 7A
★ **flush** /flʌʃ/	v.	（使脸）发红；（被）冲洗 5BII
	n.	脸红 5BII
★ **flush** /flʌʃ/	vi.	脸红 4BII,5BII
forbid /fəˈbid/	vt.	禁止，不许 2BII,7BI
formula /ˈfɔːmjulə/	n.	公式；原则；配方 2BI
★ **foul** /faul/	n.	犯规 8BI
frame /freim/	vt.	给……镶框；陷害；制定 5BI
	n.	镜框，框架；构架 5BI
franc /fræŋk/	n.	法郎 7BI
frank /fræŋk/	a.	坦白的，直率的 4BII
frankly	ad.	坦白地，直率地 4BII
freshness	n.	气味清新，精神饱满 5BI
frustrate /frʌsˈtreit/	v.	使感到灰心；挫败，阻挠 2BII

functional /ˈfʌŋkʃənl/	a.	职责的，功能的，机能的；有作用的，有功能的 1A,3A	
fuss /fʌs/	n.	大惊小怪，忙乱，小题大做	
	vi.	小题大做；（为琐事）烦恼，过于忧虑 4A,5A	
gas /gæs/	vt.	用毒气杀伤（人）5BII	
	n.	气体，煤气；汽油 5BII	
gaze /geiz/	n.	凝视，注视 2BI	
	v.	凝视，注视 2BI,4BII	
geographically /ˌdʒiəˈgræfikli/	ad.	地理地 1A	
★ **glare** /glɛə/	v.	发射强光，发出刺眼的光线；怒目而视 7BII	
	n.	强光；怒视，瞪眼；炫耀，张扬 7BII	
★ **gleam** /gliːm/	n.	闪光 7A	
glimpse /glimps/	vt.	一瞥，一看 5A	
★ **gloom** /gluːm/	n.	黑暗 4BII	
gloomily /ˈgluːmili/	ad.	黑暗地 4BII	
gloomy /ˈgluːmi/	a.	黑暗的，昏暗的；沮丧的，愁容满面的 4BII	
glory /ˈglɔːri/	n.	光荣，荣誉 4A	
glorify /ˈglɔːrifai/	vt.	颂扬，美化，使增光 4A	
glorious /ˈglɔːriəs/	a.	光荣的 4A	
glow /gləu/	n.	发光，激情，兴高采烈	
	vi.	发光；发热 5A,8BII	
gob /gɔb/	n.	[pl.] 大量 8A	
golf /gɔlf/	vi.	打高尔夫球 8A	
grab /græb/	vt.	抓取，攫取；赶紧做；抓住（机会）6A	
	vi.	抓住，夺得 6A	
	n.	抓，夺 6A	
grammar /ˈgræmə/	n.	语法（书）1BI	
grand /grænd/	a.	重大的；宏伟的；傲慢的 8A	
grandson /ˈgrændsʌn/	n.	孙子 5BI	
grant /grɑːnt/	vt.	授予；同意	
	n.	拨款，授予物 1BII,6BII	
grateful /ˈgreitfəl/	a.	感激的，感谢的 5A	
grave /greiv/	n.	坟墓 7BI	
	a.	严重的；严肃的，庄严的 7BI	
graveyard /ˈgreivjɑːd/	n.	墓地 7BI	

▲ gravel /'grævəl/		n.	碎石 4BII
grievance /'gri:vəns/		n.	委屈，冤情，不平 8BII
★ grim /grim/		a.	讨厌的，糟糕的；严厉的；严酷的，无情的 4BII
grimly /'grimli/		ad.	不愉快的 4BII
grind /graind/		n.	苦差事；枯燥乏味的工作 8BII
		v.	磨（碎），碾（碎）；折磨 8BII
grocer /'grəusə/		n.	食品杂货商 1BII
▲ gulp /gʌlp/		vi.	哽住 6BI
		vt.	狼吞虎咽地吃，吞咽；大口地吸；抑制，忍住 6BI
		n.	吞咽；一大口（尤指液体）6BI
guy /gai/		n.	家伙，伙计 1BII, 2BII
▲ habitat /'hæbitæt/		n.	（动植物的）栖息地 8A
hallway /'hɔ:lwei/		n.	走廊 6A
▲ hamburger /'hæmbə:gə/		n.	汉堡包；碎牛肉 1BII
hammer /'hæmə/		n.	锤，榔头 6BII
		vt.	锤击，敲打 6BII
handful /'hændful/		n.	少数，少量；一把 1BI
hangdog /'hæŋdɔg/		a.	惭愧的，自觉有罪的 5BII
hardware /'hɑ:dwɛə/		n.	五金器具；（计算机）硬件 5BI, 6BII
harmonious /hɑ:'məunjəs/		a.	和谐的，协调的 3BI
harmony /'hɑ:məni/		n.	协调，融洽 3BI
▲ harp /hɑ:p/		n.	竖琴 7A
harpsichord /'hɑ:psikɔ:d/		n.	大键琴 7A
harsh /hɑ:ʃ/		a.	粗糙的，刺耳的，刺目的；严厉的，严酷的 6BII, 8BI
harshly		ad.	粗糙地，刺耳地 6BII
haste /heist/		n.	急速，匆忙 2A
hastily /'heistili/		ad.	急速地，轻率地 2A
★ hasty /'heisti/		a.	匆忙的，草率的 急忙的 2A
haul /hɔ:l/		v.	拖，拉；拖拉，拖运 8BII
		n.	拖，拉，拖拉 8BII
haunch /hɔ:ntʃ/		n.	腰腿部分 7A
headquarters /'hed,kwɔ:təz/		n.	司令部，指挥部；总部 5BI
heal /hi:l/		v.	治愈，医治 8A
hell /hel/		n.	地狱；极不愉快的经历（或事）1BII

Glossary

★ heritage /ˈheritidʒ/	n.	遗产，传统 1A,4A	
hey /hei/	int.	嗨！（用于引起注意或表示疑问、惊奇、赞许或喜悦）6A	
hind /haind/	a.	后面的 7A	
hint /hint/	n.	暗示，提示，线索 2A	
	v.	暗示 2A	
holy /ˈhəuli/	a.	神圣的，圣洁的 8BII	
homeland /ˈhəumlænd/	n.	祖国，故乡 1A	
honesty /ˈɔnisti/	n.	诚实，正直 4BII	
▲ hood /hud/	n.	车盖，引擎罩；风帽；排风罩 6A,6BII	
hoop /huːp/	n.	篮筐 8BI	
hopeful /ˈhəupful/	a.	怀有希望的，有希望的 2A	
hopefully	ad.	有希望地，有前途地 2A	
horrible /ˈhɔrəbl/	a.	可怕的，恐怖的；讨厌的 5A,7BI	
horsehair /ˈhɔːsheə/	n.	马毛，马毛织品 1BII	
hospitable /ˈhɔspitəbl/	a.	殷勤的 7BI	
housebound /ˈhausbaund/	a.	不能离家的 8A	
hubbub /ˈhʌbʌb/	n.	吵闹声，喧哗 5BII	
humanitarian /hjuːˌmæniˈteəriən/	n.	人道主义者，慈善家，博爱主义者 1BII	
humanity /hjuː(ː)ˈmæniti/	n.	博爱，仁慈；人性；人类 8A	
humble /ˈhʌmbl/	a.	简陋的；谦逊的，谦恭的；地位（身份）低下的，卑贱的 5BII	
▲ humiliate /hjuːˈmilieit/	vt.	使蒙羞，羞辱，使丢脸 6A	
humorist /ˈhjuːmərist/	n.	有幽默感的人；幽默作家，滑稽演员 7BI	
hundredfold /ˈhʌndrədfəuld/	a.	百倍的 8A	
	ad.	百倍地 8A	
▲ hurdle /ˈhəːdl/	n.	障碍；跨栏 2BII	
	v.	跳过（栏栅）；克服（障碍）2BII	
▲ hustle /ˈhʌsl/	vi.	催促，催赶 8BI	
	n.	忙碌，奔忙 8BI	
ideal /aiˈdiəl/	a.	理想的，完美的	
	n.	理想 4A,5BI	
idealistic /aidiuˈlistik/	a.	理想主义的，唯心主义的 4A	
ignore /igˈnɔː/	vt.	不顾，不理，忽视 6BI	

273

illustrate	/'iləstreit/	vt.	说明，阐明；图解，加插图于 3BII
imagination	/i,mædʒi'neiʃən/	n.	想象（力）；空想，幻觉 5BI
★imitation	/imi'teiʃən/	n.	模仿，仿制；赝品 2A
▲immortal	/i'mɔːtəl/	a.	不朽的 7BI
imply	/im'plai/	vt.	暗示，意味 5BII
impose	/im'pəuz/	vt.	(on) 把……强加于；征税等，处以（罚款，监禁等）
imposing	/im'pəuziŋ/	a.	使人难忘的，壮丽的 6BII,7BI
impress	/im'pres/	vt.	留下印象；印，盖印 3A,8A
impression	/im'preʃən/	n.	印象，感想；印记，压痕 7BI
improperly	/im'prɔpəli/	ad.	不正确地，不适当地 2BII
inadequate	/in'ædikwət/	a.	不充分的，不适当的 7BI
inappropriate	/inə'prəupriit/	a.	不适当的，不相称的 2BII
incident	/'insidənt/	n.	事件，事变 5BII,8BI
★incidentally	/,insi'dentli/	a.	附属的，随带的；微不足道的 4BI
inclined	/in'klaind/	a.	倾向……的 7BI
incompetent	/in'kɔmpitənt/	a.	不合格的，不胜任的 8BII
increasingly	/in'kriːsiŋli/	ad.	日益，愈加 2BII
incredible	/in'kredəbl/	a.	难以置信的；不能相信的 2BI
index	/'indeks/	n.	索引；标志；[数学] 指数 3BII
		vt.	编入索引中 3BII
indifferent	/in'difrənt/	a.	无关紧要的 4A
individualism	/indi'vidjuəlizəm/	n.	个人主义，利己主义 4A
infinite	/'infinit/	a.	无限的，无穷的 5BI
the Infinite			上帝
initial	/i'niʃəl/	a.	最初的，初始的 8BII
		n.	词首大写字母 8BII
injury	/'indʒəri/	n.	受伤处；伤害 8A
innocent	/'inəsənt/	a.	清白的，无罪的；幼稚的；无害的，没有恶意的 5BII
inquire	/in'kwaiə/	v.	打听，询问；调查，查问 5A
inspiration	/,inspə'reiʃən/	n.	灵感 8BI
instance	/'instəns/	n.	例子，实例，事例 6BII
instantly	/'instəntli/	ad.	立即地，即刻地 2A, 5BII
institute	/'institjuːt/	n.	学会，学院，协会 3BI
		vt.	建立，设立 3BI
insult	/in'sʌlt/	v.	侮辱，辱骂，对人无理 3BII

Glossary

/'insʌlt/	n.	侮辱，凌辱 3BII
interact /intər'ækt/	vi.	互相作用，互相影响 4A
interrelated /intə'rileitid/	a.	互相联系的 3A
interrupt /ˌintə'rʌpt/	vi.	打断，打扰 4BI
	vt.	打断，打扰；中止，阻碍 4BI,8BII
interval /'intəvl/	n.	间隔，间距；幕间休息 5A,7BI
intimacy /'intiməsi/	n.	亲密，隐私 8BII
intimate /'intimit/	a.	亲密的，隐私的
	vt.	暗示 3BI
	n.	密友 3BI
▲intrude /in'truːd/	vi.	侵入，侵扰；打扰 4A
intrusive /in'truːsiv/	a.	打扰的 4A
intuitive /in'tju(ː)itiv/	a.	直觉的 3BI
invisible /in'vizəbl/	a.	看不见的，无形的 1BII,6BI
inwards /'inwədz/	ad.	向内地，向内部地 6BI
irrational /i'ræʃənəl/	a.	不合理的，荒谬的 6BI
irrelevant /i'relivənt/	a.	不相关的 2BI
▲ivy /'aivi/	n.	常春藤 6BI
jail /dʒeil/	n.	监狱 8A
	vt.	监禁 8A
jealous /'dʒeləs/	a.	唯恐失去的；嫉妒的；羡慕的 4BI
jealousy /'dʒeləsi/	n.	妒忌；嫉妒 4BI
juicy /'dʒuːsi/	a.	多汁的；有趣的 7BI
junior /'dʒuːnjə/	n.	（美国大学或中学）三年级学生；年少者；晚辈2BII
	a.	年少的，下级的 2BII
keen /kiːn/	a.	热心的，渴望的；激烈的，强烈的；敏锐的，敏捷的 7BII
label /'leibl/	vt.	将……分类；贴标签于 1A
	n.	标签，标记；称号 1A,3A
laboratory /lə'bɔrətəri;'læbərətɔːri/	n.	实验室 2A
lad /læd/	n.	男孩，小伙子 8BII
lark /lɑːk/	vi.	嬉耍 8BII
latter /'lætə/	a.	后者的；末了的 1A
	n.	后者 1A

laud /lɔːd/	vt.	赞美，称赞	6BI
layout /ˈleiaut/	n.	布局，安排，设计	3A
leader /ˈliːdə/	n.	领导者	5BI
leap /liːp/	v.	跳，跃	2BI
	n.	跳跃；飞跃，跃进	7A
leap /liːp/	vt.	跃过	6A
	vi.	跳、跃，跳动	2BI
	n.	跳，跳跃；激增，骤变	2BI
▲*legacy* /ˈlegəsi/	n.	遗产；遗留下来的东西	4A
legal /ˈliːgəl/	a.	法律的；合法的	3BI
legally /ˈliːgəli/	ad.	法律上，合法地	3BI
legendary /ˈledʒəndəri/	a.	传说中的	5BII
▲*lenient* /ˈliːnjənt/	a.	宽大的，仁慈的，慈悲为怀的	2A
liable /ˈlaiəbl/	a.	可能的；(*for*) 有义务的	8A
lightning /ˈlaitniŋ/	n.	闪电	5A
	a.	闪电似的	5A
likable /ˈlaikəbl/	a.	可爱的	8A
limitless /ˈlimitlis/	a.	无限的，无界限的	2BI
literacy /ˈlitərəsi/	n.	识字，有文化，读写能力	1BI
loan /ləun/	n.	贷款	1BI
	vt.	借出，贷给	1BI
★*locomotive* /ˌləukəˈməutiv/	n.	机车，火车头	2A
	a.	运动的	2A
longtime /ˈlɔŋtaim/	a.	(已持续) 长时间的，为时甚久的	5BI
loose /luːs/	a.	宽松的；不精确的；自由的	2BI
lord /lɔːd/	n.	[the L-] God 上帝；领主，君主；贵族	6BI,7BI
luncheon /ˈlʌntʃən/	n.	午宴，正式的午餐	7BI
★*lure* /luə/	n.	吸引力，趣味	5BI
manageable /ˈmænidʒəbl/	a.	易管理的，便于管理的	8A
manliness /ˈmænlinis/	n.	刚毅	4BII
manly /ˈmænli/	a.	有男人刚强气质	4BII
★*mansion* /ˈmænʃən/	n.	大厦	4BII
▲*mar* /mɑː/	v.	弄坏，毁坏，损害	8BI
	n.	损伤，毁损，障碍	8BI
marine /məˈriːn/	n.	(often M-) 海军陆战队士兵	6A

Glossary

		a.	海洋的，海生的；海军的；海运的，海事的 6A
▲marital /ˈmærɪtl/		a.	婚姻的 3BII
▲marvel /ˈmɑːvəl/		n.	令人惊奇的事物 7BI
marvelous /ˈmɑːvələs/		a.	绝妙的，了不起的 8BII
mastectomy /mæsˈtektəmi/		n.	乳房切除术 8A
mat /mæt/		n.	席子，垫子 1BII
maturity /məˈtjuərɪti/		n.	成熟 8BII
mechanical /mɪˈkænɪkl/		a.	机械似的，呆板的；机械的；力学的 8BII
mechanics /mɪˈkænɪks/		n.	（用作复数）结构；技工；(-s) 机械学、力学 2A
media /ˈmiːdjə/		n.	新闻媒介，传播媒介 1BI
medium /ˈmiːdjəm/		n.	方法，手段；媒体；媒介 2A
		a.	中间的，中等的 2A
▲melancholy /ˈmelənkəli/		a.	忧郁的，悲伤的 8BII
membership /ˈmembəʃɪp/		n.	会员身份；会员数 4A
merchant /ˈmɜːtʃənt/		n.	商人，批发商，贸易商，店主 5BI
		a.	商业的，商人的 5BI
★merge /mɜːdʒ/		v.	合并；结合 5A
messy /ˈmesi/		a.	肮脏的，凌乱的 6BI
microscope /ˈmaɪkrəskəup/		n.	显微镜 2A
milky /ˈmɪlki/		a.	牛奶的，乳状的，乳白色的 2A
★minimize /ˈmɪnɪmaɪz/		vt.	把……估计得最低；使减到最低程度 2BI
mission /ˈmɪʃən/		n.	使命，任务；使团，代表团 8A
mobile /ˈməubaɪl/		a.	运动的，活动的；流动的，机动的；多变的，易变的 6BI
		n.	移动电话 6BI
moderate /ˈmɔdərɪt/		a.	温和的，稳健的，适中的，适度的 7BII
		ad.	适度地 7BII
mohair /ˈməuheə/		n.	安哥拉山羊毛，安哥拉山羊毛仿制品 1BII
moonlight /ˈmuːnlaɪt/		n.	月光 7A
moose /muːs/		n.	麋（长有粗毛及厚角的一种大鹿，产于北美洲森林地带，北欧及北亚，在北欧及北亚被称为elk）1BII
motion /ˈməuʃən/		n.	运动，动作；手势；提议 3BII
		v.	示意 3BII,6BII
▲motto /ˈmɔtəu/		n.	座右铭 5BI
mouthful /ˈmauθˌful/		n.	一口，满口 7BI

multimillionaire /ˌmʌltiˌmiljə'neə/		n.	拥有数百万家财的富翁，大富豪 6BI
multiply /'mʌltipli/		v.	增加，繁殖；乘 8A
★ mutter /'mʌtə/		v.	轻声低语，咕哝 2BI
▲ mutton /'mʌtn/		n.	羊肉 7BI
mystery /'mistəri/		n.	神秘；神秘的事物 8BII
mystify /'mistifai/		vt.	使迷惑；使困惑 5A
nasty /'næsti/		a.	令人厌恶的；困难的；恶劣的 8A
nativity /nə'tiviti/		n.	出生，[the N-] 耶稣诞生 6BI
negative /'negətiv/		a.	反面的，消极的；否定的；负的，阴性的 6BI
neighborhood /'neibəhud/		n.	邻近地区，附近；四邻，街坊 1A,2BII
nevertheless /ˌnevəð'les/		conj.	然而，不过 2BI
		ad.	仍然，不过 1BII,2BI
nevertheless /ˌnevəð'les/		ad.	然而，虽然如此，依然 1BII
★ nickname /'nikneim/		n.	诨号，绰号，昵称 8BI
notebook /'nəutbuk/		n.	笔记本 2BI
notion /'nəuʃn/		n.	观念，意见 4A
nourish /'nʌriʃ/		vt.	怀有（希望，仇恨等）；滋养，使健壮 8BII
novelist /'nɔvəlist/		n.	小说家 2BI
★ novelty /'nɔvəlti/		n.	新奇感；新奇的事物 8BII
nowhere /'nəuhweə/		ad.	无处，到处都无 2BII
nurturant /'nɜːtʃərənt/		a.	养育的 4BI
nurture /'nɜːtʃə/		vt.	养育；教养 4BI
observer /əb'zɜːvə/		n.	观测者，观察员 5BI
obstacle /'ɔbstəkl/		n.	障碍，阻碍，干扰 2BI
obviously /'ɔbviəsli/		ad.	明显地，显而易见地 1A,2BI
occasion /ə'keiʒən/		n.	场合；时机，机会 5BII
		vt.	引起 5BII,8BII
occupational /ˌɔkju'peiʃənl/		a.	职业的；占领的 6BI
odd /ɔd/		a.	奇特的；临时的；单数的 3BI,6BI
ode /əud/		n.	颂歌 2BI
offhand /'ɔːfhænd/		ad.	立即 5A
		a.	随便的 5A
oppose /ə'pəuz/		vt.	反对，反抗 3BI
★ optimism /'ɔptimizəm/		n.	乐观，乐观主义 5BI

Glossary

organization /ˌɔːgənaiˈzeiʃən/	n.	组织；机构，团体 3A	
outline /ˈautlain/	vt.	略述，描画轮廓 2BII	
	n.	要点，概要；轮廓，外形 2BII	
outsider /autˈsaidə/	n.	外来者，外人 3A	
outstanding /autˈstændiŋ/	a.	突出的，显著的，未解决的 2A	
overcome /ˌəuvəˈkʌm/	vt.	战胜，克服；（感情等）压倒 2BI	
overload /ˈəuvəˈləud/	vt.	使超载，超过负荷 7BI	
	n.	超载，负荷过多 7BI	
overlook /ˌəuvəˈluk/	vt.	俯瞰，俯视，忽略，看漏；宽容 1BII,7BI	
overrate /ˈəuvəˈreit/	vt.	估计（估价）过高 6BI	
oversee /ˈəuvəˈsiː/	vt.	监视，监督 1BII	
overshadow /ˌəuvəˈʃædəu/	vt.	遮蔽，使蒙上阴影 5A	
★ overwhelming /ˌəuvəˈwelmiŋ/	a.	巨大的；势不可挡的 8A	
owner /ˈəunə/	n.	所有者，业主 3BI	
painful /ˈpeinfəl/	a.	困难的，令人不快的；疼痛的，引起疼痛的 2BI	
painless /ˈpeinlis/	a.	无痛的，不痛的 8A	
palate /ˈpælit/	n.	味觉 7BI	
panic /ˈpænik/	n.	恐慌，惊慌，慌乱 6A	
	v.	（使）恐慌，（使）惊慌失措 6A,7BI	
parade /pəˈreid/	n.	游行；检阅 4BII	
	v.	（使）列队行进，（在……）游行 4BII	
★ paradox /ˈpærədɔks/	n.	逆说，反论（如"欲速则不达"）；自相矛盾的人（或事物）1BII	
pardonable /ˈpɑːdənəb(ə)l/	a.	可原谅的，难怪的 7BI	
parkway /ˈpɑːkwei/	n.	公路，大路，林阴干道，风景区干道 1BII	
partner /ˈpɑːtnə/	n.	伙伴，合伙人；配偶 3BI	
passport /ˈpɑːspɔːt/	n.	护照 8BI	
paste /peist/	vt.	粘，贴 2BII	
	n.	糊，浆糊 2BII	
pat /pæt/	v./n.	轻拍，轻打 8BI	
	a.	非常恰当的，适时的 8BI	
patio /ˈpɑːtiəu,ˈpætiəu/	n.	院子，天井 3A	
pave /peiv/	vt.	铺砌 4A	
pavement /ˈpeivmənt/	n.	[BrE.]人行道 4A	
peach /piːtʃ/	n.	桃；年轻貌美的女子 4BII,7BI	

279

perception /pə'sepʃən/	n.	感觉，知觉；认识，观念，看法 1A
pessimism /'pesimizəm/	n.	悲观（主义）5BI
pessimistic /ˌpesi'mistik/	a.	悲观的 5BI
phenomenon /fi'nɔminən/	n.	现象 2BII
phone /fəun/	n.	电话，电话机；听筒，耳机 6BI
	v.	打电话（给）6BI
physical /'fizikəl/	a.	身体的；物质的，自然的；物理的 8BI
	n.	体格检查 3A,8BI
pine /pain/	n.	松树 1BII
	vi.	(away)（因悲哀等）消瘦，衰弱，憔悴；(for) 渴望，思念 1BII
▲*pineapple* /'painæpl/	n.	菠萝 1BII
placement /'pleismənt/	n.	放置，布置 2BI
plagiarize /'pleidʒiəraiz/	v.	剽窃，抄袭 2BII
▲*plank* /plæŋk/	a.	厚木板 5BII
playoff /'pleiˌɔːf/	n.	季后赛 8BI
★*plea* /pliː/	n.	恳求，请求；辩护；借口 8A
plead /pliːd/	v.	恳求，请求；为……辩护；提出……为理由（或借口）4BII
plural /'pluərəl/	n.	锤击，敲打；复数的 1BII
politician /ˌpɔli'tiʃən/	n.	政治家，政客 3BII
possibility /ˌpɔsi'biliti/	n.	可能（性）；可能的事 4A
potential /pə'tenʃəl/	a.	潜在的，可能的 1BI
	n.	潜力，潜能 1BI
poverty /'pɔvəti/	n.	贫穷，贫困 6BI
★*preach* /priːtʃ/	v.	鼓吹 8A
★*preacher* /'priːtʃə/	n.	说教者，鼓吹者,(尤指) 传教者；讲道者 1BII
precondition /ˌpriːkən'diʃən/	n.	前提，先决条件 2BI
predict /pri'dikt/	vt.	预言，预测，预告 6BI
predominance /pri'dɔminəns/	n.	优势，显著 5BI
★*premise* /'premis/	n.	[*pl.*] 经营场所；前提 3BI
	v.	立前提 3BI
prestigious /ˌpres'tiːdʒəs/	a.	享有声望的，声望很高的 2BII
primacy /'praiməsi/	n.	首位 3BI
primarily /'praimərili/	ad.	首先，起初，主要地，根本上 2BII

primary /'praiməri/	a.	主要的，首要的；最初的 2BII
prince /prins/	a.	王子，亲王 6BI
prior to		在……之前 3A
prior /'praiə/	a.	在前的，预先的；优先的；较重要的 3A
★privacy /'praivəsi/	n.	独处；隐私，私秘 3A
prizefighter /'praiz‚faitə(r)/	n.	职业拳击手 3BII
proceed /prə'si:d/	vi.	进行，继续下去，发生 7BI
★profound /prə'faund/	a.	极深的，深厚的；渊博的；深奥的 2A,8BII
pronouncement /prə'naunsmənt/	n.	声明 6BII
★propel /prə'pel/	vt.	推进，驱使 2A
▲proposition /‚prɔpə'ziʃən/	n.	建议，提议；家伙，事情 7BII
pug /pʌg/	n.	狮子鼻 7BII
★pumpkin /'pʌmpkin/	n.	南瓜 4A
purple /'pə:pl/	a.	紫色的 8A
	n.	紫色 8A
puzzle /'pʌzl/	v.	（使）迷惑，（使）为难，迷惑不解 5A
	n.	题，谜 5A,8A
pyjamas /pi'dʒɑ:məz/	n.	睡衣裤 7A
qualify /'kwɔlifai/	v.	（使）具有资格，（使）合格，2A
★queer /kwiə/	a.	奇怪的，异常的 5A
quicksand /'kwiksænd/	n.	流沙（区）1BII
quit /kwit/	v.	停止，放弃；辞（职）4BI,8A
ramble /'ræmbl/	vt.	漫步；漫谈 4BI
rambling /'ræmbliŋ/	a.	漫无限制的 4BI
rapture /'ræptʃə/	n.	兴高采烈，欢天喜地 8BII
rare /rɛə/	a.	稀罕的；杰出的；（空气等）稀薄的；（肉类）半熟的 5A,6A
rarity /'rɛəriti/	n.	稀有 5BII
rational /'ræʃənl/	a.	理性的，理智的；合理的 6BI
reaction /ri(:)'ækʃən/	n.	反应，反作用，反动（力）3BI
readership /'ri:dəʃip/	n.	读者群 1BI
readjust /‚ri:ə'dʒʌst/	vt.	重新调整，再调整 2A
rear /riə/	n.	后面，背后，后方，屁股 8BII
	a.	后面的，背面的，后方的 8BII
	vt.	培养，饲养，栽种 8BII

★reassure /ˌriːəˈʃuə/	vt.	使安心 7BI
reconsider /ˈriːkənˈsidə/	vt.	重新考虑，重新审议 4BII
recovery /riˈkʌvəri/	n.	恢复，痊愈；追回 8A
recreation /ˌrekriˈeiʃ(ə)n/	n.	消遣，娱乐 8BII
red-hot /ˌredˈhɔt/	a.	炽热的 1BI
ref /ref/	n.	裁判员 8BI
★refuge /ˈrefjuːdʒ/	n.	庇护，避难，避难所 3A
refusal /riˈfjuːzəl/	n.	拒绝，推却 3BI,5BII
register /ˈredʒistə/	vt.	登记，注册；（仪表等）指示，自动记下；表示，表达；注意到，记住；把（邮件）挂号 6BII
	vi.	登记，注册 6BII
	n.	登记，注册；登记表，注册簿 6BII
reinforce /ˌriːinˈfɔːs/	vt.	加强，增援 3BI
release /riˈliːs/	vt.	释放，解放；发布，发行；放开，松开 7A,7BII
relevance /ˈrelivəns/	n.	关联，中肯，适当 2BII,6BI
relief /riˈliːf/	n.	轻松，宽慰；（痛苦等）缓解、减轻；救济，救援；接替，替换 6BI
religion /riˈlidʒən/	n.	宗教，信仰 3BI,3BII
rely /riˈlai/	vi.	依赖，依靠；对……有信心 1A
▲renowned /riˈnaund/	a.	有名的，有声誉的 1BI
replace /riˈpleis/	vt.	代替，取代；把……放回原处 1A,4BI
reprint /ˈriːˈprint/	v.	再版 5BI
reputation /ˌrepju(ː)ˈteiʃən/	n.	名气，名声，名望 5BII
reread /ˈriːˈriːd/	vt.	重读，再读 2BI
resign /riˈzain/	v.	辞职，放弃，辞去；(to) 使顺从 4BII
resort /riˈzɔːt/	vi.	求助，诉诸 3BI
	n.	凭借，手段，常去之地，胜地 3BI
response /risˈpɔns/	n.	回答，响应，反应 2BII
reunion /riːˈjuːnjən/	n.	团圆，重聚 5BII
reveal /riˈviːl/	vt.	展现，显示；揭示，暴露 3A,6BI
★revenge /riˈvendʒ/	n.	报复，报仇 7BI
revolt /riˈvəult/	vi.	起义，造反，反叛 4A
	vt.	使厌恶，使反感 4A
	n.	起义，造反，反叛；厌恶，反感 4A
rodent /ˈrəudənt/	n.	啮齿动物 7A

Glossary

rosy /ˈrəuzi/	*a.*	玫瑰红色的 5BI
routine /ruːˈtiːn/	*n.*	例行公事，常规，日常事务 8BII
	a.	例行的，常规的 8BII
★ *royalty* /ˈrɔiəlti/	*n.*	版税；皇室，王族 5BI
rude /ruːd/	*a.*	粗鲁的，无礼的；粗糙的 3BI
sack /sæk/	*n.*	麻袋，包 7A
	vt.	解雇 7A
sake /seik/	*n.*	缘故，理由 8A
salesman /ˈseilzmən/	*n.*	售货员，推销员 8BII
salesmanship /ˈseilzmənʃip/	*n.*	推销术，销售 8BII
▲ *salmon* /ˈsæmən/	*n.*	沙文鱼，鲑鱼 7BI
sauce /sɔːs; sɔs/	*n.*	调味料 4A
	vt.	给……加味，调味 4A
scale /skeil/	*n.*	等级；大小；[*pl.*] 天平；刻度 2BI
	vt.	攀登 2BI
scandal /ˈskændl/	*n.*	丑行，丑闻；流言蜚语；反感 2BII
★ *scar* /skɑː/	*n.*	伤疤，伤痕；（精神上的）创伤
	v.	（给……）留下伤痕（或创伤）7BII
scholar /ˈskɔlə/	*n.*	学者 6BII
scissors /ˈsizəz/	*n.*	剪子 6BII
scissor /ˈsizə/	*vt.*	剪，剪取 6BII
▲ *scoff* /skɔf/	*v.*	(*at*) 嘲笑，嘲弄 2BI, 8A
★ *scramble* /ˈskræmbl/	*vi.*	爬，攀登；争夺，抢夺 6A
	vt.	扰乱，搞乱 6A
	n.	爬，攀登；争夺，抢夺 6A
screen /skriːn/	*n.*	屏风；遮帘；屏幕 3A
	vt.	遮蔽，隐蔽，掩护 3A
secure /siˈkjuə/	*vt.*	得到，获得；使安全，保卫；缚牢 1BI
	a.	安全的，可靠的，牢固的；安心的 1BI
select /siˈlekt/	*vt.*	选择，挑选 1BI
	a.	精选的；优等的，第一流的 1BI
semester /siˈmestə/	*n.*	学期 2BI
senator /ˈsenətə/	*n.*	参议员 7BI
sensible /ˈsensibəl/	*a.*	合情合理的；切实的；明智的，有判断力的 7BII
sensitivity /ˌsensiˈtiviti/	*n.*	敏感，灵敏（度），灵敏性 6A

★ setback /'setbæk/	n.	挫折，退步，8BI
seventeen /ˌsevən'tiːn/	num.	十七个 8BII
seventy /'sevənti/	num.	七十 2BII
severe /si'viə/	a.	严重的；严厉的；严峻的 8A
★ shabby /'ʃæbi/	a.	衣衫褴褛的；破旧的 5BII
shameful /'ʃeimful/	a.	不体面的 7BI
★ shrewd /ʃruːd/	a.	敏锐的，精明的，机灵的 1BI
sidewalk /'saidwɔːk/	n.	[AmE.] footpath 人行道 3A
signal /'siɡnl/	n.	信号 3BII
	a.	显著的；重大的；信号的 3BII
	v.	发信号 3BII, 7BI
singe /sindʒ/	n.	烧焦，烤焦 1BI
slam-dunk	n.	扣篮 8BI
slap /slæp/	vt.	拍，掌击，拍击 8BI
	n.	拍，掌击，拍击 8BI
sleet /sliːt/	n.	冰雨，雨夹雪 6A
	vi.	下雨雪，下冰雹 6A
sleeve /sliːv/	n.	袖，衣袖 2BI, 8A
slice /slais/	n.	一份，部分；薄片，切片 5A
	vt.	切（片）5A
slim /slim/	a.	（机会）少的，小的；苗条的；薄的 1BII
	v.	（用运动、节食等）减轻体重，变苗条 1BII
▲ smother /'smʌðə/	vt.	抑制 4A
★ snack /snæk/	n.	快餐，小吃，点心 7BI
▲ snarl /snɑːl/	vi.	咆哮，叫着表达；狂吠，嗥叫 6A
	vt.	咆哮着说 6A
	n.	咆哮，怒吼 6A
★ sneak /sniːk/	vi.	偷偷地走，溜 6A
	vt.	偷偷地做（或拿、吃）6A
sneaker /'sniːkə(r)/	n.	运动鞋 8BI
▲ sneeze /sniːz/	vi.	打喷嚏 5A
	n.	喷嚏（声）；打喷嚏 5A
★ soberly /'səubəli/	ad.	严肃地，冷静地 8A
soccer /'sɒkə/	n.	英式足球 8A
sole /səul/	a.	唯一的；独有的 2A, 4BI

Glossary

		n.	鞋底
solely /'səuli/		ad.	只是 2A
solemn /'sɔləm/		a.	庄严的，隆重的；严肃的 8BII
★ solidarity /ˌsɔli'dæriti/		n.	团结 3BI
sophisticated /sə'fistikeitid/		a.	精密的，复杂的，尖端的；老于世故的，老练的 6BII
sorrow /'sɔrəu/		n.	悲哀；悲痛 5A
southeast /'sauθ'i:st/		n./a./ad.	东南；东南的；向东南 3BII
spat /spæt/		vi./n.	争吵 3BI
specimen /'spesimən/		n.	标本，样本 7A
spellbound /'spelbaund/		a.	入迷的，出神的 7A
sphere /sfiə/		n.	范围，领域；球体 1A
split /split/		v.	(使)分裂；劈开；分享 5A
		n.	裂口；分裂 5A
spoil /spɔil/		vt.	损坏，破坏；宠坏，溺爱 1BI
		vi.	(食物)变质 1BI
		n.	[pl.] 战利品，掠夺物，赃物 1BI
spokeswoman /'spəuksˌwumən/		n.	女发言人 1BI
spot /spɔt/		n.	地点，处所；斑点，污点；少量 6A
		vt.	认出，发现；玷污 6A
spouse /spauz/		n.	配偶 6BI
spurt /spə:t/		n.	短促突然的爆发 6BI
stake /steik/		n.	桩，标桩；利害关系；赌本 8A
		vt.	以……打赌 8A
★ stall /stɔ:l/		v.	停止，停顿；拖延 2BI
standardized /'stændəˌdaizd/		a.	标准的，定型的 2BII
★ statesman /'steitsmən/		n.	政治家 3BII
status /'steitəs/		n.	地位，身份；状态，情形 3BII
steady /'stedi/		a.	稳定的，不变的；稳重的 7BII
		v.	(使)平稳，(使)稳定 7BII
★ stern /stə:n/		a.	严厉的，严格的 2A
		n.	船尾
sting /stiŋ/		vt.	刺痛，使痛苦；刺，蛰，叮；激怒 6A
		vi.	刺，蛰，叮；感到剧痛 6A
		n.	(昆虫的)蛰刺；刺痛，剧痛 6A
stir /stə:/		v.	搅动，移动；激起 2A

		n.	惊动，轰动 2A
strengthen	/'streŋθən/	vt.	加强，巩固 1A
stricken	/'strikən/	a.	遭殃的，患病的 5BII
string	/striŋ/	n.	弦；细绳；一串，一行 7A
		vt.	缚，捆 7A
structure	/'strʌktʃə/	n.	结构；建筑物 2A
		vt.	建筑，构成，组织 2A
★stun	/stʌn/	vt.	使晕倒，使惊吓，使目瞪口呆；打晕 3BI
		n.	晕眩，打昏，惊倒 3BI,6A
submerge	/sʌb'məːdʒ/	vt.	浸没，淹没 4A
		vi.	潜入水中 4A
submit	/səb'mit/	vt.	提交；主张
		vi.	(to) 服从，顺从 2BII,5BII
subsection	/'sʌbsekʃən/	n.	分部，分段，小部分 6BII
substance	/'sʌbstəns/	n.	物质；实质，大意 2A
subtle	/'sʌtl/	a.	微妙的；狡猾的；隐约的 3BI
sufficient	/sə'fiʃənt/	a.	足够的，充分的 5A,8BII
sufficiently	/sə'fiʃəntli/	ad.	足够地，充分地 5A
supple	/'sʌpl/	a.	柔软的，灵便的 5BI
supportive	/sə'pɔːtiv/	a.	支持的，支援的 6BI
★suppress	/sə'pres/	vt.	抑制（感情等）；镇压，查禁；阻止……的生长（或发展）6BI
supreme	/sjuː'priːm;suː'priːm/	a.	最高的，至上的；最重要的，极度的 4A
surrender	/sə'rendə/	vi.	投降；屈服于，让步 4BII
		vt.	交出；放弃 4BII
surrounding	/sə'raundiŋ/	n.	环境，周围的事物 3A
survival	/sə'vaivəl/	n.	生存，幸存 4A
survivor	/sə'vaivə/	n.	生还者，残存物 8A
suspect	/səs'pekt/	v.	怀疑；猜想 5BII
		n.	嫌疑犯 5BII
		a.	不可信的，可疑的 5BII
★suspicious	/səs'piʃəs/	a.	可疑的，怀疑的 3BI
swallow	/'swɔləu/	vt.	压制，抑制；吞，咽；轻信，轻易接受 6BI
		vi.	吞，咽 6BI
		n.	燕子；吞，咽 6BI

swear /sweə/	v.	发誓，宣誓；诅咒 2BI	
sweat /swet/	n.	汗 2BI	
	v.	（使）出汗 2BI	
sweetbread /ˈswiːtbred/	n.	[BrE.]（供食用的）牛、羊胰脏 1BII	
sweetmeat /ˈswiːtmiːt/	n.	[BrE.] 甜食，糖果，蜜饯 1BII	
sword /sɔːd/	n.	剑，刀 4BII	
swot /swɔt/	v.	用功读书，死用功 6BI	
▲syllable /ˈsiləbəl/	n.	音节	
tackle /ˈtækl/	n.	（橄榄球比赛中）擒抱对方球员；用具；滑车；辘轳 2A	
	vt.	处理；交涉 2A	
talent /ˈtælənt/	n.	天才，才干，才能 2BI,6BII	
talkative /ˈtɔːkətiv/	a.	多话的，爱说话的，多嘴的 7BI	
tame /teim/	a.	驯服的，温顺的；平淡，乏味的 7A	
	vt.	驯服，制服 7A	
tattoo /təˈtuː, tæˈtuː/	v.	刺花样 8A	
	n.	纹身 8A	
technician /tekˈniʃən/	n.	技师，技术员 3A	
temper /ˈtempə/	n.	脾气；（钢等）韧度 2A	
	v.	调和；回火 2A	
temperamental /ˌtempərəˈmentl/	a.	由于气质的 5BI	
★tempt /tempt/	vt.	引诱，诱惑；说服，劝诱 4A	
tender /ˈtendə/	a.	温柔的；嫩的；疼痛的，一触即痛的 4BII,7BI	
★terrified /ˈterifaid/	a.	恐惧的，受惊吓的 6A	
	n.	商业广告 6A	
★terrify /ˈterifai/	vt.	使害怕，使惊吓 6BI	
territory /ˈteritəri/	n.	领土，版图，（行为、知识等）领域，范围 4A,8A	
terror /ˈterə/	n.	恐怖；引起恐怖的人或事物 5A	
terrorism /ˈterəriz(ə)m/	n.	恐怖主义 3BI	
theory /ˈθiəri/	n.	理论，原理；学说；意见，看法，见解 3BI,4A	
therapist /ˈθerəpist/	n.	队医 8BI	
therapy /ˈθerəpi/	n.	治疗 8A	
threaten /ˈθretn/	vt.	威胁，恐吓；预示（危险）快要来临，是……的征兆 6A	
	vi.	构成威胁，可能发生 6A	

thrust /θrʌst/	vt.	插，挤 7BI	
	vi.	刺，戳 7BI	
	n.	戳，刺；要点，要旨；推力 7BI,8BII	
thrust /θrʌst/	vt.	插入，猛推；冲 8BII	
tide /taid/	n.	潮流，趋势；潮，潮汐 6BI	
timidity /ti'miditi/	n.	怯懦 5BI	
togetherness /tə'geðənis/	n.	团结精神；归属感 4A	
tolerate /'tɔləreit/	vt.	忍受，容忍 4BI	
tome /təum/	n.	册，卷，本；著作 7BII	
topic /'tɔpik/	n.	话题，主题 3BI,3BII	
tradition /trə'diʃən/	n.	传统，惯例 3BI,6BI	
trainee /trei'ni:/	n.	受训者，实习生 1BI	
trainer /'treinə/	n.	训练者，驯服者 8BI	
tremble /'trembəl/	vi./n.	颤抖，哆嗦 4A,7BII	
★ trench /trentʃ/	n.	沟渠，战壕 6A	
trench coat		胶布雨衣 6A	
triangle /'traiæŋgl/	n.	三角组合；[数] 三角形 8BI	
★ tribe /traib/	n.	部落；族（生物分类）1A	
troop /tru:p/	n.	军队，部队；一群，一队，一大批 4BII	
tune /tju:n/	n.	曲子，曲调；和谐，协调 7A	
	vt.	为（乐器）调音；调整 7A	
tune in (to)		收听	
twang /twæŋ/	n.	弦声 7A	
	v.	（使）发弦声 7A	
twirl /twə:l/	v.	（使）快速转动；旋转；（使）卷曲 7BII	
	n.	转动 7BII	
ultimate /'ʌltimit/	a.	最好的，最后的，最终的 8BI	
	n.	极点，顶点 8BI	
unaddressed /'ʌnə'drest/	a.	未被提出商议或解决的 6BI	
uncontrollable /ʌnkən'trəuləbl/	a.	无法控制的 6BI	
undermine /ʌndə'main/	vt.	暗中破坏，逐渐削弱；侵蚀……的基础 1BI	
uneasily /ʌn'i:zili/	ad.	不安地，担心地 2A,6BII	
uneasy /ʌn'i:zi/	a.	心神不安的，担心的 2A	
unemotional /'ʌni'məuʃnl/	a.	不诉诸感情的，不易动感情的，缺乏感情的 6BI	
unfailing /ʌn'feiliŋ/	a.	经久不衰的，无穷尽的，可靠的 5BI	

Glossary

★ unfold /ʌn'fəuld/	v.	展开,打开;显露,展现 7BII
uniformity /juːni'fɔːmiti/	n.	同样,一致,均匀 1A
unlighted /ʌn'laitid/	a.	未被照亮的;未被点燃的 7BII
unlikely /ʌn'laikli/	a.	未必的,不大可靠的 5BI
unreasoning /ʌn'riːzəniŋ/	a.	不用理智的,盲目冲动的,未加思量的 4A
unriddle /'ʌn'ridl/	vt.	解,阐明 8A
unsung /'ʌn'sʌŋ/	a.	未赞颂的 8A
urgently /'əːdʒəntli/	ad.	迫切地,急切地 1BI
utterly /'ʌtəli/	ad.	完全地,绝对地,彻底地 6A
varsity /'vɑːsiti/	n.	大学运动代表队,大学 8BI
vegetarian /ˌvedʒi'teəriən/	n.	素食者 1BII
vehicle /'viːikl/	n.	交通工具,车辆;传播媒介,手段 2A
★ verbal /'vəːbəl/	a.	用言辞的,用文字的;口头的;动词的 3BII,6BII
verbally /'vəːbəli/	ad.	口头上 3BII,6BII
veteran /'vetərən/	n.	老兵,老手,富有经验的人 4BII,5BII
vibrate /vai'breit/	v.	(使)振动,(使)摇摆 7A
view /vjuː/	vt.	看待,观察,观看 2BII
	n.	观点,见解;观察;景色 2BII
vigor /'vigə/	n.	精力;活力 5BI
vindictive /vin'diktiv/	a.	报复的 7BI
violent /'vaiələnt/	a.	猛烈的,剧烈的;暴力引起的 2A
visa /'viːzə/	n.	签证 8BI
visible /'vizəbl/	a.	看得见的,可见的,有形的 1BII
vision /'viʒən/	n.	视力,视觉,视野;想象力,幻想 1A,4A
vital /'vaitl/	n.	[*pl.*] 要害,命脉,主要部件 6BII
	a.	生死攸关的,极其重要的;有生命的,充满生机的 6BII
volunteer /ˌvɔlən'tiə(r)/	n.	志愿者,志愿兵 8A
	v.	自愿 8A
wander /'wɔndə/	vi.	漫步;离题 2A,5A
whiz /wiz/	n.	极出色的人,能手 2BI
▲ wholesome /'həulsəm/	a.	健康的 4BII
widespread /'waidspred/	a.	分布广的,普遍的 1A
wireless /'waiəlis/	a.	无线的 5BI,8BII
wit /wit/	n.	智力,才智;风趣 2BI,3BI

withdraw /wɪðˈdrɔː/	*vi.*	缩回，退出 3A	
	vt.	收回，撤销 3A	
withstand /wɪðˈstænd/	*vt.*	经受，承受，抵住 7A	
witness /ˈwɪtnɪs/	*vt.*	目击，注意到；为……作证，证明 6A	
	n.	目击者，见证人；证据，证言 6A	
▲**wizard** /ˈwɪzəd/	*n.*	奇才，男巫 8BI	
womanhood /ˈwumənhud/	*n.*	女人，女人气质 4BII	
workable /ˈwɜːkəbl/	*a.*	可经营的，可使用的 8A	
workforce /ˈwɜːkfɔːs/	*n.*	劳动力，劳动大军 1BI	
workplace /ˈwɜːkpleɪs/	*n.*	工作场所 6BI	
worrisome /ˈwʌrɪsəm/	*a.*	令人不安的 2BII	
worthy /ˈwɜːði/	*a.*	值得的，配得上的；有价值的，可尊敬的 1BI	
	a.	犯罪的，刑事的 1BI, 5BII	
wrinkle /ˈrɪŋkəl/	*n.*	皱纹 5BI	
	v.	（使）起皱纹 5BI	
writer /ˈraɪtə/	*n.*	作者，作家	
yawn /jɔːn/	*v.*	打呵欠 5A	
	n.	呵欠 5A	
yep /jep/	*ad.*	是 6BI	
▲**zeal** /ziːl/	*n.*	热心，热情，热诚 8BII	
zest /zest/	*n.*	强烈的兴趣，热情，热心 8BII	

Phrases

a fat chance	实际上不存在的机会 1BII
a handful of	少数的 1BI
a means to an end	用以达到目的的方法、事物或行动（其本身并不重要）2BII
a slim chance	可能性很小的机会 1BII
a wise guy	自以为聪明的人 1BII
account for	说明，解释；（指数量）占 4A
add to	增添；增加 4A,5A
after all	毕竟，到底，终究 4A,4BII
ahead of	在前面，领先 2BI
all the while	始终，一直 8A
and so forth	等等 3BII,7BII
apart from	除……之外，且莫说 4A,6BI
arrive at	达到，达成 2BI
as life would have it	好像命中注定一样 8BI
as long as	只要 2BI
as to	至于，关于 7A
associate with	把……与……联系在一起，联想 6BI
at first sight	初次看见时 7BI
at intervals	不时，相隔一定的距离 5A
at length	最后，终于；详细地 5BII,6BI
at one time or another	有时，又有时 4A
at one's best	处于最佳状态；（演员）达到个人最高水平；（花等）在盛开期 6A
back and forth	来回 4A
back up	支持 6BI
be ahead of	领先 2BII
be at one's best	身心俱佳，处于最好的状态 4A
be aware of	知道，觉察到，明白 3BII,7BII
be composed of	由……组成 1A
be free from	没有……的 4BII

be oneself	（人）处于正常状态 6A
be shy of	缺少 2BI
be taken aback	使某人震惊或惊奇 3BI
become of	降临，遭遇 8BI
believe in	主张 7BI
burn down	烧毁，焚毁 1BII
burn up	烧光，烧尽 1BII
burst into	突然开始，突然进入（某状态）6A
by chance	偶然地；碰巧 4BI
care for	喜欢 4BII
cast doubt on / upon	对……产生怀疑 1BI
catch one's eye	吸引某人的注意 8BII
catch sight of	看到，发现 7BI
choke up	（因激动等）说不出话来 6A
cold/hot as hell	冷/热得要命 1BII
come across	使人产生某种印象，偶然遇见，偶然发现 3BI，4BI
come to	开始……，共计为 1A,7BI
come to a head	达到紧急关头 7A
come up	被提出（起），走近，接近 5BI,6A
couldn't get over	对……感到惊奇，感到难以置信 5BI
count on	指望，依赖 2BI
cut corners	（做事）走捷径 2BII
deal with	处理，对付 6BI
die away	渐渐消失 7A
do one's best	尽其全力，尽量 2BI
drop off	睡着 7A
drop out	退出，放弃，退学 2BI
earn one's keep	挣钱维持生活 8BI
end up	结束，告终 2A
face up to	勇敢地面对、承担 6A
fall behind	落后 2BI
fall in love	爱上 8BI
fill out	填写 1BII
for all sb. knows	亦未可知，谁知道呢 3BI

Phrases

for convenience	为了方便起见 1A
for free	不要钱的 8A
for sure	确实 8BI
for the sake of	为获得或保持某事物 8A
get along	进展；过活，生活 3BII,7BII
get along with	与……相处（融洽）6BI
get into	使（自己、某人）进入（某状态）1BI
give sb. a piece of one's mind	对某人直言不讳，责备某人 6A
give up on sb.	不再相信某人会成功；对某人失望 8A
go off	进行；爆炸；（闹钟）响起来 1BII
hand out	分发 2BI
hang out	闲荡，厮混 8BI
have a habit of	有……的习惯 6BII
heat up	变激烈，加剧 6A
if need be	如果有必要 4BI
in (many) respects	在（许多）方面 5A
in addition to	除……外（还），加于……之上 3BII,7BII
in case	假使，以防万一 7A,8A
in contrast to /with	与……形成对比，和……对照 3A
in many ways	在许多方面 1BI
in no sense	决不（是）1A
in order to	为了 1BI
in person	亲自 4BII
in season	当令 7BI
in some respects	在某些方面 8BI
in store	存储着；预备着 2BI
in the habit of	有……的习惯 7BI
in the least	一点，丝毫 7BI
in time	后来，最后，终于；及时；按时 1A,5BII
keep down	控制，限制，压缩 2BI
keep sth. up	不让（精力等）衰退，保持 8BII
keep the ball in the air	让球尽可能滞空 3BI
keep up with (sb.)	与……的速度一样，跟上（某人）2A
lay off	解雇（通常用于被动语态）6A
leave off	不再使用 8BI

leave out	省去；漏掉，冷落，忽视	3A
leave over	留下，剩下	7BI
lend to	增添	3A
let it go at that	谈论到此为止，就此罢休	6A
let off (steam)	排放（废蒸汽），放走，放过	2A
let out	发出（某声音）	6BI
long for	渴望	2BI
look down one's nose	轻视，瞧不起	7A
look down upon	蔑视，瞧不起	2BI
make a fuss about	大惊小怪，小题大做	5A
make contact (with)	与……接触；通电（流）	3A
make no distinction	同等对待	2BI
make no reply	未做答复	5BII
make sure that/ of sth.	确信，使有把握；查明	4BI
make up	捏造，临时编造	6BII
make up one's mind	打定主意，决定	7BI
merge into	合并，结合	5A
more ... than	倒，倒不如说	7BI
needless to say	不用说	4BI
no sooner...than	一……就，刚……就	7A
now and again/then	时而，不时	5A
now that	既然，由于	5BII
on a scale of	在……等级	2BI
on one's own	独自地；独立地	2BI
on one's person	随身携带	5BII
on one's premises	在某人的经营场所	3BI
on the part of sb.	就某人而言	2BII
on the whole	大体上，基本上	6BI
or rather	或者更准确地说	2A
out of the question	不可能的	4BII
pat sb. on the back	对某人表示祝贺、鼓励或赞扬	8BI
pay heed to	注意，留心	6BI
pay off	还清（债务）	1BI
pick out	选择	6BII
pick up	捡起	5BI

Phrases

prior to	在……之前 3A
pull out	（车、船等）驶出，开上路 6A
put sth. to the test	使某物受检验，受考验 2BI
refer to	提到，谈到 1BI
rely on	依靠 1A
resort to sth.	求助于 3BI
right off the bat	立即 3BI
ring a bell	听起来耳熟，模糊地记得 3BI
roll up one's sleeve	卷起袖子（准备工作或战斗）8A
round off	完成，圆满结束 2A
run off with	与人私奔 8A
see to sb. or sth. that	照料 4BI
serve as	充当，用作，当作 3A
serve meals to sb.	招待某人，帮助上菜 4BI
settle in	（使）定居在……1A
settle on sth.	选择某事物，决定做某事 8A
show up	出现 8A
shower sb. with sth.	大量地给某人某物 7A
shut off	阻断，排除；拒之门外，与世隔绝 3A
side by side	一个接一个 1A
sit on its haunches	蹲着 7A
slap sb. five	双手平伸互相击掌 8BI
split into	（使）分裂 5A
stake out	用桩标出地界 8A
start off	开始活动 3BI
start up	突然站起，惊起 7BI
strike out	独立闯新路，开辟（道路等）2BI
swallow down	压制，抑制（感情等）6BI
take a hand in	插手，影响 7BI
take away from	减损 2A
take on	具有，呈现；承担 2BI
take sb. to task	责备某人，申斥某人 7BI
take...for granted	认为……理所当然 1BII
to a large degree	在很大程度上 8BI
to begin with	首先，第一 5A

295

to serve as	作为，用作	4BI
to this end	为达此目的	3BI
turn down	拒绝，驳回	1BI
turn into	走进	8BII
turn out	证明为，结果；腾空，倒出	5BII
under the sun	天下，世界上	5A
up to	（数目上）一直到，多达	1BI
wait upon/on sb.	照料或伺候某人	8BII
wear off	逐渐消失或除去	8BII
wear out	穿破，用坏	4A
week in and week out	每个星期都	8A
wind up	上（钟）弦；结束	1BII
with regard to	关于	6BI
with the exception of	除……以外	1A
work on sth.	从事于，致力于	8BI
worthy of	值得的，应得的	1BI